Ba

Hiking Humboldt
Volume 2

101 Shorter Walks, Road Walks, and Urban Walks

Rees Hughes

Maps by Jason Barnes

Lupines in the Bald Hills, Redwood National Park.

©Copyright 2017 • Backcountry Press
First Edition - second printing
Text pages printed on paper with post-consumer and recycled content

All rights reserved. No part of this publication may be reproduced, stored, or transmitted in any form or by any means—electronic, mechanical, photocopying, recording, or otherwise—without written permission from Backcountry Press.

All photos by Rees Hughes except where noted
Cover photos by Allison Poklemba (Petrolia in top center), and Rees Hughes (Black Lassic top left, Road Walkers top right, and Schoolhouse Peak panoramic)
All maps by Jason Barnes
Book layout and cover design by Backcountry Press

Published by Backcountry Press • Kneeland, California
ISBN 978-1-941624-06-7
Library of Congress Control Number: 2016933425

Order this book online: www.backcountrypress.com

Printed in the United States of America.
SUSTAINABLE
FORESTRY
INITIATIVE

Contributing reviewers:
  Jason Barnes
  Ron Berman
  Michael Kauffmann
  Keith McCloghrie
  Michele McKeegan
  Carrie Peyton-Dahlberg
  Allison Poklemba
  Aiko Uyeki

BACKCOUNTRY PRESS
Humboldt County, CA

❧Dedication❧

To Amy, the love of my life, who has supported, no...embraced, my passion for walking in every imaginable way. For all the footsteps we have shared. And, for those we haven't when you made it possible for me to be out hiking. For embracing trail stewarding and nurturing my writing about walking and encouraging my advocacy efforts. Thank you.

Acknowledgments

I want to thank the many friends and family who were willing to join me on the roads and trails of Humboldt County. Their good company made it difficult to end the 'research' for this book. They included:

Amy Uyeki
Ann Wallace
Annie Bolick-Floss
Annie Diver-Stamnes
Brooke Bisel
Carol Ralph
Dennis Rael
Emily Sinkhorn
Fortuna Senior Hiking Group (Lynn Crosthwait and Nancy Spruance)
Harvey Kelsey
Jerry Rohde
John Palmquist
Kay Sennott
Keith McCloghrie
Larry Buwalda
Mark Sommer
Mei Lan Hughes
Michael Proulx
Michele McKeegan
Rich Ridenhour
Rick Vrem
Riley Quarles
Sue Cashman

No one was more instrumental than Keith McCloghrie who joined me for countless walks and was so very helpful in refining and reviewing the book content. I also was inspired by Lynn Crosthwait and the Fortuna Senior Hiking group whose walking adventures have taken them to virtually every corner of the county. The extensive experience of Rich Ridenhour and gracious support and encouragement from Jerry Rohde were invaluable.

And a special thank you for all those who championed, built, and maintained the diverse network of rural roads and trails we have inherited. May our legacy for *those that follow us be one of which we can be proud.* ❧

Guthrie Creek by Nancy Spruance

Table of Contents

Section 1: Humboldt County

- 9   Introduction
- 10   An Ode to Walking
- 12   What to Bring Checklist
- 13   Safety
- 13   Using this book

Section 2: Hikes

- 16   **Region A • Redwood National and State Parks**
  - 18   Ossagon Trail • hike 1
  - 19   Carruthers Cove • hike 2
  - 21   Hope Creek – Ten Taypo Trail Loop • hike 3
  - 23   Big Tree – Elk Prairie Loop with many options • hike 4
  - 25   Davison Trail • hike 5
    - 28   a. Streelow Creek Trail
    - 29   b. Trillium Falls Trail
  - 30   Fern Canyon • hike 6
  - 31   Lady Bird Johnson Grove • hike 7
  - 32   Tall Trees Grove • hike 8
  - 33   Lyons Ranch Loop (and Schoolhouse Peak Lookout option) • hike 9
  - 35   Redwood Creek Levee Walks • hike 10
  - 38   Freshwater Lagoon – Old State Highway • hike 11

- 40   **Region B • Trinidad Area**
  - 42   Kane Road and the Stagecoach Hill Azalea Nature Trail • hike 12
  - 43   Big Lagoon to Patrick's Point • hike 13
  - 45   Patrick's Point • hike 14
  - 48   Trinidad • hike 15
    - 49   a. Trinidad Head
    - 50   b. Old Home Beach Loop
    - 50   c. Elk Head
  - 53   Houda Point to Moonstone Beach • hike 16

- 56   **Region C • Urban Corridor - Arcata (Indianola Road) North**
  - 58   McKinleyville Mid-Town Trail Loop • hike 17
  - 59   Hammond Trail • hike 18
    - 61   a. Hiller Park –School Road Loop
  - 62   Chah-GAH-Cho Trail • hike 19

	63	Azalea Park Natural Reserve • hike 20
	64	Mad River/Arcata Bottoms (Several Options) • hike 21
	66	Potawot Health Village • hike 22
	67	Arcata Historical/Architectural Walk • hike 23
	71	Arcata Community Forest • hike 24
	73	Arcata Ridge Trail – South Fork Janes Creek Loop Trail • hike 25
	75	Arcata Ridge Trail -- Beith Creek Loop Trail • hike 26
	77	Humboldt State University – Campus Walk • hike 27
	79	Jacoby Creek Forest Trail (by permit only) • hike 28
	81	Arcata Marsh • hike 29
	83	Bay Trail North (Arcata City Trail) • hike 30
	84	Ma-le'l Dunes • hike 31
	86	Humboldt Coastal Nature Center • hike 32
	87	Manila Dunes Recreational Area • hike 33
	88	Samoa Loop • hike 34
	90	North Jetty Area – Samoa Dunes Recreation Area • hike 35
92		**Region D • Urban Corridor - Eureka (Indianola Road) South**
	94	Hikshari' Trail • hike 36
	95	Eureka Waterfront Trail • hike 37
	97	Fay Slough Wildlife Area • hike 38
	98	Freshwater Farms Nature Reserve • hike 39
	99	Sequoia Park to Buhne Loop • hike 40
	101	a. Sequoia Park to Henderson Center
	101	McKay Community Forest • hike 41
	103	Eureka Architectural Walk • hike 42
	106	Eureka Old Town Mural and Historical Walk • hike 43
	108	Elk River Covered Bridges and Berta Road Loop • hike 44
	110	Elk River Trail to Falk • hike 45
	111	Humboldt Bay Wildlife Refuge – Shorebird Loop • hike 46
	113	Humboldt Bay Wildlife Refuge – Hookton Slough • hike 47
	114	College of the Redwoods (CR) Campus • hike 48
	115	a. Humboldt Botanical Garden
	117	Tompkins Hill Road • hike 49
118		**Region E • Fortuna/Ferndale/Rio Dell**
	120	Loleta – Singley Road/Table Bluff Cemetery • hike 50
	121	a. Loleta Railroad Tunnel
	123	Table Bluff Loop • hike 51

125	Cannibal Island – Crab Park – Cock Robin Island • hike 52	
127	Centerville Beach South and Fleener Creek Loop • hike 53	
129	Guthrie Creek Trail • hike 54	
129	Poole Road • hike 55	
130	Russ Park • hike 56	
132	Ferndale Architectural and Historical Walk • hike 57	
135	Ferndale Bottoms – Goble, Camp Weott, Port Kenyon, Fulmor, and Dillon Roads • hike 58	
137	Williams Creek Road • hike 59	
138	Bear River Ridge • hike 60	
140	Upper Bear River Road • hike 61	
141	Headwaters Forest - Salmon Pass Trail • hike 62	
143	Fortuna – Riverwalk North and Riverwalk South • hike 63	
144	Fortuna Architectural Walk • hike 64	
145	a. Rohner Park Trails	

146 Region F • Southern Redwoods

- 148 Drury – Chaney Groves Trail • hike 65
- 149 High Rock Trail and the Five Allens Trail • hike 66
- 150 Founders Grove and Mahan Plaque Loop • hike 67
- 152 Bull Creek – Addie Johnson Trail – Homestead Trail – Albee Creek Loop • hike 68
- 153 Squaw Creek Road – Baxter – Hamilton Barn – Homestead Loop • hike 69
- 155 Look Prairie • hike 70
- 156 Rockefeller Loop – Women's Federation Grove and Options • hike 71
- 157 Williams Grove – Hidden Springs • hike 72
- 159 Garden Club of America Grove Loop Trail • hike 73
- 160 Southern Humboldt Community Park Trail System • hike 74
- 161 **Others:** Thrap Mill Trail and the Pioneer Trail (Benbow Lake State Recreation Area), East Branch Road, Fleishmann Grove Trail, and Gould Grove Loop Trail.

162 Region G • King Range and Shelter Cove Area

- 164 Steamboat Rock to Sugar Loaf Island (Cape Mendocino) • hike 75
- 165 McNutt Gulch/Creek • hike 76
- 166 Conklin Creek Road • hike 77
- 167 Mattole River to Punta Gorda • hike 78
- 169 Shelter Cove • hike 79

	170	a. Short Loop
	170	b. Bill Franklin Nature Trail and Sea Foam option
	172	Sinkyone – Needle Rock Visitor Center to Bear Harbor • hike 80
174		**Region H • Inland – Northeast**
	176	Blue Lake Industrial Park and Mad River Levee • hike 81
	177	Upper Fickle Hill Road • hike 82
	178	Mountain View Road • hike 83
	179	Bald Mountain and Snow Camp Road • hike 84
	181	Walking in the Horse Mountain Area • hike 85
	182	a. Indian Butte Loop
	183	b. Trinity Alps Vista
	184	c. Horse Mountain Mine
	185	Cold Springs Wander • hike 86
	187	Spike Buck Mountain • hike 87
	188	East Fork Willow Creek • hike 88
	189	Lacks Creek • hike 89
	189	a. Pine Ridge
	191	b. Mid-Slope Road/Pine Ridge Loop
	192	Willow Creek Walks • hike 90
	192	a. Veterans Park and Camp Kimtu
	193	Brush Mountain Fire Lookout • hike 91
	194	"Prospect" Trail • hike 92
	195	Bluff Creek Historical Trail • hike 93
	197	Shelton Butte • hike 94
200		**Region I • Inland – Southeast**
	202	Summer Bridge Options • hike 95
	202	a. Shively Road
	204	b. McCann Ferry and Low Water Bridge
	205	Van Duzen County Park (Pamplin Grove-Swimmer's Delight) • hike 96
	207	Grizzly Creek Redwoods and Cheatham Grove • hike 97
	209	Redwood House Road and Kneeland Road alternative • hike 98
	210	Extra: Kneeland – Bridgeville Road
	210	Fort Seward Road • hike 99
	211	Southern Dyerville Loop Road • hike 100
	212	Mount Lassic (aka Signal Peak) and Black Lassic • hike 101
	215	Conclusions
	216	Author and Cartographer

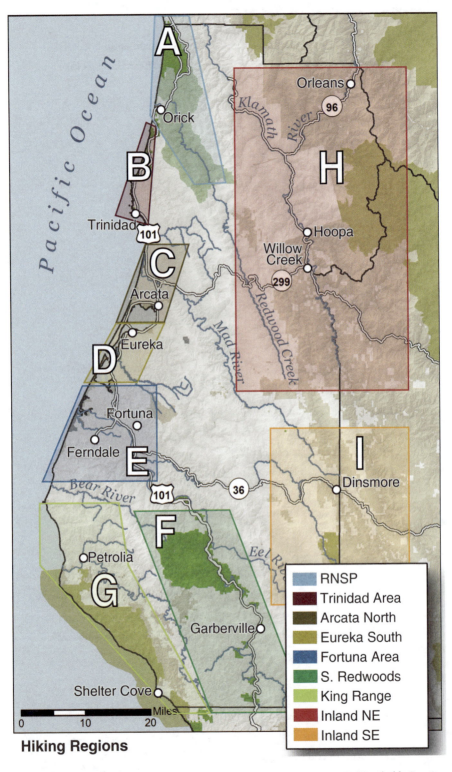

Introduction

Humboldt County includes over 4,000 square miles of coastal mountains, redwood forests, dynamic rivers and pristine bays, oak woodlands and stunning coastline. From sea level to just shy of 7,000 feet on the top of Salmon Mountain, we are blessed with an incredible diversity of landscapes and public parklands.

The growing network of trails is supplemented by nearly 1,300 miles of paved and unpaved public roadways that often serve as wonderful walking paths including rural roads with evocative names like Redwood House, Bear River Ridge, and Bald Mountain. For most of us who live in or near Humboldt County's population centers, urban walks offer a convenient way to get exercise while sampling some of the region's historical and architectural buildings, enjoying Eureka's waterfront, Fortuna's river walk, or Arcata's Marsh and Wildlife Sanctuary.

The guiding spirit of this book of modest exploration is to push yourself a little farther, to try out the unfamiliar, to marvel at the unanticipated, and to celebrate both the ordinary and the extraordinary.

This guide is intended to complement the selection of longer day hikes featured in Ken Burton's *Hiking Humboldt: Volume 1* (referred to as *Volume 1* throughout). Readers will find that there is some overlap especially on those walks where longer options are possible even though their locations are often associated with shorter walks (e.g., the Arcata Marsh, Patrick's Point State Park, Russ Park).

Although the two volumes taken together cover many hikes and walks in Humboldt County, it is not a complete listing for several reasons. First, a number of new trails are coming on line (e.g., McKay Community Forest, Bay Trail). Second, when you include road and urban walks as I have, the potential walks are nearly infinite. Consider commenting on v2.hikinghumboldt.com with your favorite Humboldt County walk that may have been omitted.

Houda Point looking at Camel Rock, photo by Ann Wallace

It is also important to note that some details describing these walks are in a constant state of flux. Common sense must prevail when reality does not match the trail or walk description. Similarly with regard to safety – care should always be exercised regarding high water, high tide, downed trees, and, perhaps most importantly in remote, rural parts of Humboldt County, awareness of marijuana cultivation. For that reason, some potential walks in southeastern and northeast portions of the County have not been included.

Be aware of weather forecasts, bring sufficient water and food, additional clothing, maps/directions, and a cell phone, although parts of Humboldt County remain without coverage. However, the most important safety measure you can take is to hike with someone else.

Although this guide highlights 101 different walks, a number of options are noted to lengthen a particular trip. In addition, there are variations on other walks with minimal description noted as 'Extras'. Walks within 30 minutes of Humboldt Bay are disproportionately represented.

I have tried to highlight road walks that typically have limited traffic and offer distinctive features (I have a weakness for panoramic views). Even though all the road walks included in this book are on public thoroughfares, in some places you will be greeted by intimidating signs that warn of patrols, forbid trespass, and discourage visitors. These are often along county roads bordered by open range private ranch lands. What are your rights and responsibilities along these roads?

A visit to the Humboldt County Land Use Division of the Department of Public Works was very illuminating. Manila folders for each county road included a variety of documents, often hand-written, from survey maps to easement language. It became clear that from mile to mile along the same road, the right-of-way may vary widely. Although the general minimum right-of-way is 40-feet, there are exceptions and, in some situations, the road may be located on one edge of the right-of-way. The best advice is to walk or ride within the maintained roadway. Make sure that you park outside of the traveled lane and do not block gates or roadways and, preferably, in a well-used pullout. I strongly encourage an ethic of accommodation and civility if ever confronted. Explain your purpose and destination and keep your dog on a leash (especially if there are open-range cows and sheep). Be walking ambassadors, gentle advocates for a leave-no-trace approach and respectful guests in neighborhoods, pasturelands, and ecosystems.

An Ode to Walking

In the course of mankind's 200,000 generations of existence, Homo sapiens developed longer legs with thicker bones and hip structures designed to facilitate walking. Being bi-pedal enabled us to use tools and was far more energy efficient than walking with four legs.

And walk we did. Until the advent of the train and the popularization of the automobile a handful of generations ago, walking was the primary means of locomotion for the vast majority. Joseph Amato (2004), called this a "revolution ... in the use of the human body and mind." For millions of years we dedicated half of our time and bodily energy to walking (and similar forms of locomotion).

However, for many Americans, walking is becoming a lost art. Overwhelmed by the convenience of car travel. Struggling to compete with the lure of extreme sports. Forgotten in the midst of busy calendars, home entertainment options, and work done in front of a computer. In 2014, the Nielsen media ratings company released data that indicated that the average American watches more than five hours of live television every day, another 32 minutes a day of time-shifted television, an hour using the Internet on a computer, an hour and seven minutes on a smartphone and two hours, 46 minutes listening to the radio. Perhaps it shouldn't be a surprise that a recent study monitoring the activity levels of people in a variety of cultures revealed that Americans, on average, took 5,117 steps a day, far below the averages in western Australia (9,695 steps), Switzerland (9,650 steps) and Japan (7,168 steps).

Amy Uyeki

Our increasingly sedentary lifestyle has had consequences. In the past 30 years, the occurrence of obesity in children has more than tripled [National Health and Nutrition Examination Survey (NHANES)] and more than one third of all adults in the U.S. are considered obese. There has been a parallel explosion in cardiometabolic health issues (e.g., Type II diabetes, cardiovascular disease).

While walking is no panacea, it is certainly part of the answer.

Walking is a gentle, low impact exercise. No expensive spandex pants, protective helmets, or licensing is required. No special training or expertise is needed. Walking facilities are truly everywhere. You can manually adjust the speed and the length of the workout to fit your time and energy levels. Walking provides reflective time or, if you are like me, walking lends itself to a social component. And, as advocated in this book, walking takes you to locations with aesthetic or historical significance.

Walking engulfs the senses. I have driven around Humboldt Bay countless times over the past thirty years. Even at 50 mph I notice the broad expanse of tidal flats or the flocks of shore birds and sometimes the magenta of blooming owl's clover. But, when I walk from Arcata to Eureka, I become aware of so much more. I see paths worn by river otters and the small pile of shell fragments that mark their 'latrine'. I have time to stop and watch a Northern Harrier silently glide just above the outstretched arms of young willows. I notice the subtle change in the tides as they climb the shoreline. I feel a change in the wind. Smell the salted air. Rub a frond of yarrow between my fingers and lift the fragrance to my nose. You miss all this from the seat of a car.

Each time I venture out for a walk in Humboldt County, I own this place as my home just a bit more. My roots extend a little deeper into the land. I appreciate the nuance and subtlety along with the glorious and the overwhelming. Sitting on a sunny hillside gazing out over upper Bull Creek appreciating late fall colors.

Stopping on Mountain View Road near Kneeland Airport and being able to distinguish landmarks now familiar from my explorations. The thrill of seeing a pod of whales as I round the southwest corner of Trinidad Head. How can you not feel a sense of belonging?

And, the spiritual dimension of walking. As professional wanderer Paul Theroux observed, "There is a reason that all serious pilgrims go on foot to their holy destinations." Walking can have a rhythmic, meditative quality. It is humbling, simple, and close to the earth. When you walk, there is time to think, reflect, and refresh the mind.

Lastly, the pragmatic side to pedestrianism. It IS very possible to get from here to there on foot. Whether it is a stroll to the store to purchase currants to complete the scone recipe or for a lunchtime rendezvous or for your doctor's appointment, walking is more often an option than we admit. If you wish, you can also go farther. I should know as I have walked from the Mexican to the Canadian border.

"Walking", Rebecca Solnit summarizes in her wonderful book, *Wanderlust: A History of Walking* (2001), "shares with making and working that crucial element of engagement of the body and the mind with the world, of knowing the world through the body and the body through the world." Amen.

What to Bring Checklist

Everyone has their own reminder list for day hikes. Here is mine:
1) Water
2) Food
3) Camera
4) Binoculars
5) Extra layer of clothing and rain jacket if precipitation is a possibility
6) For road walks, visible clothing and/or reflective vest
7) Extra pair of socks if the hike is long
8) Directions/maps/guidebook/fieldguide(s)/GPS
9) Reading glasses (otherwise the maps and guides may be useless)
10) Sunglasses
11) Hat
12) Sunscreen
13) Cell phone
14) ID, money, license (etc.)
15) Small first aid kit
16) Headlamp
17) Matches
18) Pocket knife
19) Toilet paper

Depending upon the length and remoteness of your walk, there may be other items to include. I often welcome the addition of hiking poles. Some may want insect repellant or Tecnu (for poison oak) or a swimming suit during certain times of the year. On some walks I will bring hand clippers if I suspect that the route could be overgrown. And don't forget to let someone know your general itinerary.

Safety

Safety is an important consideration in all outdoor activities. No guidebook can alert you to every hazard or anticipate the limitations of every reader. Therefore, the descriptions of roads, trails, and natural features in this book are not guarantees that a particular walk will be safe for your party. When you follow any of the routes described in this book you assume responsibility for your safety.

When walking along the beach, be sure to consult tide tables and plan appropriately. Keep in mind that inland summer temperatures can necessitate more water to stay hydrated. Poison oak can be an issue on a number of trails. Be prepared for weather changes and other possibilities (see "What to Bring Checklist"). Sadly, while many may worry most about wild animal encounters, I consider some of the greatest threats to hiker safety occur as a result of marijuana cultivation. The paranoia that seems to typify the industry makes it very important to use common sense, avoid inadvertently trespassing on private land, and steer clear of confrontation.

Since roads are incorporated into many of these walks, exercise caution when walking even seldom-traveled roads. Wearing visible colors, walking on the left so as to face oncoming traffic, and stepping well to the side when vehicles approach are among the good safety measures.

Using This Book

The hikes are grouped into nine regions, each section with its own brief introduction to the region and a map of the hikes in the region. The description of each hike includes an information box, driving and walking directions, and, for most, a map or shared map. Sidebars scattered throughout the book highlight topics of special interest.

Information boxes: Most of the information in these boxes is self-explanatory, but a few items may need clarification. Length is round-trip unless noted otherwise. Total ascent is a general approximation of the cumulative total of all the uphill portions of the hike. Elevations noted are also approximate. Many of the hikes may be inaccessible or impossible for one reason or another under certain conditions (snow, road closures, high water, etc.); access constraints are listed in the box and described in more detail in the text. Pay attention to these to avoid disappointment and safety risk. As a rule, seasonal bridges are in place from approximately Memorial Day through Labor Day and snow may be a factor from November to May in the higher country.

The US Forest Service Trail Accessibility Guidelines (USFS, 2013) wisely discourages the use of the term "**accessible trail**" given the range of abilities among those with mobility challenges. I have noted trails (with a wheelchair symbol) that are considered accessible using the California State Parks standards. These require "firm and stable" surfaces (often compacted soil), minimum width and clearance, resting and passing spaces, and gradient and slope limits. Trail obstacles such as rocks or roots are limited to 2 vertical inches. These still may be impractical for some users. Many are working to improve the quality and quantity of accessible trails (see http://access.parks.ca.gov for current state park information).

Routes: I have tried to provide sufficient detail to complete each walk but my descriptions should never trump good judgment. Changes occur. What you encounter may not precisely match my description; please report discrepancies on the web site (see below). Since I utilize distances in the route description, there may be value in having a way to measure your mileage as you walk (e.g., GPS app on a smart phone).

Getting there: All driving distances originate at the county courthouse, US 101 and J Street in Eureka. Approximate driving times are based upon beginning at the courthouse.

Maps: Each route map is oriented either North up or East up, depending on the hike's layout. Be sure you're holding it correctly! Several hikes may share one map and for a number of simple hikes I have dispensed with the map. Read the descrip-

Houda Point, photo by Ann Wallace

Symbol Key

♿	Accessible	🐎	Suitable for horses
⛱	Beach access	🎋	Picnic area
🚴	Biking allowed on trail	✨	Point of interest
🚣	Boating access	🛂	Ranger Station/Visitor Center
⛺	Campground	🚻	Restroom
🅿	Hike start - parking	🏊	Swimming hole
👪	Family Friendly	🔭	Viewpoint

tion for map-less walks carefully as that should be adequate for successful navigation. Take note of symbols at the bottom of each map too.

www.hikinghumboldt.com

This is the book's companion web site and has links to additional information not included in the printed copy. Hike #43 online, for instance, has additional details about the murals and history of Old Town Eureka. For smartphone hikers, we recommend a QR Code Reader app for quick links from the book. The website also has a forum for hikers to share observations, experiences, and comments along the trail. Users are urged to post notes on their impressions of hikes, trail conditions, unexpected access issues, and observations of natural and human history.

Hiking Humboldt Volume 2

Region A:
Redwood National and State Parks

From a handful of coast redwoods trailing south along Big Sur to a few outliers just north of the Chetco River in southwestern Oregon, the Sequoia sempervirens survives in a narrow northern California coastal band. Of the 1.6 million acres of redwoods in the current range, only about 6 percent is old growth. About 80 percent of the large trees – old growth (virgin forest) and second growth – are protected in public and privately held conservation lands. Some of the most accessible and spectacular deep redwood forests are in Humboldt County – Prairie Creek Redwoods State Park, Redwood National Park, Humboldt Redwoods State Park, Arcata Community Forest, Headwaters Forest, and the diminutive Grizzly Creek Redwoods State Park. This volume includes walks from all six locations beginning with the Redwood National Park and Prairie Creek Redwoods.

Although many of the longer walks are described in *Volume 1*, I have emphasized interesting shorter walks in and around Redwood National and State Parks in this section. Walks range from the popular Fern Canyon and Lady Bird Johnson hikes to the lesser known, but equally deserving Lyons Ranch trail high in the Bald Hills. There are accessible walks around Elk Prairie and along Prairie Creek and road walks east of Freshwater Lagoon or along the Redwood Creek levees near Orick. There is the relatively new trail to Trillium Falls and another along Streelow Creek. This section begins with several walks near the Del Norte county line.

In Prairie Creek Redwoods, photo by Michael Kauffmann

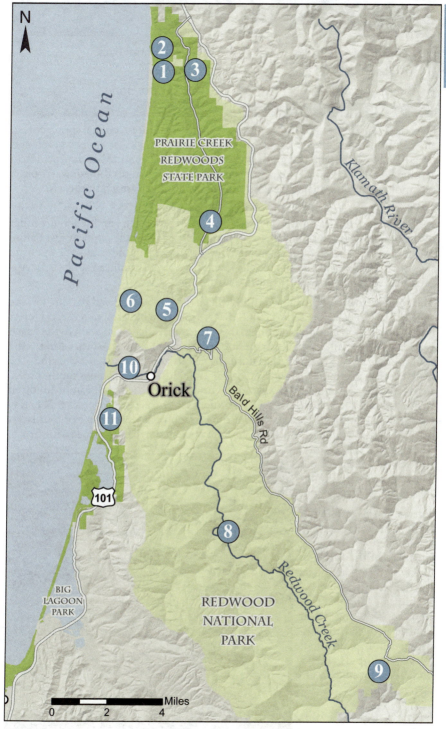

Region A: **Redwood National and State Parks**

1 · Ossagon Trail

Length: 3.6-7.6 miles
Total ascent: 800 feet
Elevations: 0-820 feet
Type: out and back
Dogs: no
Restrooms: none

Description: This walk includes old growth redwood forest, coastal spruce forest, alder-dominated wetlands, the landlocked Ossagon Rocks, as well as beach and ocean access. Although well graded, the trail back up from the beach provides an aerobic workout with its 800 feet of elevation gain. In winter though water often accumulates in the wetlands necessitating some wading to reach the beach.

Getting there: Proceed north on US 101 47 miles to Exit 753 (Newton B. Drury Parkway). Turn left (0.2 mile) on the Parkway and proceed north for about 7 miles to the signed Ossagon trailhead, located on the left side of the parkway just before the road begins a series of steep, uphill curves to the top of the grade (the opposite side of the Parkway is the Hope Creek and Ten Taypo trailhead, Hike #3). Approximate driving time, a little more than 1 hour.

The route (shown on the map with Hike #2): From the trailhead parking lot, the trail immediately begins a short climb (0.3) through an old growth redwood forest before leveling off along a high ridge (0.6). The remainder of the walk to the beach is a steady downhill dropping about 800 feet through a coastal spruce forest. The trail follows an old roadbed that until the 1960s accommodated car traffic. The trail intersects with the California Coastal Trail (1.8) that continues south toward Fern Canyon or can be taken west to the beach (2.1). The beach can be followed north 1.7 miles to the base of the Carruthers Cove trail (see separate trail entry) or to the less ambitious destination of the Ossagon Rocks, a cluster of four large, grey rocks rising dramatically from the sandy bench north of the trail to the beach. These rocks have spiritual significance to the Yurok people and should be treated with respect.

Extras: The Ossagon Trail hike can easily be lengthened by walking north from the Ossagon Rocks to Carruthers Cove or south along the California Coastal Trail and back. Using a car shuttle between the Ossagon and Carruthers Cove trailheads makes for a pleasant hike of under 5 miles.

Elk at Ossagon Rocks. Photo by Nancy Spruance

2 · Carruthers Cove

Length: 1.6 miles
Total ascent: 500 feet
Elevations: 0-500 feet
Type: out and back
Dogs: no
Restrooms: none

Description: Although this section of the California Coastal Trail begins in Del Norte County it soon crosses the county line. The trail descends on an old logging road through a spruce forest to the northern end of Gold Bluffs Beach. At moderate and low tides, the beach can be followed south around a jumble of large rocks to a broad, flat shoreline. Off-shore rocks in this area are populated by large numbers of pelagic birds. The foreshore between the ocean and the bluffs can hold considerable water during the winter and spring and may necessitate careful wayfinding to locate the bridge over Ossagon and Butler Creeks. Once across, walkers can link with the Ossagon Trail to Newton B. Drury Parkway or continue south on the Coastal Trail to Fern Canyon and beyond. To walk from the Carruthers Cove trailhead to the west end of the Ossagon Trail and back is 5.6 miles. By arranging a car shuttle, it is about a four and a half mile walk from the Carruthers Cove trailhead to the Ossagon trailhead on the Newton B. Drury Parkway.

Getting there: Proceed north on US 101 47 miles to Exit 753 (Newton B. Drury Parkway). Turn left (0.2 mile) on the Parkway and proceed north for about 8.5 miles. Turn left on the Coastal Drive and continue west for 1.0 mile. The easy-to-miss Carruthers Cove trailhead and parking area is on the left. Approximate driving time, 1 hour 10 minutes.

The route: From the trailhead parking lot, the trail immediately begins its steady descent (0.6). The final route to the beach follows the eroded high bank of diminutive Johnson Creek (0.8). Although

> ## ∞ Gold at Gold Bluffs Beach
>
> Time layers different people, activities, even structures over the same physical space. The tree-lined trail that descends to Gold Bluffs beach once led to a gold mining operation near the mouth of Ossagon Creek, one of several along the aptly named beach stretching south for several miles. The beaches, the source of gold bearing sand, were narrower in the late 1800s than they are now. Waves washed against the bluffs at high tide limiting harvesting the sand to periods of low tide. It was not until the 1870s that technology had improved enough to make separating the gold dust from the sand practical. The sand would be washed in sluice boxes "which caught the gold on copper plates charged with quicksilver" (Rohde and Rohde, 1994).
>
> In 1965, when this land was purchased for inclusion in Prairie Creek Redwoods State Park, a county road followed the route of the current Davison Road along the length of the beach north, past the current end at Fern Canyon to Ossagon Creek, where it made the steep climb up to an intersection with Drury Parkway (then US 101) not far north of the Ossagon trailhead. The beach was populated by squatters camps and had been severely trashed by years of mining operations. The transfer to the California State Parks began a long process of restoration and clean-up and, as a result, walking the trail today requires some imagination to visualize this past. ∞

the trail is not dangerous it does necessitate some care. The trail emerges onto a beach. This is your turnaround spot for the shorter hike. For those going farther, this forest portal is obscure but, fortunately, is marked by an obvious yellow trail sign mounted high above a stump. The beach south is passable in moderate and low tides and widens considerably after slightly more than a mile. In dry conditions, it is possible to angle southeast to intersect the California Coastal Trail as it crosses Ossagon and Butler Creeks. In wetter conditions, stay on the beach for roughly 1.7 miles from the point where Carruthers Cove trail reaches the beach, then turn east (2.5). A reflective highway sign is mounted several hundred yards east of the shoreline that marks the location of the continuation of the Coastal Trail. Once

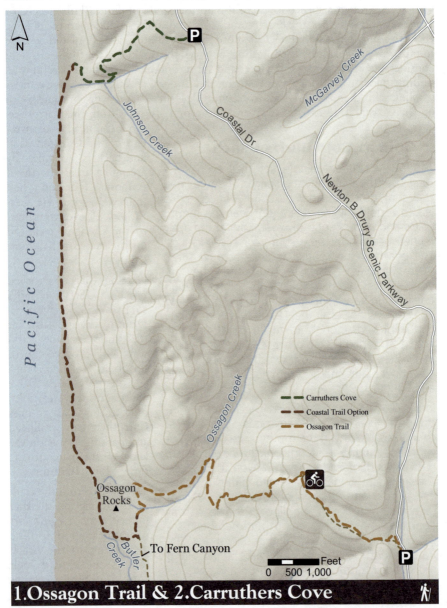

1. Ossagon Trail & 2. Carruthers Cove

across the creeks, the trail splits with the right branch continuing south toward Fern Canyon and the left branch continuing north toward the Ossagon trail (0.3 mile from the shoreline to the trail junction).

From here, as outlined above, there are several options including walking the Ossagon trail to Newton B. Drury Parkway (4.6), retracing your steps to the Carruthers Cove trailhead, or heading toward Fern Canyon.

Note: Rohde and Rohde (2004) comment that both Carruthers and Johnson are inappropriately being perpetuated as place names. The road the Carruthers Cove trail follows once led to the summer home of J.H. Crothers, editor of the *Humboldt Times* newspaper during the early 1900s. Johnson Creek was (mis)named for the Johnston family, who settled this area in 1851.

3 · Hope Creek and Ten Taypo Trail Loop

Length: 3.8 miles	**Access**: steep trail with uneven tread
Total ascent: 950 feet	
Elevations: 700-1300 feet	**Dogs**: no
Type: partial loop	**Restrooms**: none

Description: This trail meanders steeply up the Hope Creek drainage providing an aerobic workout in the midst of magnificent groves of old growth redwoods, Douglas-fir, and Sitka spruce. The trail crests a ridge before dropping down to use the abandoned East Ridge Road. When the Park Bypass was built, it cut through sections of the East Ridge Road leaving only short isolated remnants (Rohde and Rohde, 1994). The trail then departs from the East Ridge Road and makes a long gradual descent, returning to Hope Creek near the end of the circuit. As an oft-overlooked trail it offers a sense of seclusion until disturbed by distant traffic sounds in the middle of the loop and nearer at the beginning and end.

Getting there: Drive north on US 101 47 miles to Exit 753 (Newton B. Drury Parkway). Take a left (0.2 mile) on the Parkway and proceed 6.8 miles to the Hope Creek/Ten Taypo trailhead. Parking is available on both sides of the Parkway (the opposite side is the Ossagon

Trail trailhead, Hike #1). Approximate driving time, just over 1 hour.

The route: From the trailhead the trail climbs to the intersection of the Hope Creek and the Ten Taypo trails (0.4). Turn left (Hope Creek). The trail crests at just over 1,300 feet (1.0). The trail briefly follows the ridgeline before dropping down and joining the old East Ridge Road which it follows for about one half mile (1.5). The trail leaves the road and begins a gradual descent over the next two miles (3.4) although for much of the way stays high in the Ten Taypo drainage before rounding the west side of the ridge and dropping down to cross Hope Creek and rejoin the trail to the Parkway (3.8).

3. Hope Creek and Ten Taypo Trail

4 · Big Tree – Elk Prairie Loop

Length: 5.2 miles (or shorter)	accessible to California State Park standards except the Circle Trail.
Total ascent: relatively flat	
Elevations: 270-390 feet	
Type: loop	**Dogs:** no
Access : All trails are considered	**Restrooms:** yes

RNSP

Description: With the exception of some of the road walks (and by late 2017 the Eureka Waterfront Trail), the most extensive accessible trail system in Humboldt County is in the Elk Prairie/Big Tree areas of Prairie Creek Redwood State Park and Redwood National Park. This trail system offers many ways to mix and match the trails that network this area. Included in the route are magnificent old growth redwoods, picturesque Prairie Creek, the open grasslands of Elk Prairie, a nature trail, and miles of accessible trail.

Getting there: Proceed north on US 101 47 miles to Exit 753 (Newton B. Drury Parkway) and on through Redwood National and State Parks. Turn left (0.2 mile) on the Parkway and proceed north for about 2.0 miles to the Big Tree Wayside, a signed right turn into a spacious parking lot that often fills during the peak summer tourist season. It is also possible to park at the Prairie Creek Redwoods Visitor Center and in identified pull-outs along Newton B. Drury Parkway. Approximate driving time, 55 minutes.

The routes: *The Big Tree Wayside – Prairie Creek Trail – Davison Trail and/or Elk Prairie Trail – Foothill Trail Loop* (5.2 miles). This hard-packed gravel accessible trail may be slightly easier to follow in a clockwise direction. From the trailhead on the east side of the Big Tree Wayside parking lot, turn right joining the Foothill Trail, an old wagon road built in 1894 to connect Crescent City and Arcata. Cross the Cal Barrel Road continuing south until you intersect with the Cathedral Trees Trail (0.7). Turn left on the Cathedral Trees Trail. At the intersection with the Elk Prairie Trail (0.9) turn right following the Elk Prairie Trail, much of which was widened in 2015 to improve accessibility. Continue south crossing Newton B. Drury Parkway (2.1). You soon reach Davison Trail (2.3), more of the old wagon road. [Davison Trail continues 4.3 miles to the south.] Turn right (north) on Davison Trail. You can either follow Davison Trail and the Campground Road all the way to the Visitor Center (3.2) or turn left on the Elk Prairie Trail (2.4) and follow it along Prairie Creek through the south end of the Elk Prairie Campground and on again from the north end (called the Redwood Access Trail). This is a very pleasant alternative to the road walk (3.6). From the Visitor Center the Prairie Creek Trail crosses Prairie Creek and follows the creek north through this primordial landscape (4.6 using the road; 5.0 using Redwood Access Trail). Take a right turn leaving Prairie Creek Trail and almost immediately crossing Newton B. Drury Parkway staying right to Big Tree (4.7; 5.1) and on to the parking lot (4.8; 5.2).

The Big Tree Wayside – Prairie Creek Trail – and returning via Cathedral Trees Trail (3.3 miles) or Foothill Trail Loop (2.7 miles). From the parking lot trailhead, turn left to the Big Tree continuing on (veer left) soon crossing Newton B. Drury Parkway (0.2). The connector trail from the Parkway soon reaches the Prairie Creek Trail. Turn left following this trail as it winds its way to the Prairie Creek Redwoods Visitor Center (1.6). Just after crossing Prairie Creek, the Cathedral Trees Trail can be reached by turning left or by continuing to the Visitor Center and catching the trail as it parallels the entrance road back toward the Newton B. Drury Parkway. Just across the Parkway (1.8), Foothill Trail offers the shortest and quickest return to the Big Tree Wayside. Cathedral Trees Trail goes a little farther east passing Elk Prairie Trail (2.0) and the Rhododendron Trail (2.3) staying left at each junction. After continuing north and paralleling Foothill Trail, the Cathedral Trees Trail connects with Circle Trail (3.1). Go left to Big Tree and left again to the Big Tree Wayside parking lot (3.3).

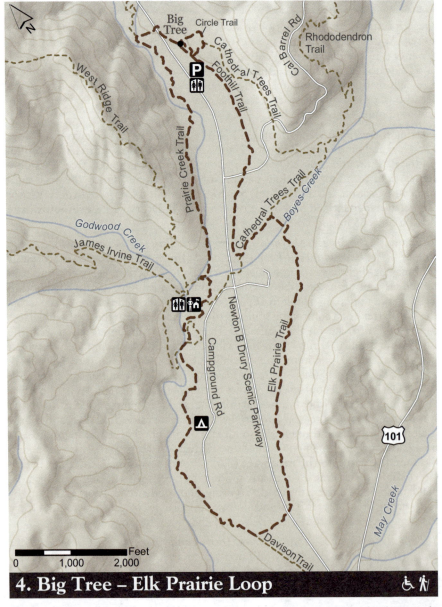

4. Big Tree – Elk Prairie Loop

Nancy Spruance

Prairie Creek Redwood Visitor Center – Davison Trail and/or Elk Prairie – Cathedral Trees Trail (2.6 – 2.9 miles). This hard-packed gravel, accessible trail is a variation of the above walks and circumnavigates the large prairie once the preferred home to the Park's elk herd. In more recent years you are more likely to spot deer than elk here. For the most part the trail hugs the trees along the perimeter offering views across the prairie.

Extras. *Revelation Trail.* This accessible loop trail (0.3 mile) is located a short distance south of the Prairie Creek Redwoods Visitor Center. It is a signed nature trail that focuses on redwood forest ecology and the spiritual and philosophical dimension of the natural world.

Circle Trail. This loop trail (0.3 mile) begins at Big Tree and makes a short circuit through a section of redwood forest. This is a choice for walkers with limited range (stamina, desire, or attention span) best made to get a little more of the forest experience than just admiring Big Tree.

Nature Trail (0.3 mile one-way). This short trail crosses Prairie Creek on a seasonal bridge a short distance downstream from the Revelation Trail. It intersects with the James Irvine and West Ridge Trails just before reaching the Prairie Creek Trail. A right turn would take you to the Visitor Center.

5 · Davison Trail

Length: 6.1 miles (one-way)
Total ascent: 250 feet (N-S)
Elevations: 190-390 feet
Type: out and back

Access constraints: none
Dogs: no
Restrooms: yes

While the Davison Trail is a pleasant trail in its own right as it stretches from Lost Man Creek to Elk Prairie Visitor Center, it also serves as the backbone from which a number of other trails diverge: Elk Prairie Trail (Hike #4), Streelow Creek, Trillium Falls, and Berry Glen Trail.

Description: Davison Trail incorporates roads used in the commercial logging operations between the Elk Prairie area and the Lost Man Creek access road. The roads and trail tend to be well-drained with durable surfaces that make for good winter walks when other trails are too wet. The 1.1 miles on the east side of US 101 are paved.

Aside from the highway noise from nearby US 101 the walk is very pleasant—passing through stretches of prairie, riparian areas, healthy second growth forests, stands of alder and spruce, with a high probability of seeing elk.

Getting there (options): There are three trailhead options for walking Davison Trail. Approximate driving time, 50 - 55 minutes.

1) Mid-Trail. Proceed north on US 101 44.8 miles to the Davison Road exit. Turn left on Davison Road and proceed for a quarter mile to the Elk Meadows Day Use Area. Ample parking exists at the trailhead. This option places you nearer the middle of the trail (2.4 miles to Lost Man Creek Picnic Area; 3.7 miles to Prairie Creek Redwoods Visitor Center).

2) Lost Man Creek End of Trail. Proceed north on US 101 45.3 miles to Lost Man Creek Road. Turn right and proceed either 0.1 mile to the intersection with Davison Trail (limited parking) or 0.8 mile to the Lost Man Creek Picnic Area with ample parking and restroom facilities. This option places you at the south end of the trail.

3) North End of Trail. Proceed north on US 101 47 miles to Exit 753 (Newton B. Drury Parkway) through Redwood National and State Parks. Turn left (0.2 mile) on the Parkway and proceed north for about 1.2 miles. Turn left on the access road to the Visitor Center and Campground (0.1 mile). Parking is available. This option places you at the north end of the trail.

The route: The trail is well signed. From the south end, if starting at the Lost Man Creek Picnic Area, walkers must follow the access road back to the beginning of the Davison Trail (0.8). The road crosses Lost Man Creek and Little Lost Man Creek under a green canopy. As in many places in these parks, you cannot help but admire the many shades of green represented in this landscape. Davison Road, which can be popular with cyclists, is paved en route to a crossing of US 101 (1.9). Shortly after crossing the highway the trail continues west over Prairie Creek and along an elk-viewing platform. The trail reaches the Elk Meadows Day Use Area (2.4) where it crosses Davison Road and parallels Prairie Creek for the next 2.5 miles (4.9). Turn right at the Wolf Creek Environmental Center access road crossing back over Prairie Creek. Davison Trail soon separates (5.1) and pushes north to Elk Prairie Campground and Prairie Creek Redwoods State Park Visitor Center (6.1).

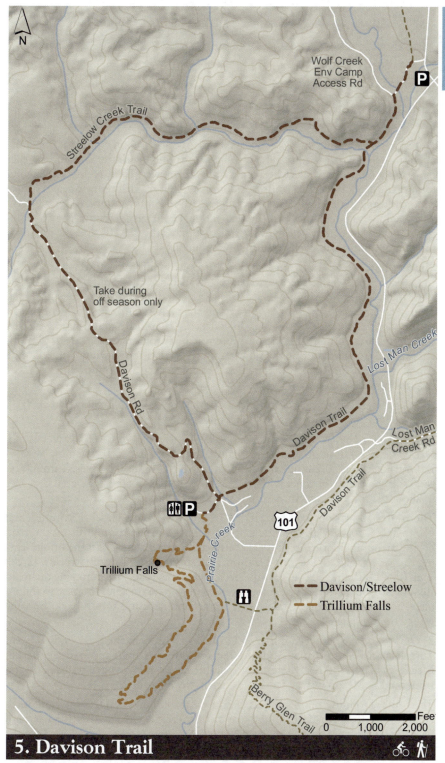

5. Davison Trail

5a Streelow Creek Trail

Length: 4.8 miles
Total ascent: 280 feet
Elevations: 250-390 feet
Type: out and back
Dogs: no
Restrooms: yes

Description: Most of this walk occurs on roads once used in commercial logging operations. The roads and trail tend to be well drained with durable surfaces that make for good winter walks when other trails are too wet. The Streelow Creek Trail follows the creek through a landscape dominated by an alder, redwood, and spruce canopy dotted beneath with massive old growth redwood stumps. The trails have been well maintained and gently graded and make for easy walking. The most significant drawbacks may be the traffic noise from nearby US 101 and the potential for greater numbers of cyclists during the summer.

The Streelow Creek Trail runs westwards from the middle of the Davison Trail to Davison Road. Since there is no parking available at either of its ends, this hike must include another trail/road at both its start and its end with Streelow Creek Trail in the middle. The shorter option is to start and to end on the Davison Trail and is good at any time of the year. In contrast, Davison Road during the heavily trafficked times of the year is too busy and too dusty to be part of a safe or pleasant alternative. However, during the slow season (late fall through winter) the 1.7 mile trip along Davison Road is preferable to back-tracking and can be incorporated into the off season loop.

Getting there: There are two trailhead options for walking Streelow Creek Trail. Approximate driving time for both, just under one hour.

1) *The Shorter Option.* Proceed north on US 101 47 miles to Exit 753 (Newton B. Drury Parkway) through Redwood National and State Parks. Turn left on Newton B. Drury Parkway (0.2 mile) and proceed north for about 0.2 miles. Turn left on the Wolf Creek Environmental Camp access road. The road is restricted by a gate in about 0.2 mile where a turnaround and limited parking exist. Park here.

The route (shown on map for Hike #5): From the Wolf Creek Environmental Camp access road, walk past the gate on the access road soon crossing the road bridge spanning Prairie Creek (0.2). Turn left a short distance past the bridge leaving the access road. Following Davison Trail south, turn right on Streelow Creek Trail (0.5). Initially the trail uses the bed of a logging road. After crossing the main stem of Streelow Creek (1.3), the trail becomes single track all the way to the intersection with Davison Road (2.4). Turn around here and return back the same way to the trailhead.

2) *Off-season Loop.* Proceed north on US 101 44.8 miles to the Davison Road exit. Turn left on Davison Road and proceed for a quarter mile and park at the Elk Meadows Day Use Area where there is ample parking. (The out-and-back option from the Elk Meadows Day Use Area is a lengthy 8.4 miles.)

The route: From the Elk Meadows Day Use Area, follow the Davison Trail north crossing Davison Road (0.2) and paralleling Prairie Creek. This road is hard packed and virtually flat the entire way to the Streelow Creek Trail (2.3). Turn left on Streelow Creek Trail as with shorter options. The trail uses the bed of a logging road, crosses the main stem of Streelow Creek (3.1), and continues as a single track all the way to the intersection with Davison Road (4.2). Turn left on Davison Road climbing steadily and continue until it descends and emerges out from under the trees (5.9). Turn right and proceed into the Elk Meadows Day Use Area (6.0).

5b · Trillium Falls Trail

Length: 3.1 miles
Total ascent: 400 feet
Elevations: 200-450 feet
Type: 90% loop

Access constraints: none
Dogs: no
Restrooms: yes

Description: It is amazing that just a stone's throw from Arcata Redwood Company's Mill B these old growth redwood groves would survive. Much of the credit must go to the efforts of the Save the Redwoods League. A number of the leaders and benefactors are memorialized on the plaques on this walk. This trail passes 10-foot Trillium Falls and spends more time in the forest before gradually dropping back toward the wetlands along Prairie Creek. These wetlands are one of the most dependable locations for viewing Roosevelt elk.

Getting there: Proceed north on US 101 44.8 miles to the Davison Road exit. Turn left on Davison Road and proceed for a quarter mile to the Elk Meadows Day Use Area. Ample parking is available at the trailhead. This option places you near the middle of the Davison Trail that links Elk Prairie and the State Park Visitor Center to the Lost Man Creek Picnic Area, a distance of almost 6 miles. Approximate driving time, 50 minutes.

As interpretative displays in the Elk Meadow Day Use Area illustrate, from 1948 until restoration in the 1990s this was the location of Arcata Redwood Company's Mill B and its massive 8-acre asphalt-covered log deck.

The route (shown on map for hike #5): From the Elk Meadow Day Use Area proceed south (right) on Davison Trail. Trillium Falls Trail departs to the right (0.2) and quickly switchbacks up the hillside and enters the redwoods. There are 19 named groves over the next several miles with plaques and a number of benches scattered along the route. The trail makes a bridge crossing some 100 feet from Trillium Falls (0.6), a 10-foot cascade distinctive not so much because of its size as the paucity of falls in these parks. The trail continues to climb before cresting (1.1). Then the trail undulates through more redwood groves before dropping back down to Davison Trail (2.8). Turn left on Davison Trail and follow it 0.3 mile to the Day Use Area (3.1). This trail has been linked with the Davison, Berry Glen, and Lady Bird Johnson Trails in *Volume 1* to create a more ambitious and lengthy hike.

Indian Pipe (Monotropa uniflora), photo by Nancy Spruance

6 · Fern Canyon

Length: 1.2 miles	bridges (generally June to September), it can be difficult to walk the canyon without getting wet feet.
Total ascent: 180 feet	
Elevations: 5-160 feet	
Type: 80% loop	
Fee: $8 per vehicle	**Dogs:** no
Access: Without the seasonal	**Restrooms:** yes

Description: Fern Canyon, with its winding, fern-covered walls stretching far above, is among the most popular attractions in the Park. The primeval setting has been used in the filming of *The Lost World: Jurassic Park*, BBC's *Walking with Dinosaurs* and IMAX's *Dinosaurs Alive*. It is an easy walk up through Home Creek with much to see; this has made it very popular for families.

Getting there: Proceed north on US 101 44.8 miles to the Davison Road exit. Turn left on Davison Road and proceed 6.9 miles to the parking area at the road's end. Davison Road can be dusty in the summer and slow going year round. Cross Squashan Creek just after the turn to the Gold Bluffs Beach Campgound which can require some care during periods of high water. Allow 75 minutes to reach the parking lot.

The route (no map for this hike): From the parking lot and picnic area, the trail proceeds north along the base of the bluff before descending to the floodplain of Home Creek (0.2). The trail turns east entering the mouth of the canyon following a well-trod path that crosses a series of plank bridges put in place as water flow permits. The canyon walls, blanketed by the delicate five-finger fern, become more dramatic. All too soon it is over (0.6) as the canyon broadens and the trail exits up the northern rim. At the intersection with the James Irvine Trail turn left (0.8 mile). Follow the trail through the spruce forest as it descends back down to a crossing of Home Creek (1.0) and returns to the trailhead (1.2).

∞ Roosevelt Elk

By 1860, the eastern elk had been completely eradicated and the slaughter in the West was quickly decimating elk populations, much as white man had dealt with the buffalo and the passenger pigeon. Teddy Roosevelt spearheaded a movement to protect the plummeting population of the western subspecies (later named Roosevelt elk in his honor) but by 1912, just over 100 elk were estimated to remain in Northern California. The creation of Prairie Creek Redwoods State Park in 1923 and subsequent efforts on the part of the Save the Redwoods League that resulted in the creation of the 1,600-acre Madison Grant Forest and Elk Refuge (see the plaque just off the Newton B. Drury Parkway in the middle of Elk Prairie) in 1948 were key to the preservation of this last remaining herd. Under the management and protection of Prairie Creek Redwoods State Park the population grew. Currently there are seven Roosevelt elk herds in Redwood National and State parks that can be seen in any number of locations from Elk Meadows to Big Lagoon to the Bald Hills to Gold Bluffs Beach (but, ironically, rarely in Elk Prairie). The largest band, some 250 animals, roams the Bald Hills. ∞

Extras. The California Coastal Trail extends along the foot of the Gold Bluffs both north and (using the beach) south. This is an easy way to add to the walk. Even more ambitious options are covered in *Volume 1* via Friendship Ridge or the James Irvine Trail. Gold Bluffs Beach is also open to equestrians.

7 · Lady Bird Johnson Grove

Length: 1.8 miles	accommodate wheelchairs using a brief, steep ramp from the parking lot.
Total ascent: 100 feet	
Elevations: 1,350-1,440 feet	
Type: 70% loop	**Dogs:** no
Access: The trail is hard-packed, broad, and well graded and can	**Restrooms**: yes

Description: This short walk through a magnificent stand of old-growth redwoods is one of the most popular trails in Redwood National and State Parks. It is a broad, well-graded nature trail without much elevation gain.

Getting there: Drive north on US 101 43.3 miles to Bald Hills Road. Turn right and follow Bald Hills Road for 2.5 miles to reach the parking lot and trailhead. The lot is just off the right side of the road. Approximate driving time, 55 minutes.

The route: From the parking lot, the trail begins by crossing a pedestrian bridge that spans Bald Hills Road. Shortly after crossing the bridge there is a box for the nature trail guides. When the trail splits (0.3), stay left and you will return via the other fork. The trail then reaches the site of the dedication of Redwood National Park in 1968 (0.6). Soon the Berry Glen Trail (see *Volume 1* for a more detailed description) forks to the left and begins its 3.5-mile descent to US 101 (0.8). The Lady Bird Johnson Grove trail continues back to the parking lot (1.5). Turn left to retrace your steps across the footbridge and reach the parking lot.

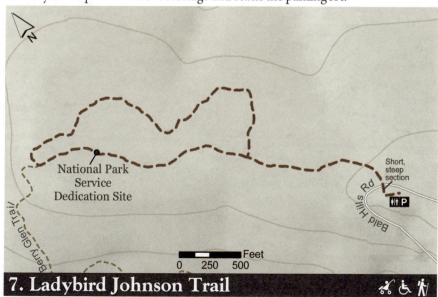

7. Ladybird Johnson Trail

8 · Tall Trees Grove

Length: 3.5 miles
Total ascent: 700 feet
Elevations: 180-840 feet
Type: 10% loop
Access: A free permit and gate combination must be obtained in person at the Thomas H. Kuchel Visitor Center (hours are 9am – 4pm in winter and 9am – 5pm the rest of the year). The number of permits is limited to 50 daily.
Dogs: no
Restrooms: yes

Description: Although accessible by the much longer Redwood Creek Trail and the Dolason Prairie/Emerald Ridge Trails, this relatively short walk offers the easiest way to reach the Tall Trees Grove. The trail drops steeply to Redwood Creek where it loops around an alluvial bench, home to this extensive redwood grove. There are spur trails to Redwood Creek and the Redwood Creek Trail.

Directions: Drive north on US 101 40.2 miles to the Kuchel Visitor Center to obtain a permit. Continue north on US 101 through Orick for 3 miles. Turn right and follow Bald Hills Road for 7 miles to the Tall Trees Access Road. Unlock the gate, and follow this sometimes dusty, sometimes muddy road for nearly six miles to the trailhead. Approximate driving time 1 hour and 45 minutes.

The route: The trail almost immediately reaches an intersection with the Emerald Ridge Trail. Continue on the Tall Trees Access Trail dropping steeply past several benches to the Tall Trees Grove Loop Trail (1.3). The loop trail meanders through the majestic stand of redwoods (2.2) before making the return trip back up to the parking lot (3.5). From the loop trail you can connect to the Redwood Creek Trail and find easy access to the creek itself.

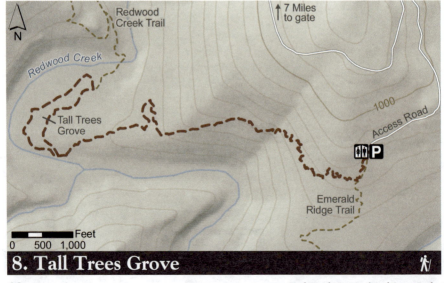

8. Tall Trees Grove

∞ A Brief History of Redwood National Park

Rohde and Rohde (1994) provide an excellent summary of the history of efforts to protect the redwoods. The story is tainted by greed and sullied by dishonesty, but has its heroes too. The idea of a redwood national park was first proposed in 1852 and again in 1879. Efforts continued sporadically over the ensuing decades with the sole success being Teddy Roosevelt's designation of Muir Woods as a national monument. It was really the creation of the Save the Redwoods League in 1918 by a group of prominent preservationists that elevated the possibility. Their purchases became a core component of the land included in the Humboldt Redwoods, Prairie Creek, Del Norte Coast, and Mill Creek/Smith River state parks. The elusive idea of a national park struggled to gain traction until it was revived in the early 1960s. In 1963, Secretary of the Interior Stuart Udall proposed a national park, and Congress considered legislation to do just that in 1966. North Coast timber companies and supporters were in strong opposition and it was not until October 2, 1968 that President Johnson signed the bills authorizing the creation of a 58,000-acre national park. The compromise legislation included considerable acreage already protected in the state parks and much of the land it did add had been cut over or was part of 'the worm', a narrow 8-mile strip along Redwood Creek that ended just upstream from the Tall Trees Grove. A decade after its creation, 48,000 acres were added to the park, much of it having been aggressively logged by timber companies since the park's establishment. Even then, the legislation had survived a firestorm of protest including a logging truck convoy that journeyed to Washington, D.C. Since that time, considerable money and effort have been expended on restoration of these lands and protection of the fragile ecosystem and the opposition to the park has dissipated. ∞

9. Lyons Ranch Loop

Length: 4.8miles	**Access:** The Bald Hills receive some snow in the winter at the higher elevations.
Total ascent: 800 feet	
Elevations: 2,150-2,600 feet	
Type: 80% loop	**Dogs:** no
	Restrooms: none

Description: This is a delightful hike through prairies and oak woodlands high in the Bald Hills, a long ridge separating the Redwood Creek and the Klamath River drainages. The hike ultimately reaches the barn and a few remaining buildings marking the century-long presence of Jonathan and Amelia Lyons and their descendents who, at one time, operated four ranches stretching across ten miles of these hills. The panoramic views across the Redwood Creek valley are magical. In the spring the prairies can be rich with wildflowers. In the summer, this walk offers a welcome escape from the cool fog of the coast. In the fall, you may, as I have, witness black bears nosing through the woodland understory in search of food.

Consider also the walk up to and around Schoolhouse Peak with its added views north. Schoolhouse Peak, overlooking Lyons Ranch and Redwood Valley, was named for Bald Hills School that had been built in 1876 by area sheep ranchers at the base of the modest peak. The deteriorated structure was burned in the 1950s because it was considered unsafe.

Getting there: Drive north on US 101 43.2 miles to Bald Hills Road. Turn right and follow Bald Hills Road for 16.8 miles (passing en route the turns to Lady Bird Johnson Grove, the Redwood Creek Overlook, the Tall Trees Grove access road, and the Dolason Prairie trailhead). Turn right at the signed Lyons Ranch trailhead road and continue 100 yards to the parking area. Approximate driving time, 1 hour and 32 minutes.

The route: The only route noted in the National Park signage at the trailhead

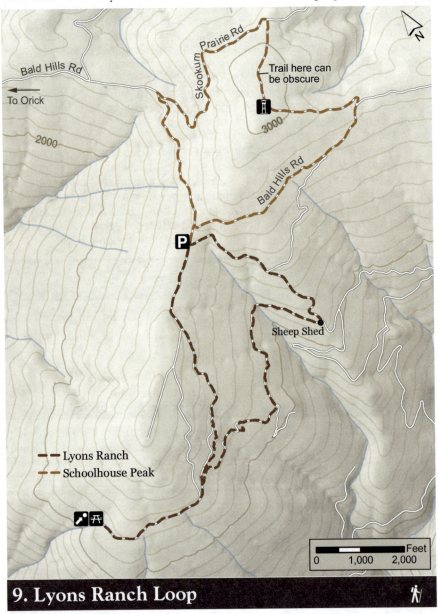

9. Lyons Ranch Loop

involves following the graveled Lyons Ranch access road for two miles to the remnants of the ranch. While that is a very pleasant out-and-back walk, I prefer the wonderful loop option detailed here that is about a mile longer.

Immediately on the south side of the gate restricting vehicular access to the trail, turn left and follow the road that drops steadily to a large metal-roofed structure (0.9), formerly used as a sheep shed. Here the road forks. Turn right following the road that passes between the shed and the rusting shell of an old trailer. This road contours through oak woodlands until it intersects with Lyons Ranch Road (2.4). Turn left and follow this road as it drops gently until reaching the old ranch site (3.0). The old Lyons Home Place barn is on the left and deteriorating bunkhouses are across a small draw. There is a shaded picnic table and a pleasant, grassy flat.

For the return trip, follow the gravel Lyons Ranch Road as it climbs back to the parking lot (4.8). There are several intersections with other roads (including the one you walked down) but the proper route is signed and obvious.

Schoolhouse Peak Lookout Option: From the Lyons Ranch parking area, walk further east on Bald Hills Road to the junction with the access road up to Schoolhouse Peak Fire Lookout (0.8). Turn left at the intersection with the fire lookout access road (1.1) The Lookout is up this road (1.5). It is possible to continue northeast from the fire lookout on an overgrown road that becomes more obvious as it begins to descend. Veer left at an intersection with a somewhat more established dirt road that quickly reaches the well-established Skookum Prairie Road (1.9). Turn left and follow the road as it skirts the wooded northwest side of Schoolhouse Peak intersecting with Bald Hills Road (2.8). By taking a left on Bald Hills Road, you return to the Lyons Ranch entrance road (3.4). Although my enthusiasm is dampened by the half of this route that uses Bald Hills Road, the views are dramatic and the walk is a nice alternative for those interested in a variation on the Lyons Ranch loop.

10·Redwood Creek Levee Walks

Length: 4.4 miles	water can make portions of this walk unsafe.
Total ascent: flat	
Elevations: 0-40 feet	**Dogs:** yes
Type: out and back	**Restrooms:** yes
Access: It is possible that high	

Description: The management of high water in Redwood Creek has been controversial and more changes may be made to the final miles of the watercourse. In the meantime, the levees on both the north and south sides of Redwood Creek offer a broad, level, and pleasant walk past pastures to the mouth of the river. Most of the year the only option is an out-and-back hike but during the low-flow summer and fall months when the mouth of Redwood Creek often closes, it is possible to pick your way around the mouth and make the trip a loop (for the adventurous). It is also possible to walk the north levee and return on adjacent Hufford Road.

Getting there: Drive north on US 101 42 miles to the bridge over Redwood Creek in Orick. Parking is readily available on the north side of the bridge either near the large redwood monument, in the small commercial center, or, if you plan to stop at the Palm Café, in front of that eatery. Approximate driving time, 45 minutes.

Nancy Spruance

The route: There is very little to differentiate the north and south levees of Redwood Creek. They both offer views of pastures, mountains, the backs of a few houses and businesses (more on the south side), and periodic visual and physical access to Redwood Creek. The north side does offer a road alternative (Hufford Road) and access to the beach north of the mouth of the creek. The south side offers access, although wading is often involved, to the Redwood Park Kuchel Visitor Center.

Out-and-back Options. Both levees are accessed from the US 101 bridge over Redwood Creek, though the north side is more cumbersome. They are both flat, gravel pathways, and 2.2 miles long one-way.

Loop with Wading Option. When the mouth of the creek is closed, the water of Redwood Creek backs up as water is unable to reach the ocean. The complexity of making the route a loop depends upon just how much water has ponded behind the sand dam. The higher the water the more you are forced into the driftwood on the north side of the estuary and the more daunting it is to wade the south side. From the Visitor Center, make your way northeast following the informal network of trails or cross-country to the oxbow channel (0.2). I have crossed when the chan-

ꕤ Redwood Creek Levees

During the great flood of 1964, the waters of Redwood Creek submerged nearly every home and business establishment in Orick. Residents were evacuated, much of nearby agricultural land was inundated, roads were damaged, and a layer of mud was deposited in buildings. In response, the Army Corps of Engineers excavated and enlarged the channel and created two earthen levees along the lower 3.4 miles of Redwood Creek. The highlight of the 1968 ceremony to christen the completed project was a mop parade to the mouth of Redwood Creek where participants tossed their well-used mops into a bonfire.

These flood control efforts have been devastating to the health of the estuary. The change in the natural movement of sediment has reduced the estuary volume by over half and fish habitat and water quality have been severely impaired. Additionally, no longer is there replenishment of fertile sediment onto the floodplain pastures. As a result, nearly half a century later, a number of public agencies and private landowners are involved in the Redwood Creek Estuary Restoration and Levee Rehabilitation Project.

The goal of this initiative is to find an acceptable balance between agricultural productivity, ecological restoration, and flood protection benefits. The vetting of design alternatives began in 2015. The options generally involve removing some of the westernmost sections of the existing levees, replacing some portion of those levees (but more broadly spread) and restoring some of the sloughs and meanders formerly part of the estuary. The project is still in the early stages. ꕤ

nel has been dry and in ankle deep and waist deep water. Aim generally toward a thicket of small trees. Once under the tree canopy there is minimal undergrowth making it relatively easy to walk to the south levee (0.5). If the water level is low, there may be some exposed beach to walk. It is important to understand that this segment does not have an established trail and good judgment should be exercised.

Loop with no wading option. For those who, like me, prefer to walk a loop and either the mouth is open or you are deterred by the thought of wading and route finding, it is possible to walk the north side levee and either return or begin on Hufford Road (1.8 miles between the west end of the levee and US 101). The west 0.5 mile of Hufford Road has a pleasant feel, ambling by aging barns.

10. Redwood Creek Levee Walks

11 · Freshwater Lagoon – Old State Highway

Length: 7.2 miles or shorter
Total ascent: 250 feet
Elevations: 50-290 feet
Type: out and back

Access constraints: none
Dogs: yes
Restrooms: no

Description: When US 101 was straightened and rerouted to the west side of Freshwater Lagoon, this three and a half mile stretch of highway was left to serve but a handful of houses. As a result, there is minimal traffic (I encountered one car in two hours of walking). The road offers a pleasant walk under the canopy of coastal forest with frequent views over Freshwater Lagoon to the open ocean. The walk lends itself to a car shuttle or key exchange to avoid the necessity of walking out and back the same route. This walk can be combined with a stop at Orick's "World Famous" Palm Café for a meal or just a piece of pie.

Getting there: Proceed north on US 101 37.9 miles to the signed intersection with US 101 and Old State Highway. Turn right onto the Old State Highway. The turn occurs shortly after US 101 crests following its climb from Stone Lagoon and is easy to overlook.

∞ The Old State Highway

For some 70 years, between the middle of the 1880s and the 1950s, the main route up and down the coast went around the east side of Freshwater Lagoon before dropping into Redwood Creek valley. Until 1919, the route trended even farther east than the current Old State Highway. Even though the state's engineers investigated the possibility of utilizing the sandspit as early as 1914, the cost of getting around Lookout Point at the north end of the spit was deemed prohibitive. However, in the years before World War II, the increased traffic, the steep grades, and the continuous succession of curves of the Old State Highway made it imperative to revisit this obstacle. By the mid-1950s, the current alignment of US 101 was complete.

Among the casualties of this final re-route was Conrad and 'Pinky' Zuber's Lookout Lunchroom. Located north of Lookout Point, the eatery provided patrons with a view of the ocean and, for 25 cents, an opportunity to drive their cars down a steep road to the beach below. However, motorists often found themselves "forced to engage the services of an old Dodge truck, conveniently operated by Mr. Zuber, to haul them up the grade." (Rohde and Rohde, 1994) ∞

Freshwater Lagoon before 1956 from the Boyle Collection, Humboldt State University Library

Parking exists on the north side of the road shortly after turning onto the Old State Highway and at a number of locations along the length of the road. The north end of Old State Highway intersects with US 101 just east of the entrance to the Humboldt County Transfer Station on the west of Orick. Approximate driving time, 45 minutes.

The route: If the route is hiked out and back, its length can easily be adjusted to fit the time and energy of the walker. The Lagoon Weekenders Club, a private fishing and recreational club, occupies some prime waterfront about a mile from the south end. About a mile from the north end is Lookout Point, once the site of the Lookout Lunchroom and a steep road down to the beach.

11. Freshwater Lagoon – Old State Highway

Region B:
Trinidad Area

The predominantly public lands of Region A give way to increasingly private ownership around California's second smallest incorporated city, Trinidad. Because of this, hikes in this region are all on or near the coast. In addition to popular walks in the Patrick's Point and Trinidad area, included in this section is a road walk along the old stagecoach road and azalea preserve above the north end of Big Lagoon, a walk around the south end of Big Lagoon, and a delightful low tide walk from Houda Point to Moonstone Beach.

These lagoons and the rocky headlands are some of the most distinctive features of the Humboldt County coastline. Although the North Coast lagoons constitute the largest lagoon system in the United States, they have been altered significantly by human intervention. Only Stone and Big Lagoons still experience the fluctuations in water level caused by the periodic breaching of the narrow sand spit that separates them from the ocean.

In addition to Humboldt Lagoons State Park, the dramatic coastline has been protected by public ownership of Patrick's Point, Elk and Trinidad Heads, and some of the beautiful beaches south of Trinidad. Trinidad serves as one of five gateways to the California Coastal National Monument, a designation that protects the reefs, rocky outcroppings, and small islands along the entire 1,100-mile length of California's coastline. For good reason, this area includes some of the most popular walks in Humboldt County.

Pewetole Island, photo by Ann Wallace

Region B: **Trinidad Area**

12 · Kane Road - Stagecoach Hill

Length: 0.5 mile loop around the Stagecoach Hill Azalea Nature Trail; Kane Road and Old Wagon Road is 6.0 miles (shorter options)
Total ascent: 600 feet
Elevations: 320-600 feet
Type: out and back or short loop
Dogs: only on road
Restrooms: no

Description: The 40-acre Stagecoach Hill Azalea Reserve is one of Humboldt County's hidden secrets. From late April to early June, this concentration of azaleas adorns a hillside already glorious because of its spectacular view of the Pacific Ocean. Although the trails aren't long enough for you to break a sweat, the much longer road walk option can be an excellent choice any time of the year although it is particularly nice when the skies are clear enough to enjoy the panoramas.

Kane Road, named for Federic and Belle Kane who owned a ranch in the area beginning in 1914, follows the route of the old stagecoach/wagon road that once passed around the east side of Big Lagoon. Owners of property near the south end of Kane Road have spread larger rock that makes for more difficult walking.

Getting there: Drive north on US 101 33.8 miles. Turn right on Kane Road and proceed uphill 0.5 mile to a T-junction. The left turn option, a gravel road, leads 0.5 mile to the small parking area for the Stagecoach Hill Azalea Nature Trail. The right turn, which is a continuation of Kane Road is paved for the first 0.15 mile. At 0.3 mile the road splits. Take the right fork and follow the single track unpaved road for 0.8 mile past the intersection. There is a small parking area just as Kane Road reaches the first panoramic view of Big Lagoon.

The route: The beginning of the Stagecoach Hill Azalea Nature Trail (0.5) is signed and starts just south of the dirt parking area. The short loop begins where the trail splits 100 yards from the start. The east side of the reserve is a Sitka spruce forest. The west side opens up into view-filled hillside abundant with azalea that bloom in late spring. Watch for Douglas iris during that same time period.

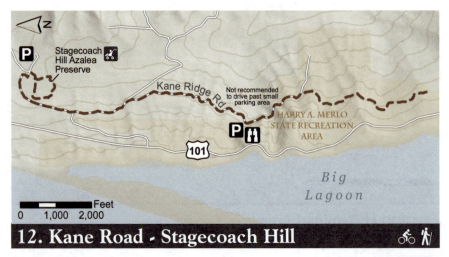

The Kane Road walk can be started from the Stagecoach Hill Azalea Nature Trail parking area (north end) or the small parking area near the gate (south end). From north to south, the unpaved road descends across a panoramic hillside to the intersection with the paved road as it climbs up from US 101 (0.5). Continue on south, staying on the contour, as the road is briefly paved but becomes gravel (0.65). The road soon splits (0.8) with the left branch climbing the hill and the right branch continuing on the same general contour. Stay right soon passing a home on the left. The road stays relatively level as it winds through a spruce and alder forest. The road crosses a short paved pad (1.5) and continues to an informal parking area (1.6). The views of Patrick's Point and Big Lagoon from the small parking area and just south are among the highlights of this walk (2.1). The public-access road continues crossing the edge of two private parcels before entering the Harry A. Merlo State Recreation Area (3.0). Here the road forks. The more established option climbs left to private property. The public right of way, which is much more overgrown, veers right along the power line. Although the views diminish, the walk is pleasant. During wet times, the road becomes much muddier as it descends toward Tom Creek.

13 · Big Lagoon to Patrick's Point

Length: options include 1 mile to 4.8 miles (shorter options too)
Total ascent: flat-300 feet
Elevations: 0-300 feet
Type: out and back or shorter loop

Access: $2 at Big Lagoon; $8 Patrick's Point
Dogs: not in state park
Restrooms: yes

Description: There are several ways to explore the Big Lagoon and Agate Beach area ranging from a short stroll to an extended beach walk. The Short Loop Option routes you through the Sitka spruce forest overarching the Big Lagoon County Park campground before circling back along the shoreline of Big Lagoon. The Agate Beach Option is an out-and-back walk along the beach from the county park and up to the turnaround point at the Agate Beach Overlook. The Agate Beach Car Shuttle Option is just a one-way walk beginning at the Overlook in Patrick's Point State Park. Although the car shuttle requires more logistical planning, it benefits from the 300-foot descent (versus climb) to Agate Beach. This beach is ideal for beachcombers and agate hunters. There are stretches of soft sand and tougher walking.

> ### ∞ Agates
> Agates are semi-precious gemstones that, for the diligent and the fortunate, are to be found on the aptly named Agate Beach. Their distinctive layered appearance occurs when an empty pocket in a host rock, generally ancient volcanic lava, fills in layer-by-layer with a silica-rich solution that forms agates' characteristic concentric bands. Silica is one of the most abundant materials on earth (most commonly found in nature as quartz). The colors and arrangement of agates are influenced by changes in pressure, temperature, and mineral content that occur during the formation process. Most of the agates found along the North Coast are milky, light-colored stones. ∞

Getting there: Drive north on US 101 29.5 miles. Turn left on Big Lagoon Park Road and proceed for 0.3 mile past Big Lagoon School. Take the next right turn after passing the school and follow that road (Big Lagoon Park Road) for 0.4 mile before veering left at a split in the road [with the right fork leading to the campground and the left fork leading to the Day Use parking and boat launch (0.1 mile)]. There is ample parking and a bathroom at this location. For the Car Shuttle Option you will also drive to Patrick's Point State Park (see Hike #14) and proceed to the Agate Beach Overlook parking lot after leaving a second car at the Big Lagoon County Park Day Use area. Approximate driving time to Big Lagoon County Park, 35 minutes.

13. Big Lagoon to Patrick's Point

The route: Short Loop Option. This short walk from the Big Lagoon County Park Boat Ramp parking lot begins by walking east out of the lot. It joins the Big Lagoon Park Road (0.1). Follow the Park Road through the campground (0.5). Turn left just past the restrooms for access to the shoreline. Unless the Lagoon is unusually high, it is possible to walk along the shoreline until the way is blocked by willows (0.7). At this point, the options are to retrace your steps or take one of the paths back into the campground to the Park Road and back (1.0).

Agate Beach Option. Walk southwest from the Big Lagoon County Park Boat Ramp/Day Use parking lot veering to the beach before reaching the first house (0.2). Walk south under the eroding bluffs that rise steeply above the beach (1.9). Be sure to look up to the top of the bluffs for evidence of homes that once enjoyed the magnificent cliff-edge views. This beach is subject to notorious undertow so it is very important to keep a watchful eye on the waves and an awareness of the tides. At the south end, it is possible to make the climb to the Agate Beach overlook, high above the beach below (2.4). The return trip involves retracing your steps unless you arrange for a key exchange or the car shuttle option.

Extras. It is easy to extend your hike south to the trails in Patrick's Point State Park or north along the lengthy sand spit between Big Lagoon and the ocean. There is also the opportunity to wander through the community of Big Lagoon with its collection of cabins, vacation cottages, and homes or venture up to Roundhouse Creek Road along the high bluffs above Agate Beach.

14 ·Patrick's Point

Length: 4.0 miles including a Wedding Rock side-trip	**Type:** loop
	Access : $8 per vehicle
Total ascent: 420 feet	**Dogs:** no
Elevations: 50-330 feet	**Restrooms:** yes

Description: Perched high above the ocean on 640 forested acres, Patrick's Point State Park offers ocean views, rocky headlands, a traditional Yurok village and native plant garden, access to Agate Beach, tide pools, and a network of trails. Although the hike described here is a simple loop circumnavigating most of the features of this compact park, many variations are possible (encouraged). In the summer the park can be quite crowded. In the winter, you may have the entire park virtually to yourself.

Getting there: Drive north on US 101 27.6 miles taking Exit 734 (Patrick's Point Drive). Turn left onto Patrick's Point Drive proceeding 0.5 mile to the park entrance. Turn right on the park access road to the entrance station (0.3 mile). Parking is available at a number of features throughout the park. If you intend to do the loop, it's easy to park in the lot just north of the entrance station near the Visitor Center. Approximate driving time, 35 minutes.

The route: It is worth a stop at the Visitor Center before you begin your walk. Proceed north from the trailhead several hundred feet east of the Visitor Center. On your left, immediately after beginning the trail, is a traditional hand-dug canoe. The trail splits with a right turn leading to the Sumeg Village and the native plant garden (0.1). The left option bypasses the Village continuing north to parking for the Red Alder Group Picnic area (0.3). From Red Alder it is possible to make a 0.2 mile detour and climb Ceremonial Rock, an old sea stack now much removed from the ocean. Trails from Ceremonial Rock cross the meadow in several directions allowing walkers to shorten their walk by cutting through the center of the park. My recommendation for loop walkers is to follow the road out of the parking area for Red Alder Group Picnic area, take a right at the stop sign and turn immediately left (signed for traffic as one-way the opposite direction). This road winds through the Agate Beach Campground to the overlook (0.7). From the overlook there is trail access to Agate Beach far below. Our loop route however, continues along the main campground road (stay right). A distinct but un-signed trail leads from the road north to the Rim Trail with a view out over the ocean, Agate Beach, and distant Big Lagoon (1.0). (If you miss this access, additional trails departing on the right from the road also connect with the Rim Trail.) From here the route

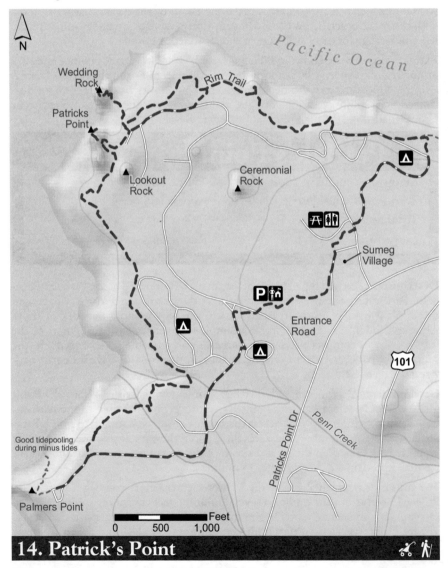

14. Patrick's Point

Sumêg Village. Photo by Michael Kauffmann

follows the Rim Trail as it hugs the forested lip of the Park high above the crashing waves below. The Rim Trail reaches the side trail to Wedding Rock (1.6), a must-see diversion (0.3 mile roundtrip). Wedding Rock offers a stunning view of this rugged coastline and a great spot for whale watching or just being hypnotized by the waves as they roll landward. Back on the Rim Trail a short walk further south is another short but worthy detour to Patrick's Point.

The Rim Trail continues to Palmers Point (2.9). The Rim Trail is quite vulnerable to erosion and the State Park is regularly faced with re-routing the trail further from the rim itself. Palmers Point offers trail access to a great tide pooling area during minus tides. The loop route from Palmers Point follows the park road past Abalone Campground and Penn Creek Group Campground to the Entrance Road (3.6). A brief right turn takes you to the Visitor Center (3.7).

∞ The Yuroks

Yurok means "downriver people" in the neighboring Karuk language, befitting since the historic land of the Yurok people stretched from the mouth of the Klamath River to Bluff Creek and down the coast south to Little River. Permanent settlements concentrated along rivers and lagoons with the largest being Rek-woi (Requa), a modest 25 houses. During the summers, the Yuroks would venture into the high country for hunting and gathering. However, the arrival of white settlers changed everything. By the end of the gold rush era it was estimated that three-quarters of the Yurok population had died from disease or massacre. The Lower Klamath River Indian Reservation, created in 1855, was considerably smaller than the ancestral territory. The federal land allotment system, predatory land acquisition, and inter-tribal land disputes further dismembered the integrity of Yurok territory. As a result, land issues have continued to more contemporary times. In 1988, the Hoopa-Yurok Settlement Act partitioned the reservation between the two tribes, creating a distinct Yurok Reservation and tribal government.

The Sumêg (the place name for the Patrick's Point area) Village is the re-creation of a seasonal Yurok encampment - consisting of traditional style family houses, a sweat house, changing houses, a redwood canoe, and a dance house. ∞

15 · Trinidad Area

Three popular short hikes in the Trinidad area can be walked individually or customized by taking elements of two or all three, much as Ken Burton has done in *Volume 1*. The shortest alternative descends to Old Home Beach from the Trinidad Lighthouse and returns via the Parker Creek Trail. The spectacular loop trail up Trinidad Head with its 360-degree view of this magnificent stretch of coastline is a well-known destination for locals. The extended walk from Trinidad State Beach to Elk Head with options to drop down to College Cove passes through spruce forest to this coastal headland. The most ambitious could easily spend an entire day wandering the trails and streets of the Trinidad area topped off with wine tasting, food, or a stop at the small but worthwhile Trinidad Museum.

Getting there: Drive north on US 101 22.2 miles to Exit 728 (Trinidad). Take a left on Westhaven Drive S./Main Street proceeding west underneath US 101 for 0.2 mile. For the Trinidad Head and Old Home Beach walks turn left on Trinity Street and proceed for 0.2 mile to the T-junction. Parking is available in several locations in this area. If you wish to drive all of the way to the Trinidad Head parking areas, turn right on Edwards Street (0.2 mile) and left on Lighthouse Road. Lighthouse Road descends steeply for 0.1 mile. Paved parking is available to the left and copious unpaved parking is straight ahead from the end of Lighthouse Road.

For the Elk Head walk, continue west on Main Street for 0.2 miles. At the T-junction, turn right on Stagecoach Road and take an immediate left on State Park Road. Proceed west 0.2 mile to the parking lot. And to park in the Elk Head parking lot, turn right on Patrick's Point Drive and proceed north for 0.5 mile. Turn left on Anderson Lane turning right on Stagecoach Road (0.3 mile). Continue on Stagecoach Road (0.2 mile) turning left into Elk Head parking lot (0.1 mile). ***Be careful not to leave valuables in your car as the Elk Head trailhead is notorious for vehicle break-ins.*** Approximate driving time for all options, 25 minutes.

Trinidad Lighthouse. Photo by Ann Wallace

15a · Trinidad Head

Length: 1.8 miles
Total ascent: 450 feet
Elevations: 10-330 feet
Type: 70% loop

Dogs: leashed
Restrooms: yes, near restaurant and parking lot

Description: Walking the Trinidad Head has long been one of Humboldt County's most popular short hikes. The views in every direction from the Head are stunning almost no matter what the weather. Although the initial climb up the Head is steep, it is short. There are several highly recommended ways to extend the walk including a walk out on the Trinidad pier, perhaps a visit to the Seascape restaurant adjacent to the pier, and a walk to the Memorial Lighthouse at the intersection of Trinity and Edwards Streets.

The route: From parking near the Trinidad Memorial Lighthouse, walk west on Edwards Street taking a left on Van Wycke Street that deteriorates to a narrow footpath after passing several houses. Stay on Van Wycke until reaching Galindo Street (0.2). Turn left at Galindo following a grassy footpath south. In a block, steps take you down to the edge of a boat ramp and associated parking lot. Cross the parking lot and proceed south next to the Seascape Restaurant to explore the pier. To reach the access to the Headlands, walk west through the parking lot (0.3). The trail around the Headlands can be started either on the paved road that leaves from the border of the paved and unpaved lots or by climbing the stairs at the south end of the unpaved parking lot. The only real decision that must be made comes at the top of the steep climb (0.5) on the paved road that serves as the trail and the access road to the functioning lighthouse on the south side of Trinidad Head. Do you go left and clockwise around the Head or straight (on the dirt trail) and counterclockwise around the Head (1.5)? The route has benches regularly spaced along the way and several spur trails with nice views. I recommend going counterclockwise in order to have the prevailing northwest winds at your back on the less protected side of the walk. From the end of your loop, return to your vehicle.

∞ Global Air Monitoring Station

At the top of Trinidad Head is an unremarkable collection of towers and buildings sheltered behind a phalanx of fences. It is one of only six global monitoring stations maintained by the National Oceanic and Atmospheric Administration to measure the baseline conditions of air quality. With others in remote locations like the top of the Greenland ice sheet, Barrow, Alaska, the top of Mauna Loa in Hawaii, and Antarctica, why Trinidad Head? Because Trinidad Head experiences prevailing winds off the ocean and there are no nearby population centers (especially to the west), it is perfectly suited for basal atmospheric measurements. The instruments sample the presence of aerosols, radiation, methane, hydrocarbons, and much more. These data help us assess climate change, atmospheric quality, and ozone depletion. ∞

Extras. Extend your return to the car if you are so inclined. If the tide allows, exit the Trinidad Head parking lot on the west side to reach Trinidad State beach and walk the beach northwards to the unmarked trail up to the Trinidad State Park parking area (you will encounter other trails on your way to the parking lot, stay right at the first two intersections and left at the third) and on east to Trinity Street. Turn right on Trinity Street to return to the Memorial Lighthouse. It is also possible to walk along Lighthouse Road as it climbs north from the unpaved parking lot, turning left on Ewing Street (past Humboldt State University's Telonicher Marine Lab), and continuing on the trail at the end of Ewing Street to the Trinidad State Park parking area (as above). And the third possibility is to walk out along the pier.

15b · Old Home Beach Loop

Length: 0.7-0.9 mile	Type: loop
Total ascent: 220 feet	Dogs: leashed
Elevations: 0-200 feet	Restrooms: no

Description: This is another short, pleasant walk in 'greater' Trinidad that can easily be combined with other walks in the area. It drops quickly to Old Home Beach and climbs back up Parker Creek Trail with two options for returning to the Memorial Lighthouse with its commanding views of Trinidad harbor and the coastline south to distant Cape Mendocino.

The route: From the Memorial Lighthouse just below the intersection of Trinity and Edwards Street a path (Axel Lindgren Memorial Trail) drops steeply down (0.1) to Old Home Beach (also known as Indian Beach). The final six or seven steps are eroded and caution must be used. The Parker Creek Trail, east (left) along the beach (0.3), climbs up crossing Groth Lane and continuing (0.4) to an intersection with a left and right trail option. The left turn option (no dogs are allowed) climbs on the south side of the homes lining Wagner Street eventually reaching Wagner through a non-descript easement. For this reason, it is easier to walk this trail in this direction rather than beginning on Wagner and then trying to locate the trail's entrance. Turn left on Wagner and left again on Edwards following it back to the Memorial Lighthouse (0.7). The right turn option soon connects with Parker Street. Follow Parker Street to View Street (0.7). Turn left on View and right on East and left on Ocean Avenue (0.8). Turn a final right on Edwards returning to the Memorial Lighthouse (0.9).

15c · Elk Head

Length: 1.3-3.1 miles	Type: partial loop
Total ascent: variable	Dogs: leashed
Elevations: 20-260 feet	Restrooms: yes

Description: The 159 acres of Trinidad State Beach are spread over a marine terrace cloaked in beach pine and Sitka spruce split by Mill Creek. With easy side trips to Trinidad State Beach and College Cove, the longer options of this hike involve crossing Mill Creek and climbing to the Elk Head trail. The popular Elk

Head trail offers wonderful views of Pewetole Island, College Cove, and Trinidad Head to the south and rugged, windswept coastline to the north. If you park near the Trinidad Library and Museum, you can also include a quick stroll around Saunders Park and the native plant garden before heading toward Elk Head.

The route: From the Trinidad State Beach parking lot, descend past the restroom and connect with the trail that contours above the south side of Mill Creek. As the trail approaches the beach (0.2), it splits with the left fork continuing to the beach and the right fork turning abruptly back east routed lower along Mill Creek. The trail crosses a railed bridge and angles left and west (0.3). The undulating trail

15. Trinidad Area

Whale on slip by Little Head (near current pier), Trinidad, 1920s. Photo from the Boyle Collection, Humboldt State University Library.

travels through a largely Sitka spruce forest to the Elk Head parking lot (0.9). Several unmarked braids to the trail including some options that lead to College Cove or out to Stagecoach Road can cause confusion. In general, trails dropping down to the left are headed to College Cove.

The trail on to Elk Head begins at the west end of the parking lot. As it proceeds west it passes a trail down to College Cove and its sheltered beach and a number of overlooks with panoramic views of College Cove, Pewetole Island, and Trinidad Head. The trail emerges from the trees to the windswept west end of Elk Head (1.4) and continues on to Megwil Point (1.6) with its views north. On the return, there is an alternative path that splits to the left shortly after passing the wooden portal. This path soon rejoins the main trail (1.8). I always take this option as I love the dense canopy and the dark, ethereal atmosphere it creates. From this

∞ Whaling in Trinidad

For about six years, beginning in September 1920, the California Sea Food Products Company operated a whaling station in Trinidad. Some sources reported that 800 whales, mostly humpbacks, were processed in just two of those seasons. Whaling during this time was done using powerful steamers armed with 150-pound harpoons attached to a six-inch manila line 2,000 feet in length. When the harpoon struck the whale, a bomb on the end exploded opening four claws that would anchor the harpoon in the whale. If not killed immediately, the animal had to be "played" gradually, exhausting the whale until it could brought aside the steamer.

Air would be pumped into the whale carcass to make it float until it could be towed to the whaling station for processing. According to Andrew Genzoli, there "it was stripped of all meat which was cut in small pieces and cooked 12 to 16 hours. Then it was dried and ground into chicken feed. The bones were cooked and ground into fertilizer and bone meal. Even the blood was dried and converted into fertilizer. The whale's tail was always cut, sliced and shipped to Japan, where it was welcomed as a delicacy." The smell from this process was intense and one of the reasons that processing was eventually moved to factory ships where no deodorizer was necessary and refuse could be disposed of overboard.

Soon the whaling station was closed. The last remaining building from the station was razed in 1961. ∞

point, the return trip follows the same route back (3.1).

Extras. Consider taking the short walk to Saunders Park, home to the small but worthwhile Trinidad Museum and native plant garden. Follow Main Street east toward US 101 (west of the Chevron Station and across the street from Murphy's Market and the Trinidad Shopping Center). The Museum is open 12:30 – 4 pm, Wednesday – Sunday. Parking is available.

16 · Houda Point to Moonstone Beach

Length: 2.0 miles
Total ascent: 0-150 feet
Elevations: 20-260 feet
Type: loop
Dogs: leashed
Restrooms: yes

Description: This is a very special walk that combines some spectacular coastline with tide pools, sandy beaches, and interesting coastal features. It is only possible to walk this loop during very low (ideally minus) tides so keep an eye on your tide chart for opportunities to take this delightful walk. I typically park at the Camel Rock/Houda Point parking area in case the route is inaccessible for some reason that requires turning back. The area around Houda Point and Houda Cove is more interesting and less crowded than Moonstone Beach. However, parking and beginning at Moonstone Beach works equally well and much better if someone in the party is unsure on their feet.

Getting there: Drive north on US 101 19.5 miles taking Exit 726A (Westhaven Drive) after crossing Little River. At the intersection with Westhaven Drive South (0.1 mile), turn left proceeding under the 101 overpass. At the intersection with Scenic Drive, turn right and proceed 0.5 mile to the Camel Rock/Houda Point parking area. Approximate driving time, 22 minutes.

Exceptional tide pooling on Hike #16. Photo by Ann Wallace.

The route: From the parking area at Camel Rock/Houda Point in front of the big chain, the trail drops to a narrow ridge using a series of steps. The first option encountered is a trail that drops steeply off to the right in a series of steps that eventually ends at the broad, flat Luffenholtz Beach South. The second option encountered is a trail that drops steeply off to the left to Houda Cove on the south side of the Point. The current solution – stairs using cabled together wooden steps – appears to be functioning effectively although, over the years, this route has proven particularly vulnerable to erosion. The third option is to continue straight which provides access to several benches and views from the top of Houda Point but also continues to the west edge of the Point requiring a scramble to reach the beach. This is more safely done coming up from the beach but is unmarked and the route is ambiguous. All three get you to the beach.

During minus tides of the late spring, summer and fall, it is generally possible to

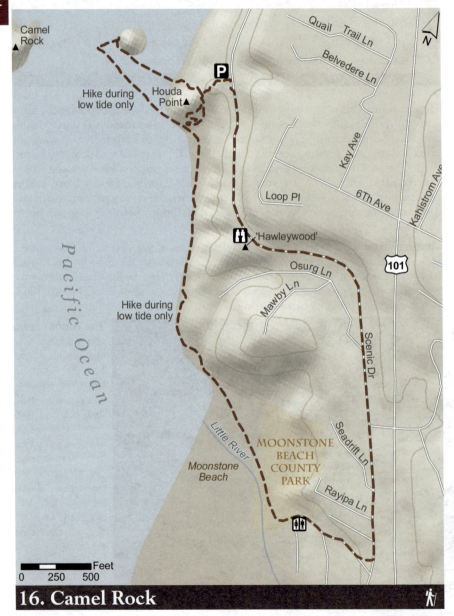

16. Camel Rock

venture to the shallows that stretch to Camel Rock (aka Little River Rock, 0.3). This area along the west side of the massive sea stack that anchors the beach often offers good tide pooling opportunities and, depending upon sand erosion, allows for walking into a cave on that side. Once exploring this area is complete, walk south along the beach or at the base of the bluffs rising 150 feet above the beach. You reach Pilot Point (just past the private home located on a rocky bench above the beach) where you turn left (0.9) and walk across Moonstone Beach to the parking lot for the County Park (1.1). Depending upon the current location of the mouth of Little River, you may have to remove your shoes and wade. There have been a few times in nearly 30 years of walking this route when beach erosion has left a more daunting chasm. In the unlikely event that has happened, you will need to return to Houda Point. Otherwise, from the parking lot, the access road climbs steeply back to Scenic Drive (1.2). Turn left and carefully follow Scenic Drive back to the Camel Rock/Houda Point parking area (2.0).

It is worth noting that as Scenic Drive leaves the trees and returns to the coastal bluffs, the vantage point now occupied by a home with a large paved pullout was once the location of 'Hawleywood'. This was a view-endowed tourist trap dating from that era when Scenic Drive was US 101.

∞ The Seasonal Cycle of Beach Sand Erosion and Deposition

Significant amounts of sand come and go on area beaches seasonally. Winter patterns tend to erode beaches. The higher waves, shorter wave periods, and shorter wavelengths move sand onto offshore bars where it is stored until the following summer. Major winter storms exacerbate this pattern. In the summer, the low wave heights, and long periods and wavelengths move the sand onshore re-building the broad sandy terrace. Offshore bars diminish, the foreshore becomes steeper, and the beaches larger.

If sand supplies change, this can result in permanent beach erosion. The construction of any new dams on the Klamath, Mad, or Eel River would further reduce the quantity of sand. The addition of jetties or breakwaters affects sand movement and availability. Climatic events like El Niño cause sea level rise for extended periods and more frequent and intense storms result in beach loss. Winter storms in the El Niño years of 1982-1983 and 1997-1998, in particular, caused severe beach erosion along California's shoreline.

As a result, from season-to-season and year-to-year, Moonstone and Luffenholtz beaches can look very different. Rocks once exposed are covered. Rocks once covered are now exposed. Camel Rock may be connected with the mainland by a sandy spit or it could require rubber boots to make the crossing in low tide. ∞

Extras. From the Camel Rock/Houda Point parking lot, continue north on foot or by car 0.3 mile to Luffenholtz Beach County Park. The first left turn opportunity enters a small parking area with a closed restroom, a picnic table, and a short trail out to a dramatic headland. Just beyond this attraction is an area where the roadway regularly subsides. Once across that dip is a pullout and the beach access for Luffenholtz Beach North, another very pleasant pocket beach.

CAUTIONARY NOTE: Petty theft has become increasingly common in this area. Do not leave valuables visible in your car. Many regulars have even chosen to leave their car unlocked so that they don't end up with a broken window.

Region C:
Urban Corridor – Arcata North

Arcata, McKinleyville, and the Samoa Peninsula offer a rich array of trails complemented by some surprisingly pleasant urban and road walking opportunities. In addition, several new trails are in the planning stages, such as the McKinleyville Community Services District efforts to extend the Mid-Town Trail or formalize the existing social trail that follows the Mad River south from the end of Ocean Drive. Soon the Arcata Ridge Trail will link West End Road with Sunny Brae and the Bay Trail will forge on south along the North Coast Railroad Authority right-of-way. And Manila has been funded for a multi-modal path along the north side of CA 255. These are all exciting developments.

The bay and beaches, dunes and marshes, bottomlands, and redwood forests make for a variety of settings for the many walking options in this Urban Corridor. While the beloved Hammond Trail, the Ma-le'l Dunes, the Arcata Community Forest, and Arcata Marsh are the most widely known walking resources, many other possibilities exist. A spring walk among the blossoms of Azalea Park Natural Reserve or an evening on the grounds of Potawot Village or a weekend stroll through the beautiful Humboldt State University campus are unique resources rarely considered. Enjoy the recently completed South Fork Janes Creek Loop or the surprisingly strenuous Beith Creek Loop.

Ann Wallace

Region C: **Arcata North**

17 · McKinleyville Mid-Town Trail Loop

Length: 2.8 miles
Total ascent: flat
Elevations: 90-140 feet

Type: loop
Dogs: leashed
Restrooms: yes

Description: This rather unspectacular urban loop begins at Pierson Park in McKinleyville, passes the World's Tallest Totem Pole in the McKinleyville Shopping Center, and includes the Mid-Town Trail. Most of the route meanders through residential McKinleyville.

Getting there: Take Exit 718 (Central Avenue) 11 miles north on US 101. Pro-

ceed north to either Gwin or Pickett Road (2.0 miles), turning right (east) to Pierson Park, approximately 0.2 mile. Parking is available at Pierson Park. Approximate driving time, 20 minutes.

The Route: The route will be described clockwise. Walk west through Pierson Park or on Gwin Road to the crossing light on Central Avenue (0.2). Proceed west on City Center Road taking a left at the World's Tallest Totem Pole (0.3) to Hiller Road (0.4). Although Hiller Road does not have a sidewalk, a substantial shoulder makes the walk relatively pleasant as you walk west to McKinleyville Avenue (0.8). Turn right on McKinleyville Avenue. Follow the sidewalk on the west side until Railroad Avenue (after which there are sidewalks on both sides of McKinleyville Avenue) and proceed to Parkside Drive (1.5). Turn right (east) on Parkside Drive. The Mid-Town Trail begins at the east end of Parkside Drive (1.7). Note an obvious spur trail on the left (north) side of Parkside that begins with a couple of steps down and soon crosses Widow White Creek on a footbridge and winds its way to McKinleyville High School. The Mid-Town Trail generally follows a right-of-way between housing developments that limits its aesthetic appeal. At Railroad Avenue (2.2), turn left (east) and proceed to Central Avenue (2.5). Turn right on Central and then left (east) on Pickett (2.7) crossing Pierson Park to the parking lot (2.8).

Extras: An additional 0.6 mile can be added to this loop by continuing west a further 0.3 mile to Thiel Avenue. Thiel parallels but has less traffic than McKinleyville Avenue and offers several right (east) turns back to McKinleyville Avenue with Adkins Road being the final option. In all cases turn left once you reach McKinleyville Avenue to resume the original route.

18 · Hammond Trail

Length: 2.8 miles (longer options)
Total ascent: 250 feet
Elevations: 10-100 feet
Type: out and back
Dogs: leashed
Restrooms: yes

Description: This multi-use trail has the distinction of being Humboldt County's most popular and for good reason. It is convenient, well-maintained, and offers views of Clam Beach and the Mad River. It includes a picturesque crossing of the Widow White Creek along a short interpretive segment and offers a variety of points of access. This portion of the California Coastal Trail follows much of the railroad right-of-way used by the Hammond Lumber Company to transport logs to its Samoa mill until 1961.

Getting there: There are innumerable points of access for the trail with five primary options: Clam Beach County Park just north of Strawberry Creek at the north end of the trail, Letz Avenue north of the intersection of Airport Road and Letz Avenue, at the west end of Murray Road, at Hiller Park, and on the south side of the Hammond bridge on Mad River Road. Each has parking available.

Full-length Option: This option is a one-way hike that utilizes a car shuttle. Leave the car at the northern trailhead and begin the hike at the southern trailhead. Getting to the northern trailhead involves driving north on US 101 for 16.9 miles to Exit 723 (Central Avenue). Turn left at the stop sign at the bottom of the off-ramp and proceed under US 101 for 0.1 mile. To reach the southern trailhead, drive 9.9 miles north on US 101 taking Exit 716B (Giuntoli Lane). At the end of the off-ramp, take the third exit from the roundabout (Giuntoli Lane) heading west back over the freeway. Turn right on Heindon Road (0.3) and left on Miller Lane. In 0.8 mile turn right on Mad River Road and remain on Mad River Road as it bends through the Bottoms for the next 1.7 miles. Watch for the Mad River bridge and a parking area just to the right of the ramp up to the bridge. Approximate driving time, 20 – 25 minutes.

The Recommended Shorter Option: This option begins and ends at Hiller Park which can be reached by driving US 101 north for 11 miles taking Exit 718 (Central Avenue) just as you cross the Mad River bridge. Continue north for 1.8 miles to Hiller Road. Turn left onto Hiller Road and continue west for 1.0 mile. Turn right on Fischer Road into the Hiller Park complex.

The Full Route: The trail immediately climbs to the crossing of the Mad River with views of this normally languid river. The trail joins Fischer Road (0.1) which it follows up above the flood plain of the Mad River to a junction with School Road (0.7). Rogers Market, at this corner, offers the one trailside opportunity to purchase refreshments. Take care crossing School and Hiller Roads as they tend to carry a higher volume of traffic. Hiller Park (1.4) is a point of access for the Mad River Bluffs trail network. The trail continues north (passing one more point of access to the Mad River Bluffs trails just before crossing a small bridge about 0.1 north of Hiller Park) through a tunnel of overhanging trees to Knox Cove (1.9) and the Murray Road access trail (2.1). From here there are two alternatives which later rejoin. A paved trail departs to the right and the unpaved trail, continues straight hugging the bluffs above the Mad River until it reaches a T-junction (the left turn here quickly drops to the Mad River). Turn right and follow the trail east as switchbacks up and reaches an informational kiosk and stile. Pass through the stile (horses and cyclists are prohibited and should use the paved alternative) and descend the stairs to the bridged crossing of Widow White Creek and on to the reunion with the paved option. The paved alternative reaches and then follows Murray Road to

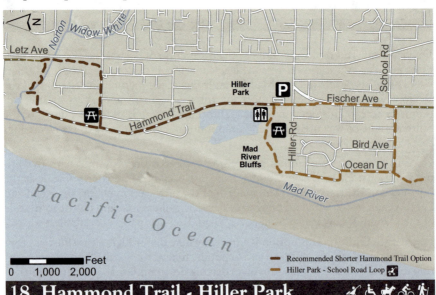

∞ Eureka and Klamath River Railroad

Originally operated as the Eureka & Klamath River Railroad, the assets were included with Andrew Hammond's purchase of the John Vance Mill and Lumber Company in 1900. The railroad, with spurs sprinkled throughout the fecund timberland from Big Lagoon soouth to Little River, was routed along Clam Beach and much of the current route of the Hammond Trail to the bridged crossing of the Mad River. It then angled across the Arcata Bottoms to an intersection with lines from the east and south. In 1945, a devastating forest fire destroyed twenty-three railroad bridges. Instead of repairing the railroad north of Crannell (Little River), Hammond concentrated on road construction and the use of trucks. In 1961, Georgia-Pacific (who had purchased Hammond in 1956) discontinued the use of trains to haul logs from Crannell to its Samoa mill. The track from Crannell to Fishers Siding (near the intersection with School Road) was dismantled in the summer of 1963, and the track from Samoa to Fishers Siding was disassembled in the spring of 1966. ∞

a signed junction with the trail's continuation north (adjacent to US 101) and thereby to the reunion.

From the junction of the two braids of the Hammond Trail, continue north along Letz Avenue past a gate and the intersection with Airport Road to the Letz Avenue trailhead (3.8). The trail again becomes single track as it enters a grove of cypress and bends west around the Clam Beach Overlook (not accessible from the trail) with its unrestricted views to the north (4.1). The trail descends to join the vegetation-covered dunes and parallels the highway to its bridged crossing of Strawberry Creek and its northern terminus (5.4).

18a · Hiller Park – School Road Loop

Length: 2.0 miles	**Type:** loop
Total ascent: flat	**Dogs:** leashed
Elevations: 5-80 feet	**Restrooms:** yes

Description: This pleasant loop begins at Hiller Park in McKinleyville, passes through the dog park and along the short Baduwat Trail. The route continues on Ocean Drive, the least satisfying portion of the walk as views to the west are limited by hedges and houses of the private landowners. Once the route reaches School Road, the panorama includes the Mad River and the bucolic pastures to the south. An optional spur extends to the river. The last 0.6 mile follows the Hammond Trail back to Hiller Park.

Getting there (map shared with Hike #18): See directions to Hiller Park in Hammond Trail description.

The Route: The route will be described counter-clockwise. Proceed from the parking lot west past the playground and small arboretum. Veer left (0.2) on the single track trail entering the Mad River Bluff trail system and continue to the Ocean Drive entrance to the Mad River Bluff trails on the Baduwat Trail (0.4). Walk through the parking area and south on Ocean Drive to the intersection with School Road (1.1). Turn left (east) on the paved walkway adjacent to School Road and walk to the intersection with Fischer Road (1.4). Rogers Market offers a convenient refreshment stop. Follow the Hammond Trail (note the entrance on the northeast corner of the intersection of Fischer and School Roads) north to Hiller Park (2.0).

Extras. The network of trails in Hiller Park and the Mad River Bluff trail system **offer** any number of ways to extend this loop. See also the separate entry for the Hammond Trail. In addition, at the corner of Ocean and School Road there is a trail down to the Mad River that follows the river southeast. The first 0.2 is well drained and reasonably maintained. After that the network of social trails can be muddy, overgrown and ambiguous as they parallel the Mad River (often leading to the river's edge). During drier times it is possible to follow the trail until it rounds a cluster of small oxidation ponds (mostly drained) fenced and owned by the McKinleyville Community Services District (0.6) and connects with the service road. At this time, the service road is not open to the public. The Community Services District has future plans to formalize the trail to these obsolete ponds.

19 · Chah-GAH-Cho Trail

Length: 0.8 mile	**Type:** loop
Total ascent: flat	**Dogs:** yes
Elevations: 190 feet	**Restrooms:** no

Description: Completed in 2016 by the McKinleyville Land Trust, these short trails loop around a 9.5-acre parcel south of Kmart with views over the Mad River Bottoms. With its hard-packed trails that meet the State Park Access Guidelines, this is a convenient location for an evening stroll any time of the year and an ideal vantage point for late fall and winter sunsets.

Getting there: Take US 101 12.6 miles north to Exit 719 (School Road). Turn right on School Road and continue east for 0.4 mile to Betty Court (just west of Mill Creek Cinema). Turn right on Betty Court and proceed to the south end of the road (0.1). Find abundant parking in the adjacent parking lot. Approximate driving time, 15 minutes.

The route: There are three entry points to Chah-GAH-Cho: at the end of Betty Court, at the southeastern corner of the adjacent parking lot, and southwest of Healthsport. The two loops, through the prairie and the woods, are each roughly .4 mile long. No map is provided for this simple walk.

View of the Arcata Bottoms from the Chah-GAH-Cho, photo by Amy Uyeki.

20 · Azalea Park Natural Reserve

Length: 1.0 mile	Type: loop
Total ascent: 280 feet	Dogs: yes
Elevations: 150 feet	Restrooms: no

Description: This short figure 8 hike is particularly stunning when the azaleas are in bloom (late April through early June). The convenient access from Arcata and McKinleyville and the varied terrain of the Reserve make it ideal for a quick evening stroll. The single-track trail weaves through inviting stands of coastal spruce, crosses several seasonal streams, and the azaleas. Although the steps on the east side loop suffer from deferred maintenance, the overall walk is very enjoyable.

Getting there: Take US 101 11 miles north to Exit 718 (Central Avenue) to McKinleyville (just as you cross the Mad River). Take the right fork and turn right on North Bank Road. In 0.8 mile, turn left on Azalea Avenue. In 0.2 mile, turn left into the parking lot. Approximate driving time, 15 minutes.

The route (no map): From the west side of the parking lot, several obvious trails begin. Since it is a loop (of just 0.4), each option works. The east side loop trail (longer at 0.6) involves crossing Azalea Avenue to reach the trail entrance.

∞ Rhododendrons & Azaleas

The forests, gardens, and landscapes of Humboldt County are adorned with azaleas and rhododendrons. Their delicate pinks, translucent oranges, rich whites, and gentle reds have become North Coast icons. But, what is the difference between azaleas and rhododendron?

When the Swedish naturalist Linnaeus established the genus, *Rhododendron*, in 1753, Azaleas were placed in a separate genus. However, in 1834 Linnaeus' taxonomy was corrected with the genus *Rhododendron* being broken into eight sub-categories of which two were azaleas (evergreen azalea bushes and deciduous azalea bushes). So, all azaleas are rhododendrons but not all rhododendrons are azaleas.

In general, rhododendrons are larger than are azaleas, and they tend to have larger leaves. Azalea flowers generally have five stamens, while the rhododendron flowers have ten stamens. Unlike rhododendrons, azaleas are often deciduous. ∞

Western Azalea

Pacific Rhododendron

21 · Mad River/Arcata Bottoms

Length: many options
Total ascent: flat
Elevations: 5-20 feet
Type: loop
Dogs: yes
Restrooms: no

Description: All walks in the Arcata Bottoms are flat, through active agricultural land on minimally travelled roads. They can be windy. You can easily design your route according to the time you have available. Notable features on the north side of the Bottoms include the Mad River, Tyee City, and Mad River Beach. However, it is more difficult to create a satisfying loop route in this direction and Mad River Road tends to have the most traffic in the Bottoms.

The routes referred to as **Arcata Bottoms South** and **Arcata Bottoms Center** both start from the parking lot near St. Mary's Church and School (or street parking far-

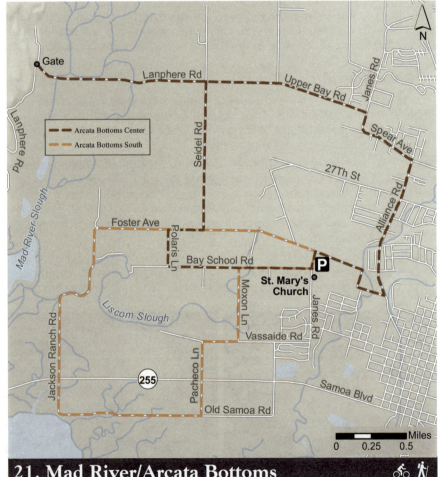

21. Mad River/Arcata Bottoms

ther south along Janes Road). The Arcata Bottoms Center route includes an optional out-and-back trip over the Lanphere Bridge that spans Mad River Slough and returns via Alliance Road in Arcata. The Arcata Bottoms South

Marbled godwits, photo by Riley Quarles

route heads west to Liscom Slough, an arm of Mad River Slough, where Jackson Ranch Road bends south and crosses CA 255. The route continues east on the Old Samoa Road, passing some old barns and pastures used extensively by Aleutian Geese, before turning back toward St. Mary's.

Getting there: Drive 7 miles north on US 101 taking Exit 714B (CA 255/Samoa Boulevard) west from Arcata (1.3 miles) to 'V' Street. Turn north on 'V', right on Vaissade at the T-junction (0.3 mile), and left on Janes Road (0.2 mile). St. Mary's Church will be on the right in 0.5 mile. Be sensitive to high use times at the St. Mary's Church and Elementary School. Approximate driving time, 16 minutes.

The Route: Arcata Bottoms Center – walk west on Bay School Road (1.0). Although this parallels Foster Avenue, Foster tends to have more vehicular traffic so Bay School Road is preferred. Turn right on Polaris Lane (1.2) to Foster Avenue. Turn right on Foster to Seidel Road (1.4). Left on Seidel (2.4) to Lanphere Road. For those interested in a longer walk, turn left on Lanphere Road and follow it 1.2 miles (one-way) to a bridge spanning Mad River Slough and on to the gated entrance to Lanphere Dunes (permit required for access). Return to the intersection with Seidel and rejoin the loop route. The shorter loop route turns right (from Seidel Road) onto Lanphere Road which becomes Upper Bay Road. Follow Lanphere/Upper Bay Road 1.2 miles to Janes Road (3.6) -- yes, different road but same name as the road that is home to St. Mary's Church. Turn right on Janes. As Janes turns left (east), it becomes Spear Avenue. Turn right on Alliance Road (4.1). Follow Alliance Road to Foster Avenue (5.1). Turn right on Foster and follow it to the original Janes Road (5.8). The Church is south on Janes (5.9).

Additional Options: I personally like to minimize my time on Foster Avenue and turn left on 'Q' Street for the home stretch. Turn right on Zehndner Avenue and right on Janes. It is just slightly farther than continuing on Foster to Janes and has the benefit of sidewalks.

The Route: Arcata Bottoms South – walk west on Bay School Road (1.0). Turn right on Polaris Lane (1.2.) to Foster Avenue. Turn left on Foster. It eventually becomes Jackson Ranch Road. The bucolic Jackson Ranch Road crosses CA 255 (2.9) and continues south and then east passing several decaying barns that are now part of the Mad River Slough and Wildlife Area. Turn left on Pacheco Lane (4.2). Pacheco is a mostly gravel road that re-crosses CA 255 (4.4) and continues on north to an intersection with Vassaide Road (4.7) which is also gravel. Turn left on Moxon Road (5.0) which intersects with Bay School Road (5.5). Turn right and follow it to Janes Road and St. Mary's Church (6.0).

22 · Potawot Health Village

Length: up to 2 miles
Total ascent: flat
Elevations: 40-60 feet
Type: loop
Dogs: no
Restrooms: no

Description: I have been walking on the Potawot Health Village network of paved and unpaved trails for years. The natural and very intentional landscaping has matured into something quite special. A sinuous series of wetlands have been created, native grasses and other plants reintroduced, and an extensive food garden and orchard established. While none of the trails are particularly long, they can be combined for a pleasant walk. By parking on Janes Road or in the Mad River Hospital parking lot and walking on the marked shoulder of the entrance parkway into Potawot the walk can be extended. A self-guided nature tour is available with numbered stops on the trails. Seating and a picnic table are spaced around the grounds.

Getting there: Drive 10 miles north on US 101 and take Exit 716B (Giuntoli exit),

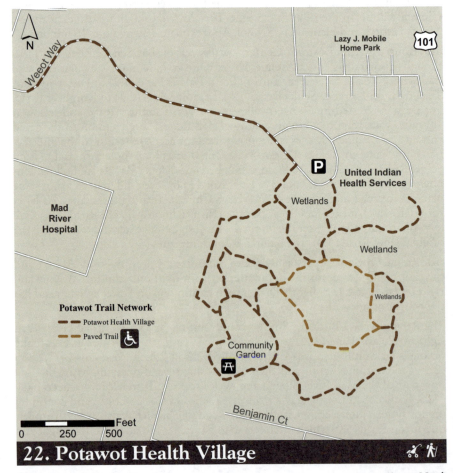

proceeding on Giuntoli Lane to the west (follow the roundabout to the third exit). The route passes over 101, rounds a traffic circle and continues on west, veering left (south) and becoming Janes Road. From the initial turn onto Giuntoli Lane to the signed entrance to Potawot is about one mile. Turn left into the entrance parkway for 0.3 mile to parking. Several access points to the trail complex exist south of the parking lot and entrance parkway. Approximate driving time, 16 minutes.

The route: A half-mile concrete path suitable for wheelchair use circles the prairie area of the grounds. A longer, partially unpaved path around the perimeter of the grounds also circles the extensive community garden. Additional trails border and connect the wetland features. A kiosk with a map of the trails is at the entrance to the trail system.

23 · Arcata Historical/Architectural Walk

Length: up to 4 miles
Total ascent: 400 feet
Type: loop
Dogs: yes
Restrooms: Corner of 'F' Street and 8th

Description: Arcata (then called Union) was established by a group of Trinity River miners led by scientist/explorer Dr. Josiah Gregg who located Humboldt Bay by land. Each of the 33 members of the Union Company was allocated 160 acres. Subdivision of these claims resulted in a flurry of property trades.

Gold, timber and agriculture shaped Arcata's development although the establishment of the Humboldt State Normal School in 1914 (which evolved into Humboldt State University) and the arrival of the Redwood Highway in 1925 have probably had far greater long-term impacts. Arcata has a rich and well preserved architectural heritage spanning 1852 to 1930 that can be viewed on this walk from downtown through the neighborhoods east and west of US 101. This includes excellent examples of Settlement, Victorian, Transitional or Craftsman homes.

Bair House

Getting there: Follow US 101 north for 6.8 miles taking Exit 713 (CA 255/Samoa Boulevard) west. This circles around to cross back over US 101 (0.5 mile). Merge onto Samoa Boulevard continuing west 0.3 mile to G Street (the first traffic light). Turn right on G Street continuing north for 0.3 mile to the Arcata Plaza. Parking is available around the Plaza or in

Hiking Humboldt Volume 2

adjacent blocks surrounding the Plaza.

The route: This is a complicated and meandering route beginning on the Plaza. The Plaza is still Arcata's hub serving as the location for Saturday Farmers' Markets, the start of the Kinetic Sculpture Race, the Oyster Festival, the North Country Fair, and more. Anchored on the southwest corner of the Plaza is the Jacoby Building (1857) and on the northeast corner is the Hotel Arcata (1914) with a number of structures dating from the late 1880s through current years (although designed to retain the architectural integrity of the Plaza). Once you round the Plaza, depart from the northeast corner heading east on 9th Street.

> ### ∞ The Name Arcata
>
> In 1856, the Humboldt County Court recognized the incorporation of 'Union' although four years later the name was changed to 'Arcata' by legislative act. However, the meaning of Arcata was unclear. An article in a Eureka newspaper in 1855 suggested that Arcata was "the Indian name of this place." However, the editor of the *Humboldt Times*, who was opposed to the name change, wrote that "it means a certain place in town where the diggers [a disparaging term applied to Native Americans] were once in the habit of congregating, which in our language would be about the same as "down thar" or "over yonder". Historian Lynwood Carranco noted that many "old-timers still insist that Arcata means 'a bright and sunny spot'". He also suggested another possible meaning, "shallow, peaceful water or lagoon." Apparently the Eureka Chamber of Commerce, following investigation, concluded that Arcata was an Indian name meaning "where the boats landed." Carranco's best guess however, was that Arcata was a corruption of "O-ke'to". This would be translated from the Yurok language as 'where it [land] is flat". ∞

Turn right on F Street passing the Arcata Ballpark (home of the Crabs) and the current City Hall (0.2). Turn left on 7th continuing east over US 101 towards Union (0.6). At 100 7th Street is Arcata's only 'Shotgun House' (1908) built with rooms in a row without a connecting hallway. Notice the cork tree before you reach 'A' Street. On the southwest corner of 7th and Union is the Phillips House (1852) which is on the National Register of Historic Places and serves as a historical museum (only open Sundays 2 – 4 p.m.).

Turn left climbing Union Street over the crest to 12th Street (0.9). Turn right on 12th, left on Spring Street, left on 13th, and left on Union back to 12th (1.1). This short loop passes a half dozen homes dating from the late 1800s through the first decade of 1900. Turn right on 12th and follow it to C Street (1.3). Note the Sobol-Rossi House (1226 B Street) which dates from 1874-5.

Turn left on C Street to 10th Street. Right on 10th for one block to D Street. Left on D Street to 9th Street. Turn left into the road that dead ends facing the Graham House, 380 9th Street, a classic Victorian built in 1888. This stretch passes several notable homes from this same era (1.6). Return to D Street and turn right to 11th Street. Turn left on 11th re-crossing US 101 and continuing to G Street (1.9). As you walk here, imagine the landscape of Arcata before the freeway split the community.

At 11th and G Street the route turns right passing the massive wood edifice of the Presbyterian Church (1911). As you climb G Street you pass the Sowash House, a beautifully restored Craftsman (1160 G Street), and several nice examples of Transitional architecture en route to 14th Street (2.1). Left on 14th for one block and right on H Street to 17th Street (2.3). The Ericson House at 1376 H Street is most notable as the home of photographer A.W. Ericson who documented on film life in the early years of this growing community. Across the street, 1395 H Street, is the Whaley House built in 1855 in the classic Settlement style.

Turn left on 17th and right on J Street entering the quiet confines of Greenwood Cemetery. The pleasant walk around perimeter of the cemetery takes you past many of the leading families of the early years of Arcata. Leave the cemetery (3.0) passing the much more cramped Catholic section that was for many years in the shadows of the imposing St. Mary's Church (destroyed by fire in 2003 after standing for 119 years).

Turn left on 16th for two blocks to I Street. Turn right on I Street for two blocks and right again on 14th Street (3.2). Note the distinctive Cullberg House at 1452 I Street (1862) and the classic Queen Anne architecture of the Lady Anne Bed and Breakfast (902 14th Street). 980 14th Street is the mirror image of the Lady Anne.

Turn left on J Street and left again on 13th to pass the Bair House (916 13th

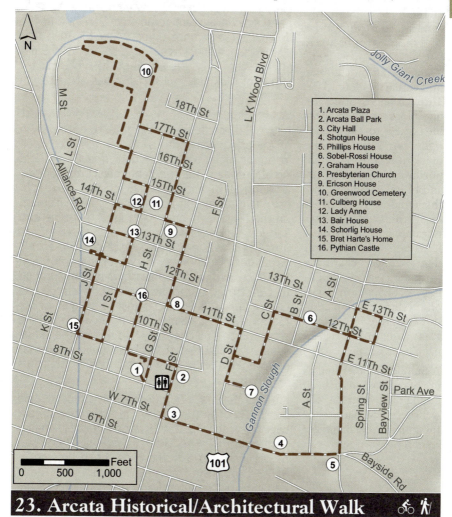

23. Arcata Historical/Architectural Walk

Street). Constructed in 1888 by the Newsom brothers, the same architects responsible for the Carson Mansion in Eureka, the Bair House is considered among the better examples of Queen Anne architecture. Turn right on I Street and right again on 12th as the route slaloms down toward the Plaza. At 1050 12th Street is the Schorlig House, another house on the National Register of Historic Places. Backtrack briefly to J Street turning right.

Bret Harte, journalist and writer, lived in the original house at 927 J Street in 1860. He courageously condemned the Indian Island massacre of between 80 – 250 Wiyot men, women, and children in February, 1860 (3.7). Turn left on 9th Street for one block and left again on I Street to 14th. Turn right on 14th for one block to H Street. On the northwest corner of 14th and H is the imposing Pythian Castle. The Knights of Pythia's North Star Encampment, a national fraternal organization that stressed charitable work, erected this building in1885. Turn right on H Street completing this circuitous route at the Plaza (4.1) in just two final blocks.

A number of other houses of note have not been highlighted here. The website www.arcatahistory.org is the definitive resource.

∞ The Arcata Plaza and William McKinley

There is no more iconic and, perhaps, ironic symbol of liberal Arcata than the statue of assassinated President William McKinley situated in the center of Arcata's Plaza. Set aside as a village green by the Union Company at the time of original settlement in 1850, for many of the early years residents shared the Plaza with loaded mule trains and grazing livestock. It wasn't until 1902 that cattle were banished from the streets and a concerted effort resulted in beautification of the Plaza. The first palm trees were planted, the radiating sidewalks were completed (1910), and the Women's Temperance Union water fountain that still exists on the Plaza's west side was erected (1912), but it was the arrival of the nine-foot tall statue of McKinley in 1906 that has come to define the Plaza.

Why McKinley? McKinley's assassination in 1901 had so affected the region that the little town of Minorville just north of Arcata renamed itself in honor of the dead president and 81-year-old Arcata resident George Zehndner commissioned a young San Francisco-based sculptor, Haig Patigian, to create a statue of McKinley for placement on the Plaza. Zehndner had met the President in San Jose some weeks before anarchist Leon Czolgosz shot McKinley twice (McKinley died nine days later of gangrene). However, the 1906 San Francisco earthquake unleashed a conflagration that destroyed the foundry where the statue had been completed. Unbeknownst to Patigian or the foundry owner the employee of a nearby machine shop and several passersby had moved the statue to relative safety. After this welcome surprise was discovered, the statue was shipped north to its new home.

I'm sure that both Zehndner and McKinley would be shocked by the statue's irreverent treatment over the years. Our 25th President has had cheese stuffed up his nose, worn a wide variety of garments including a traffic cone, been dressed as Santa Claus, held flowers and picture frames and bananas, but remains (for now) the center of the Plaza. ∞

24 · Arcata Community Forest

Length: between 2-4 miles
Total ascent: 600 feet
Elevations: 200-600 feet
Type: loop
Dogs: leashed
Restrooms: at Redwood Park

Description: With seven distinct trailheads and 19 different numbered trails in addition to the new South Fork Janes Creek Loop and the Arcata Ridge Trail, the number of walking permutations in the Arcata Community Forest can keep you busy (or lost) for some time. The 14 plus miles of trails traverse a mature second growth forest that is sustainably managed by the City of Arcata. With elevations in the forest ranging from 200 to 1100 feet there is plenty of opportunity for an aerobic workout. Given the proximity to Humboldt State University and the town of Arcata, most of the trails are well used. These two loops provide an excellent overview of the forest experience.

Getting there: Take US 101 North for 6.8 miles to Exit 713 (Old Arcata Road/Sunny Brae) staying right at fork. In .5 mile take the third exit (Union Street) from the traffic circle. Proceed up the steep hill to 12th Street (0.6 mile). Turn right onto 12th and left on Bayview (0.1 mile). Follow Bayview Street for 0.3 mile to the Redwood Park parking area.

For the Mid-Length Loop Option, instead of turning left on Bayview Street, turn right for just 225 feet before turning left on Park Avenue and continuing for 0.5 mile steeply up to a small, dirt parking area on the left. If you see Fickle Hill Lane on your right, you have just passed the trailhead. Approximate driving time, 12 minutes.

The routes (Shown on map for Hike #25):

Short Loop Option. Redwood Park – Trails #1 - #9 - #3 - #2 - #1 (2.0 miles). The trails are well signed. Cross Redwood Park to the east side where several signs mark the entrance to the Community Forest and Trail #1. Follow Trail #1 as it climbs through mature stands of second growth redwoods to an intersection with Trail #9 (0.5). Turn left on Trail #9 following it to the intersection with Trail #3 (0.9). Walk Trail #3 as it descends through the forest to an intersection with Trail #2 (1.4). Turn left on Trail #2 and follow it to an intersection with Trail #1 (1.5). By turning right on Trail #1 and crossing the bridge you quickly reach the parking lot on the northeast side of Redwood Park. By continuing left on Trail #1 the trail climbs briefly before crossing a small tributary of Campbell Creek and returning to Redwood Park (2.0).

Mid-Length Loop Option. Fickle Hill Road – Trails #9 - #8 - #9 (3.7 miles). From the small parking area adjacent to Fickle Hill Road, follow the service road north into the Community Forest. The road, also designated as Trail #9, extends into the heart of the Community Forest to an intersection with Trail #8 (1.0). You will pass Trails #1, #3, and #4 before arriving at #8. Turn right crossing under the power lines staying on Trail #8 as it loops around to a second crossing of the power line corridor (1.4). Stay on Trail #8 as it completes its large circuit of the center of the forest passing Trails #15, #12, #6, #11, #5, #14, and #16 before reaching Trail #9 again (2.8). Follow #9 back to the parking area (3.7). The intersections are clearly numbered.

Hiking Humboldt Volume 2

∞ A Brief Early History of the Arcata Community Forest

Dedicated in May, 1955 as the first municipally-owned community forest in California, the 600-acre Arcata Community Forest has provided a dependable revenue stream through sustainable timber harvests, offered a rich network of multi-use trails and roads, and until 1964 was the primary source of Arcata's municipal water supply (the empty Jolly Giant reservoir on Trail #8 remains from that period).

Much of the early history of this forestland following the arrival of white settlers was about cutting down trees. The first mill was established in 1853 and by about 1908, the last of the virgin timber had been removed from the western slopes of Fickle Hill. Before and after that era, the streams (Campbell Creek, Janes Creek, Jolly Giant Creek) emanating from these tracts of hillside were tapped as a largely inadequate solution to Arcata's water needs. Problems with water quality and erratic supply dogged the privately held Union Water Company and the Public Utilities California Corporation, which owned much of what we currently consider the Community Forest. When the City of Arcata ultimately purchased the water utility in 1935, much of the watershed came with it. But it really was not until Arcata looked elsewhere for dependable water in the early 1960s that the door was opened for much broader recreational use of the Community Forest.

It should be noted that Redwood Park had a different inception. In 1904 the Union Water Company donated 26 acres of second growth redwoods to the City of Arcata. This area was then and still is known as Redwood Park. Redwood Park also was the site of a dance platform and band shell, picnic tables, and for nearly three decades, an auto park. It is now in the midst of a comprehensive makeover. ∞

Ann Wallace

25 · Arcata Ridge Trail

Since the purchase of the Sunny Brae Forest in 2006 by the City of Arcata, it has been the intent to link this parcel with the Arcata Community Forest using a trail that would extend from West End Road to Margaret Lane in Sunny Brae. Until a solution is identified for the dangerous crossing of Fickle Hill Road, there are two delightful loop trails, one at the north (Hike #25) and one at the south end (Hike #26) of the future Ridge Trail.

South Fork Janes Creek Loop

Length: 3.3 miles
Total ascent: 700 feet
Elevations: 180-460 feet
Type: partial loop
Dogs: leashed
Restrooms: none

Description: The walk includes enough elevation gain to be aerobic, a taste of mature redwood forest, a stretch of switchbacking trail through young stands of redwood, and walking along alder-lined South Fork of Janes Creek. It is a very pleasant alternative to the more familiar trails in the Arcata Community Forest.

This trail opened during the summer of 2014 and represents a wonderful collaboration between the City of Arcata and the generosity of the Samuels family, who agreed to an easement through their timberland adjacent to the Arcata Community Forest. It is particularly important to respect the agreement with the family and stay on the signed trail. The South Fork Janes Creek Loop Trail is accessible from the Arcata Ridge Trail West End Road trailhead or the Community Forest's Diamond Drive trailhead.

Getting there: Drive 8 miles north on US 101 and take Exit 714B (Sunset Avenue). From the middle lane of the exit, turn right on Sunset Avenue (0.3 miles). At the stop sign, turn left on L.K. Wood Boulevard. Stay straight on L.K. Wood Boulevard for 0.7 miles. (Do not follow the road left back over US 101.) Turn right on Diamond Drive. Continue on Diamond Drive as it winds its way steeply at times for nearly one mile where the road makes a sharp left turn at the top. There is ample street side parking in this area. The trailhead will be on your right just as the road makes its sharp left turn. Approximate driving time, 15 minutes.

The West End Road trailhead is a short distance east of the US 101 overpass as it crosses above West End Road. Drive 9.5 miles north on US 101 and take the CA 299 exit toward Weaverville/Redding. At 0.8 mile take the Guintoli Exit. Turn right at the stop sign and right again on West End Road (.1 mile). Continue west on West End Road for 0.8 mile. On the left (south) side of the road is a pullout adequate for parking (more permanent trailhead parking is planned to be completed in 2017). The signed trailhead is about 100 yards southeast of the parking area.

The route: The Arcata Community Forest uses a system of numbers for the trail (there are associated names but none of the signs use those names). From the Diamond Drive trailhead, follow Trail #5 veering left at the junction less than 100 yards from Diamond Drive (the right fork connects with California Avenue in 0.2 mile). Continue on Trail #5 (0.3) turning on Trail #10, a single-track trail that leaves from the left side of Trail #5. This trail drops to a bridged crossing of a fork of Janes Creek before climbing to a signed intersection with the Janes Creek Loop

Trail (0.6). Continue (straight) onto the single-track South Fork Janes Creek Loop Trail. The trail begins a series of switchbacks (0.8) that descend to several crossings of Janes Creek (or tributaries). It joins an old logging road that parallels Janes Creek (1.3). [Note: The rock used on that road is large and, for several stretches, is largely composed of broken concrete chunks. This makes for somewhat difficult walking.] The route follows the road to an intersection with another logging road (1.9). Turn left on this logging road. (A right turn will take you down to the West End Road trailhead) The trail makes a relatively short but steep climb back to complete the loop (2.7 mile) at the intersection with Trail #10. Turn right on Trail #10 to retrace your steps to the Diamond Drive trailhead.

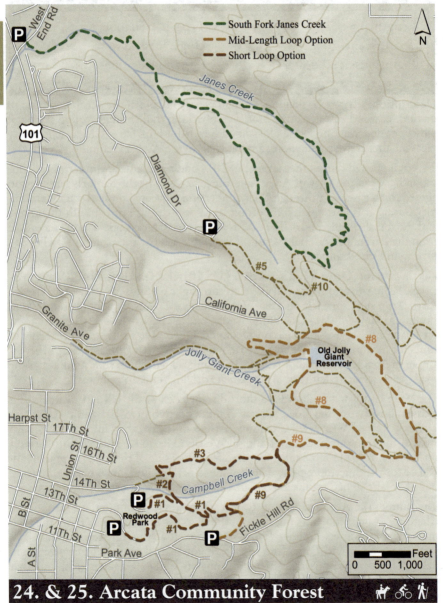

I prefer to walk the loop counterclockwise rather than to descend on the steep, gravel road. I find that the switchbacks provide more stable footing going down.

The access from West End Road trailhead follows the top of a levee separating a channelized portion of Janes Creek from an active timber operation and eventually an overgrown log pond. Take special note of the beautiful wrought iron bridge (0.1). As the single track trail merges onto a logging access road (0.5), turn right. You cross Janes Creek (0.6) and begin climbing to an intersection with the South Fork Janes Creek Loop trail (0.8). See the above directions for completing the 2-mile loop. Once back at this intersection, turn right to retrace your steps to the West End Road trailhead.

26 · Arcata Ridge Trail – Beith Creek Loop

Length: 2.6 miles
Total ascent: 640 feet
Elevations: 200-760 feet

Type: partial loop
Dogs: leashed
Restrooms: none

Description: The Sunny Brae Forest is a 'feel good' story related to walking in Humboldt County. Due an outcry from the Sunny Brae neighborhood, local fund raising efforts, and support from the city and a number of partners, this 171-acre parcel was purchased by the City of Arcata in 2006. Since then, a network of trails including the Beith Creek Loop has slowly been constructed that will culminate in the completion of the 4.5-mile Arcata Ridge Trail that will connect Sunny Brae with West End Road by climbing up and over Fickle Hill.

The Beith Creek Loop, walked counterclockwise, begins with a sweeping contour through maturing second growth, crossing fingers of Beith Creek before switch-backing and climbing steeply to an intersection with a gravel access road. The short time on the road provides some views out across Arcata and Humboldt Bay. The descent snakes through forest on its return to the Margaret Lane trailhead.

Getting there: Drive north on US 101 for 7.0 miles to Exit 713 (CA 255/Samoa Boulevard/Old Arcata Road). Stay right following the signs to Sunny Brae, merging with Samoa Boulevard/Old Arcata Road (0.3 mile). Continue on Samoa Boulevard/Old Arcata Road to the second roundabout (0.4 mile). At the second roundabout, take the 3rd exit and continue east on Buttermilk Lane for 0.7 mile to the intersection with Margaret Lane. This intersection occurs at the top of a gradual uphill grade and just before Buttermilk Lane makes a sharp turn to the right. Turn left on Margaret Lane. The trailhead is one block up just as Margaret Lane bends left. Street parking is readily available. The trail begins with a set of concrete stairs located on the outside of this turn in Margaret Lane.

The route: At the top of the stairs, directional signs separate cyclists and pedestrians, sending walkers and runners to the right until the paths reunite at the end of a graveled service road (0.1). From here you can use either the single-track trail as it continues paralleling the road or the road itself as it continues steeply uphill to a junction where the road turns left (0.2). At this turn, the signed Beith Creek Loop begins. Follow the single-track trail as it splits off to the right. Directions will be described beginning with a right turn onto this single-track trail. The Beith Creek Loop trail intersects with the bottom of a steep one-way downhill trail dedicated to mountain bikers (0.4). Stay right and continue the long contour in and out of several minor drainages. The trail switchbacks left at a corner dominated by pampas grass (1.1).

Do not eat! Photo by Ann Wallace.

The Beith Creek Loop trail turns left following an old logging road up initially and then steeply up eventually crossing some of these same small tributaries some 400 feet higher on the side of Fickle Hill. Eventually the single-track trail broadens into a graveled road (1.5) and joins a service road (1.6). Turn left (the right turn option goes steeply uphill) and follow this service road. At an easily-missed junction the single-track Beith Creek Loop trail (this also serves as a section of the Arcata Ridge Trail) veers left (1.9) from the road and meanders downhill (2.2). The trail passes the top of the one-way downhill mountain bike trail (to the left) and crosses the dirt service road as it slaloms downhill. It emerges onto a graveled service road near a new water storage tank with power lines overhead. Just before the water tank is another single-track trail that begins east of the water tank and descends to the service road near the beginning of the Beith Creek Loop. Either the trail or the road can be followed. The road and trail reach the beginning of the Beith Creek Loop (2.4) and the return to the Margaret Lane trailhead (2.6).

Extras. From the north side of the new water tank a connector trail descends from the road. It angles north down the hillside before turning southwest and making a long contour to an intersection with Panorama Court (0.5). Panorama Court leads downhill connecting with Panorama Drive. A left turn on Panorama Drive takes you back to Margaret Lane just west of the trailhead.

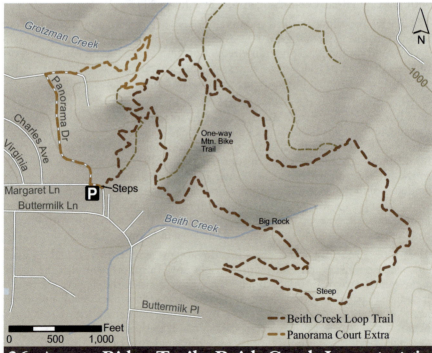

26. Arcata Ridge Trail - Beith Creek Loop

27 · Humboldt State University

Length: 2.2 miles
Total ascent: 250 feet
Access: parking is restricted M-F until 5pm
Type: loop
Dogs: leashed
Restrooms: yes, if campus is open

Description: Humboldt State University is one of the most beautiful campuses in California with views out to Humboldt Bay, groves of redwoods, and colorful landscaping. HSU's 144-acre main campus is lovingly referred to as 'Hills and Stairs University' and this walk around the campus does little to avoid the ups and downs. Although this walk remains outside of all buildings, additional exploration is certainly encouraged.

Getting there: Drive north on US 101 for 7.9 miles taking Exit 714B (Sunset Avenue). At the intersection with Sunset Avenue (0.3 mile), stay in the right lane and take the right turn onto L.K. Wood Boulevard going south. In 0.1 mile, turn left onto Plaza Avenue. After 5 p.m. on Fridays and on the weekends no parking permit is required in the large lot to the right off of Plaza Avenue. At other times, metered street parking and metered options are available or a day permit can be purchased. Other parking options exist on the streets west of US 101 (pay careful attention to signed parking restrictions). Approximate driving time, 10 minutes.

The route: It is helpful to have a campus map to best follow these directions (http://www.humboldt.edu/maps). From the parking lot near Plaza Avenue, walk east toward campus past the bus stop and left just beyond the 'Library Circle', the circular turnaround for vehicular traffic. Walk up the narrow roadway in between the Little Apartments and the Health Center past the Youth Educational Services or YES House (0.1). Stairs veer off to the left descending the hillside. At the bottom of the stairs turn right. Continue past a campus informational sign where a path splits to the right from the sidewalk (0.2). Take this path down to the residence hall parking lot. Cross the lot to Granite Avenue. Turn right on Granite Avenue and walk along the street past the Jolly Giant Commons and an open lawn (0.5). Just as the road begins a steep ascent (to Creekview Apartments), a gravel road veers right and continues along Jolly Giant Creek on the other side of a gate. Follow this gravel road for a short distance to a bridge over the creek. Turn right and cross the bridge, ascending a paved walkway that climbs back to main campus level (0.7). Turn left to cross just west of the University Center. This route will take you to a walkway between the University Center and Nelson Hall East and into the 'Quad' with its distinctive clocktower/elevator on the east side. Veer left as you cross the 'Quad' and climb the stairs to Founders Hall (0.8). From the sidewalk on the west side of Founders Hall, enjoy the nice views out over Humboldt Bay and Arcata Bottoms. (If the building is open, the interior courtyard is worth a visit.) Turn right and walk south past Founders and Van Matre Halls. The sidewalk bends around a small parking area with two staircases at its southeast end. The westernmost of those two drops to a service road (Laurel Drive). Cross the road and descend the stairs on the opposite side of the service road and slightly uphill. This leads you through the site previously occupied by the President's home. Now only remnants of the patio remain with the addition of a chainsaw sculpture garden. After crossing this area, turn left at the walkway leading into the Redwood Bowl (0.9). Walk the length of

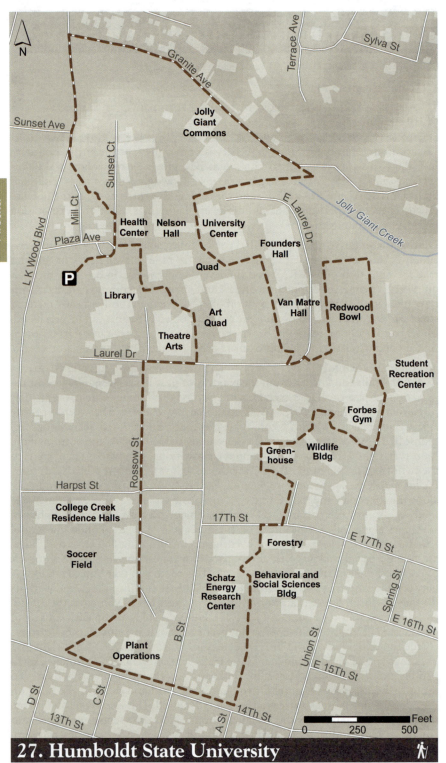

the track but instead of completing the loop, take the southeast exit past the scoreboard (1.2) climbing the stairs west of the Student Recreation Center.

Walk along Union Street to the east of Forbes Gym. On the downhill side of Forbes Gym, turn right on the service road. From the service road turn left at the second set of stairs that drop through a redwood grove to the west of the Wildlife Building (1.4). At the base of these stairs, you will be able to take a detour to the right to visit the Greenhouse (limited hours M – F) or to the left to visit the stuffed animals in the Wildlife Building. However, our route continues on south to the east of the Campus Events Field and crosses 17th Street to the Forestry Building. Go to the west side of the Forestry Building and continue on south up another set of stairs (1.5). Continue south from the top of the stairs along the road between the Schatz Energy Research Center and the Behavioral Social Sciences (BSS) building. If the BSS building is open, consider a trip to the west end of the top where a balcony offers an excellent view. Continue south to 14th Street where you will turn right (1.6).

Walk along 14th beyond 'B' Street passing the Plant Operations (aka Facilities Management) building to a walkway to your right that returns to campus (1.7). If you reach L.K. Wood Boulevard you have gone too far. Follow this walkway to Rossow Street and turn left (north) just past the College Creek Complex (residence halls). Walk north on Rossow across Harpst Street continuing past the Parking Services Booth and up yet another set of stairs (2.0). Turn right (east) on Laurel Drive until you pass the Theatre Arts Building. At the intersection of Laurel Drive and 'B' Street turn left and climb another short set of stairs to the 'Art Quad'. Cross the Art Quad, climbing no more stairs, and take the sidewalk leaving from the northwest side of the Quad (just past the Theatre Arts Building). At the Library, a right turn will take you back to the Library Circle and Plaza Avenue (2.2) where the walk began.

28 · Jacoby Creek Forest Trail

Length: 5.2 miles	**Type:** out and back
Total ascent: 370 feet	**Dogs:** with permit on leash
Elevations: 750-1050 feet	**Restrooms:** no

A "Nature Area Entrance Permit" from the City of Arcata, Department of Environmental Services is required. Contact 707-822-8184 for more information. Allow 7 – 10 days to process. Docent-led hikes or hikes with a research purpose are prioritized. In addition, there are no bridges for the multiple crossings of Jacoby Creek. At times crossings will be difficult or impossible.

Description: This walk through some of the 1,350-acre Jacoby Creek Forest and along the upper sections of Jacoby Creek is worth the extra effort required to secure a permit. The trail, for the most part, follows old logging roads that parallel Jacoby Creek. The maturing stands of second growth timber and riparian habitat make this a very enjoyable walk. There is a minimum of signage although only near the turnaround does the network of social trails create significant confusion.

Getting there: Drive north on US 101 for 5.1 miles to the Bayside Cutoff. Turn right and proceed 0.5 mile to the intersection with Old Arcata Road. Turn left on

Old Arcata Road and right on Jacoby Creek Road (0.7 mile). Proceed east on Jacoby Creek Road for 4.1 miles. At the 1.7-mile mark on Jacoby Creek Road be sure to veer left to remain on Jacoby Creek Road. In another 1.7 miles the pavement stops and the gravel begins with the final 0.7 mile being gravel surface. This stretch of road passes through a number of private holdings and traffic has been a source of concern among the neighbors. As signs reinforce, be considerate when driving to the parking area (e.g., minimizing dust in the summer) and selecting a parking spot. Ample parking exists at the trailhead although cars require a permit from the City of Arcata or vehicles will be towed.

Jacoby Creek Forest, photo by Nancy Spruance

The route: The trail begins from the east side of the parking lot along an old logging road (the old parking lot used to be about half a mile further along this old logging road). The first crossing of Jacoby Creek (0.8) is generally relatively easy in summer and fall but when water is high this could be the end of the walk. Three more crossings lie ahead with the next one arriving quickly (1.0). For the intrepid and those with good balance, it is possible to cross on what remains of an old log bridge. For the more prudent and cautious, there is a well-marked crossing just west of the downed bridge. The trail continues along the south side of Jacoby Creek, at times rising high above the distant murmur of the water. Although some side channels must be navigated, you reach the next crossing (1.7) followed in short order by the final crossing (1.8). The quality of the trail slowly deteriorates and the number of social trails created by mountain bikers increase. In general, when options exist, take the trail closer to Jacoby Creek. You will reach a clearing that seems to serve as the confluence of several unmarked trails (2.6) but any further walking will require a commitment to exploration.

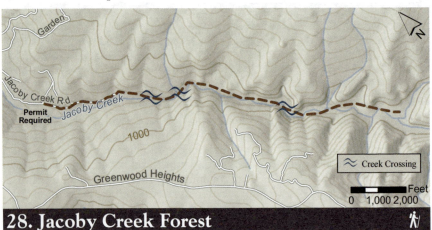

28. Jacoby Creek Forest

29 · Arcata Marsh

Length: up to 4 miles	**Type:** loop
Total ascent: flat	**Dogs:** leashed
Elevations: 6-25 feet	**Restrooms:** yes

Description: The Arcata Marsh offers a network of trails with almost infinite possibilities for the walker. All trails are flat and comprised of hard-packed gravel. A number of interpretive signs, covered 'blinds', and benches have been placed throughout the Marsh. This is not only a place ideal for bird watching and appreciating the views of shallow Arcata Bay, but also a popular location for recreational walking. The Visitor Center suggests four reasonable loop options of varying lengths: The 1-mile Shorebird Loop around Klopp Lake and Mount Trashmore; the 1.5-mile Central Marsh Circuit, the 2-mile walk from the Interpretive Center around the Oxidation Ponds, and the 4-mile Tour de Marsh, using the perimeter trails to circumnavigate the Marsh.

Getting there: Follow US 101 north for 6.8 miles taking Exit 713 for CA 255 (Samoa Boulevard) west. The first option for access to the Marsh is to turn left on South G Street and proceed south for 0.5 mile. On the right side is a large parking area. The second option is to go farther along Samoa Boulevard to I Street (0.1 mile or two blocks past G Street). Turn left on South I Street which serves as a long access road to the west side of the Marsh. Drive 1.0 miles from Samoa Boulevard to the parking area at the end of the road. Approximate driving time, 10 minutes.

The route: Shorebird Loop (1 mile) – start and end at the South I Street parking lot. From the south end of the parking lot join the trail along the south and east side of Klopp Lake until it reaches No Name Pond where you will turn left. At the top of the stairs turn right and follow this trail along the north side of Mt. Trashmore (the whimsical name given to the area that once was a landfill) until it almost reaches South I Street where you turn onto trail leading off to the left along the west side of Mt. Trashmore and Klopp Lake back to the parking lot.

Central Marsh Circuit (1.5 mile) – start and end from the South G Street parking lot near the Marsh Interpretive Center. From the south end of the lot follow the trail that continues south paralleling Butcher's Slough and crossing the unused railroad tracks. Just beyond the tracks, turn right at the T-junction crossing over Butcher's Slough. Continue west passing the south side of Allen Marsh and its covered blind. Cross South I Street and continue on the trail next to the road as it bends sharply west. In about 0.1 mile turn right on the trail that leads north between the restored salt marsh on the left and Gearhart Marsh and Brackish Pond on the right. [Consider continuing straight along the restored salt marsh to the edge of McDaniel Slough where the tide gate was removed and the levee breached and back (0.5).] Follow this trail as it circles around Brackish Pond and returns to South I Street. Cross South I Street and connect with the trail leaving from the northeast corner of the graveled parking area. Follow this trail as it crosses Butcher's Slough. Take the first right hand turn after the Butcher's Slough bridge and follow this trail to the Marsh Interpretive Center and on to the parking lot.

Oxidation Pond Loop (2 mile) – Begin as in the Central Marsh Circuit. After crossing the railroad tracks, instead of turning right at the T-junction, turn left.

This trail crosses the north side of the sometimes odiferous Primary Wastewater Treatment facility and just south of Arcata Corp Yard. Cross the access road to the facility and a small parking lot and continue the trail on the east side of that parking lot. This trail bends around the fenced Corp Yard joining a seldom-used service road. Follow the service road as it loops around the entire eastern-most oxidation pond, a .87 mile circuit. Keep your eyes open for marsh wrens, northern harriers, and countless shorebirds and gulls. When you have done enough loops retrace your steps to the South G Street parking lot.

Tour de Marsh (4 mile) – This hike basically combines elements of the first three hikes following the outermost trails around the Marsh.

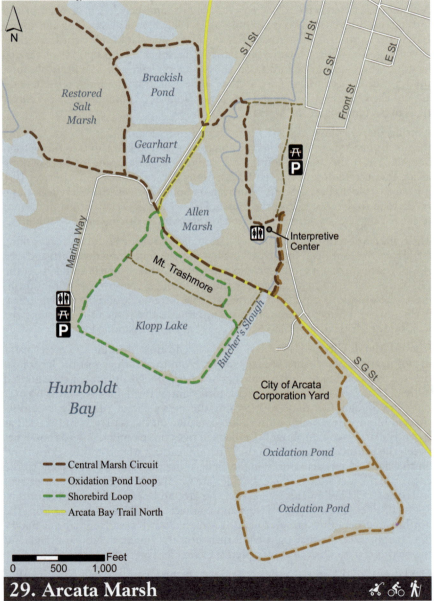

29. Arcata Marsh

30 Bay Trail North (Arcata City Trail) – Larson Park to Samoa Boulevard

Length: 2.6 miles	Type: out and back
Total ascent: flat	Dogs: yes
Elevations: 20 feet	Restrooms: yes

Description: This, the northern-most segment of the Bay Trail, is a paved, multi-modal trail. The broad pathway is well illuminated as it snakes its way from Arcata's Skate Park along Jolly Giant Creek north of the high school, and south through Arcata's Creamery District to Samoa Boulevard. Beginning in November 2017, it will connect with the continuation of the Bay Trail as it proceeds south as a paved trail through the Arcata Marsh and on several miles to just north of Bracut.

Directions to the trailhead: Drive north of US 101 for 8.2 miles taking the Sunset Avenue exit. Turn left onto Sunset Avenue for 0.2 mile. At the traffic circle, turn right on Jay Street and right again on Eye Street. In one block, turn right into the parking lot for Larson Park. Alternatively, continue on west from Sunset Avenue on the newly constructed Foster Avenue for 0.3 mile. Some off-street parking is available on the north side of Shay Park. However, with this being an urban trail, access is possible anywhere along its length.

The route: The trail is exceptionally well signed and lighted. From the Sunset Avenue/Foster Avenue traffic circle the trail proceeds south along the north and west sides of Shay Park. It is possible in several places to detour on single-track paths through Shay Park and re-connect with the Arcata City Trail. Jolly Giant Creek meanders through Shay Park until it passes under Alliance Road. The trail then parallels and later crosses (0.7) Alliance before continuing south along 'L' Street to its current terminus at Samoa Boulevard (1.3).

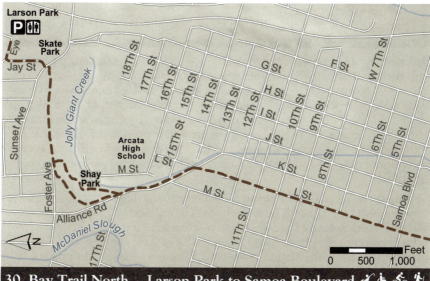

30. Bay Trail North – Larson Park to Samoa Boulevard

Samoa Boulevard to Jacoby Creek

Construction is expected to be complete of more than two miles of additional multi-user trail from Samoa Boulevard to near Bracut by the end of 2017. This trail will utilize portions of the railroad right-of-way as it passes through the Arcata Marsh and along the northeast corner of the bay. It will have multiple points of access and eventually be prepared to extend on south.

Manila – Samoa – North Jetty

Over the past several decades, the broad vegetated sand spit that is home to Manila and Samoa and remnants of Humboldt County's timber heritage has become an increasingly attractive option for walkers. Through acquisitions and improvements, the Bureau of Land Management, Humboldt Bay National Wildlife Refuge, Friends of the Dunes, and the Manila Community Services District have done much to knit together and restore the fragments of the North Spit. Well-established trails exist in Ma-le'l Dunes North and South, the Community Center, and at the Nature Center along with decent walking around Samoa and the North Jetty. The long, firm beach ocean-side and the NCRA railroad right-of-way bay-side allow for the more adventurous walker to tie together different networks in creative ways depending upon stamina and sense of direction. Here are a couple of walks to get you started.

31 · Ma-le'l Dunes

Length: 1-4 miles
Total ascent: variable
Elevations: 0-80
Type: loop
Access: Open from sunrise to one hour after sunset; the access road to the Ma-le'l North trailhead and parking area is currently limited to Friday through Monday (the Ma-le'l South trailhead is open daily).
Dogs: yes in Ma-le'l South; not permitted in Ma-le'l North
Restrooms: yes
Horses: yes in Ma-le'l South; not permitted in Ma-le'l North

Description: The landscape and the trails in Ma-le'l North are among my favorites with their unique combination of slough, high dunes, forest, and beach. There is a surreal quality to being surrounded by massive 80-foot dunes here in Humboldt County or walking along the prism of the old Hammond railroad through garlands of lichens draped from arching Sitka spruce. The dunes are an attractive destination for families with children. I appreciate the concerted efforts that have been made to eliminate invasive plant species along these beaches. The walking opportunities in Ma-le'l South are pleasant enough too, and the parking area is open more often.

Getting there: Take US 101 North for 0.5 mile to the intersection with CA 255. Turn left on CA 255 north over the bridges to the Samoa Peninsula. Continue north 4.7 miles to Young Lane where you will turn left. (If you cross the abandoned railroad tracks or the closed Sierra Pacific mill you have gone too far.) At the T-junction, turn left to the Ma-le'l South parking lot and trailhead (0.1 mile) or right 0.7 mile to the Ma-le'l North parking lot (only open Friday through Monday). Approximate driving time, 13 minutes.

31. 32. & 33. Samoa Peninsula

The route (See map for Hikes 31-33): From the Ma-le'l South parking lot take one of the trail options to the beach (the Lutguk trail leaves from the horse section of the parking lot and the Ledik trail leaves from the hiker section). The Du'k Loop trail departs from a signed trailhead a short distance north of the intersection of Young Lane and the Ma-le'l Dunes access road. Follow one of these trails to the beach and turn right. Turn inland again at the Kimuk or Hout trails, which lie between 1 and 1.5 miles north along the beach (depending upon which trail you used to reach the beach). These trails can easily be missed as they tend to be marked with solitary wood poles. These two trails, aided by wooden walkways in key spots, cross the fore dunes area and the standing water that accumulates during the wet season. Continue to watch for the poles as you make your way up the dune face. The Kimuk trail has a delightful view over the slough and the Arcata Bottoms just before it descends from the high dunes and emerges a short distance north of the trailhead for Ma-le'l North. The longer Hout trail climbs the highest dunes before dropping down the steep dune face to an intersection with the Dap Loop Trail. (There is a rope strung between poles here should you wish to ascend the dune face.) Both options take you through the spruce and pine forest rich with huckleberry, salal, reindeer lichen and bearberry. Take the Tsoutsgish trail (paralleling the slough) left to remnants of the Hammond railroad bridge across the slough (0.2) or right to the Ma-le'l North parking lot (0.5). The Viqhul trail (0.5 mile each way) meanders through the dune forest to a bench and view of the slough and Bottoms. From the Ma-le'l North parking lot walk the 0.8 mile along the access road back to the Ma-le'l South lot.

Be warned that the Tsoutsgish trail has poison oak.

32 · Humboldt Coastal Nature Center

Length: 1.8 miles
Total ascent: little elevation gain but the soft sand can make for more challenging walking
Type: loop
Dogs: leashed
Restrooms: yes
Horses: yes, on certain trails

Description: Ten short trails network the roughly 116 acres that surround the Humboldt Coastal Nature Center. From the Friends of the Dunes property it is relatively easy to walk south along the beach to the Manila Community Center or north to the Ma-le'l Dunes. The Nature Center has several fascinating exhibits including photos illustrating the evolution of the distinctive Stamps House.

Getting there: Take US 101 North for 0.5 mile to the intersection with CA 255. Turn left on CA 255 North over the bridges to the Samoa Peninsula. Continue north 4.5 miles to Stamps Lane where you turn left. Keep left following the gravel road to the parking area for the Nature Center (0.2), the distinctive, partially buried building with a cupola on top. Approximate driving time, 10 minutes.

The route (See map for Hikes 31-33): The primary trailhead is on the west side of the Nature Center. The Wildberries trail descends from the trail register near the west entrance to the Nature Center and winds through several clusters of shore pines and willows before turning toward the ocean. It soon crosses the Waterline trail near a round concrete structure. The Waterline trail parallels the ocean about 100 yards inland for the length of the Friends of the Dunes property. The Back

Dune trail departs from the south side of the staff and handicapped parking lot splitting into the Beach Access trail (which joins the Wildberries trail as it emerges from the pines and willows on the way toward the beach) and the Back Loop trail (not on map but roughly parallels the Beach Access Trail 100 yards further south). The other notable trail is the William Weaver Ridge trail which takes an interesting route through higher portions of the property before bending back toward the ocean. A pleasant loop can be crafted using the combination of Back Dune to Back Loop to Willliam Weaver Ridge to South Beach Access trails and along the beach north to return along the Wildberries trail to the Visitor Center (1.8).

Although the trails are well-marked with Carsonite-type signs, the signs do not use trail names which is confusing. The good news is that the trail system is not so complex or lengthy that you are likely to be lost for long. To help orient yourself there generally is a view of the Visitor Center or the ocean not far away. My personal favorite is to walk to the beach on the Wildberries Trail, continue north to Ma-le'l North, turn inland across the dunes to the slough, and return along the Ma-le'l access road, and back along the Waterline Trail from Ma-le'l South (5.8 miles).

33 · Manila Dunes Recreation Area

Length: 2.0 miles
Total ascent: little elevation gain but the soft sand can make for more challenging walking
Type: partial loop
Dogs: yes
Restrooms: yes
Horses: yes, on certain trails

Description: This parcel of over 150 acres of beach, dunes, wetlands, forest and trail network forms the southern boundary of contiguous public lands along this coastal strip that begins with Lanphere Dunes at the north end. In the Manila Dunes Recreation Area (MDRA) 11 short trails (e.g., Beach Pea Trail, Strawberry Dune Trail) offer a variety of walking options. Longer walks can be designed to or from the adjacent Humboldt Coastal Nature Center to the north or the longer walk to Samoa Beach (see the Manila to Samoa walk, Hike #34). It is also possible to incorporate surface streets in Manila.

In recent years, the trail signage apart from the informational kiosks has deteriorated or disappeared. This creates special challenges to locate and follow specific trails. The Blackberry Hollow Trail, which parallels the beach and can be used to connect many of the trails, can become impassable during the rainy season. Despite these negatives, this is a worthy destination for a summer evening, as a place to walk your dog, or bring your family to enjoy the beach and dunes.

The described walk includes high dunes, beach, forest, and a return on Peninsula Drive.

Getting there: The trailhead is located at the Manila Community Services District, 1611 Peninsula Drive, Manila. Take US 101 North for 0.5 mile to the intersection with CA 255. Turn left on CA 255 North over the bridges to the Samoa Peninsula. Continue north 2.9 miles to Peninsula Drive where you will turn left. In 0.6 mile the destination is on the left. Approximate driving time, 8 minutes.

The route (See map for Hikes 31-33): My favorites hikes in the MDRA are longer and involve walking either north to the Humboldt Coastal Nature Center property or south to Samoa using the Beach Pea Trail in transit between the beach and roads in Manila. However, this loop begins by walking either through the Community Center grounds to the Beach Pea Trail (or the very short Silk Tassle Forest trail which quickly reunites with the Beach Pea Trail). Either follow the Beach Pea Trail directly to the beach (0.4) or the longer Strawberry Dune Trail which passes a decaying observation deck (0.5). After walking the beach, make your way to the intersection of the Blackberry Hollow Trail and the Sunset Dune Trail (1.0). You can do this by returning to the Blackberry Hollow Trail on the Beach Pea Trail or the Strawberry Dune Trail and walking south. Or walk 0.4 mile south (0.3 from Strawberry Dune Trail) on the beach to the Sunset Dune Trail and turning inland. None of these are marked other than by a concentration of footprints. During wet times, you will have to utilize the Sunset Dune Trail as the Blackberry Hollow Trail becomes too wet. Continue inland on the Sunset Dune Trail for about 100 yards to an ambiguous split in the trail. One branch turns left and your choice veers right and inland. The trail, once leaving the sand, is well defined as it winds through a thick forest eventually emerging on Peninsula Drive (1.5). Turn left to return to the Community Center (2.0).

North Side Highway 255 Trail. Caltrans and Humboldt County received funds that would provide for a short 0.5 mile path within the right-of-way for CA 255 as it passes through Manila. The multi-user trail will parallel the north side of the highway between Pacific Avenue/Dean Street and Carlson Drive. The trail is scheduled to be constructed in 2018.

34 · Samoa Loop

Length: 5.6-6.3 miles
Total ascent: flat
Elevations: sea level – 60 feet
Type: loop
Access: High tide or surf may complicate the beach walk
Dogs: yes
Restrooms: yes
Horses: beach only

Description: This diverse hike includes a stroll through the historic company town of Samoa, developed in the late 1800s by the Vance Lumber Company (reorganized as the Hammond Lumber Company in 1912), a beach and bay walk, and a transit through the Manila Dunes Community Center. It would be easy to build in stops at the Samoa Cookhouse and/or the Humboldt Bay Maritime Museum.

Getting there: Drive north on US 101 one-half (0.5) mile to the intersection with CA 255. Turn left on CA 255 proceeding over the bridges spanning the Bay for 2.0 miles to New Navy Base Road on the north side of the Bay. Turn left on New Navy Base Road for 0.3 mile. Turn left on Cookhouse Road and in 0.1 mile turn right on Vance Avenue and quickly left on N. Bay View Road. Parking in the spacious lot for the Samoa Cookhouse is convenient and safe.

Alternatively, it is also reasonable to park at the Manila Community Resource Center. After crossing the bridges on CA 255, instead of turning left on New Navy Base Road, turn right continuing on CA 255 for 1.6 miles. Turn left on Pacific Avenue and again left on Peninsula Drive (200 feet). Proceed 0.2 mile to the Community Center. Approximate driving time, 8 minutes.

The route: From the parking lot at the Samoa Cookhouse, turn left on the unsigned road at the bottom of the short rise that leads to the parking lot. It is just before Vance Avenue and has far less traffic than Vance Avenue. Soon you will reach the Samoa Post Office and Fire Department (0.4) and other central buildings of this once robust community. These buildings, like many of the houses, are in varying states of decay. Veer right to Vance Avenue, turn right on Vance and proceed two blocks to Rideout Street (0.6). Turn left on Rideout and, as you pass the Samoa Women's Club, veer right on Sunset Avenue. At the end of Sunset (0.8), follow the dirt path departing from the right side of the road to the pedestrian tunnel that passes underneath New Navy Base Road. The path continues northwest past a building reaching the beach (1.0). Although it is certainly possible to make the beach your destination and return the way you came, turning right and walking northeast along the beach can be a much more interesting (and, perhaps, adventurous) route. There are several places to turn inland, but the best route is to continue north along the beach to the unsigned main access trail to the Manila Community Resource Center (3.0). This popular trail reaches the Community Resource Center (3.4) after it climbs up and over a set of high dunes.

For much of the length of this beach walk a trail parallels the beach a short distance east of the beach. This trail follows the old water line that serviced the two pulp mills that once dominated the North Spit landscape. Since it can be difficult at times to find the turn inland from the beach, this Waterline Trail can be a useful resource.

Option 1. From the Manila Community Center, turn left on Peninsula Drive and follow it to CA 255 (3.7). Carefully cross this busy highway and turn right on the frontage road on the south side of the highway. The road crosses the old North Coast Railroad Authority (NCRA) railroad (3.8). This railroad, which offers closer access to the Bay, can be followed the entire way back to Samoa (6.3). The railroad is usually kept brushed back by the Timber Heritage Association which uses this route for periodic "speeder" rides.

Option 2. It is also possible, and slightly shorter but less aesthetically pleasing, to turn right on Peninsula Drive. It intersects CA 255 (4.0). Turn right and walk the

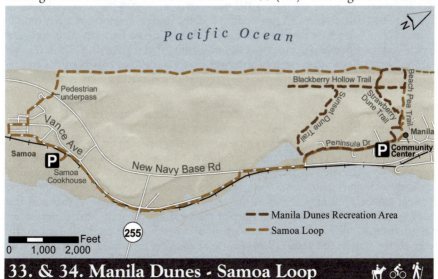

33. & 34. Manila Dunes - Samoa Loop

remaining distance to Vance Avenue along CA 255 (4.4). Although there is ample shoulder, there can be considerable traffic traveling at high speed making this a much less pleasant option. Although the railroad is quite close, it is inaccessible from CA 255 because of a tidal channel between the railroad prism and the road. The remainder of the route (5.6) can either be walked along Vance Avenue or on the railroad that can be accessed at any number of places along Vance Avenue.

35 · North Jetty Area - Samoa Boat Ramp County Park and Samoa Dunes Recreation Area

Length: 1.8 miles
Total ascent: flat
Type: out and back
Access: do not attempt during high surf
Dogs: leashed
Restrooms: yes
Horses: yes

Description: Although much of the recreational focus in the Samoa Dunes Recreation Area is Off-Highway Vehicles (OHV), the North Jetty is a popular and interesting destination for pedestrians. The jetty offers excellent views of incoming breakers and any boat traffic crossing the bar. My preferred walk begins at the Samoa Dunes Recreation Area parking/picnic area in a grove of trees on the southeast end of the peninsula and follows the jetty from the Bay to the Pacific Ocean. There are additional opportunities to walk north along the beach, incorporate the BLM access road into your route, visit the Samoa Boat Ramp County Park, and even spot (in very low tides) what little remains of the wreck of U.S.S. Milwaukee farther north on the peninsula or walk the old shipbuilding community of Fairhaven. There is no map for this straightforward walk.

Getting there: Drive north on US 101 one-half (0.5) mile to the intersection with CA 255. Turn left on CA 255 proceeding over the bridges spanning the Bay for 2.0 miles to New Navy Base Road on the north side of the Bay. Turn left on New Navy Base Road for 4.6 miles (Samoa Boat Ramp County Parking Area), 5.6 miles to the Samoa Dunes Recreation Area Picnic Area on the southeast corner of the end of the peninsula, or 0.2 mile farther to the Jetty parking area and access. Approximate driving time, 12 minutes.

The route: From the Picnic Area parking lot, walk east through the trees to the jetty as it bends around the end of the Samoa Peninsula. I like to begin the walk here for the view north to Eureka and across the Bay towards the mouth of the Elk River. Follow the jetty to the right as the jetty parallels the mouth of Humboldt Bay observing the swells as they build on their way through the mouth. Depending upon the tide and ocean conditions, it is not unusual that waves overtop the jetty. Be very careful should you choose to walk on the jetty. Because of that and the poor condition of the jetty (a number of places along the jetty have experienced extensive erosion), I am content to walk along the soft (alas) sand adjacent to the jetty all the way to the ocean (0.9). An easy extension is to walk north along this beach. Throughout this area, it is possible to encounter OHVs just about anywhere.

Extras: USS Milwaukee. During minus tides, some of the remaining skeleton of the Navy cruiser, USS Milwaukee, is still visible just off shore. In 1917, the Milwaukee was sent to assist with the rescue of a beached submarine only to experience an even more ignominious fate. The ship, a casualty of treacherous currents, ran aground and was a total loss. 1.2 miles from the beginning of New Navy Base Road, across from the pulp mill smokestack, park on the west side of the road (distinctive because of the large boulder near the pullout) and walk to the beach nearby.

Hammond Lumber Company, Shuster Collection, Humboldt State University Library

Fairhaven. 1.8 miles before reaching the Samoa Dunes Recreation Area Picnic Area turn left (east) to enter Fairhaven on Lincoln Street and then the second right (Park Street, unmarked) and follow it to the shore of Humboldt Bay. Although little evidence remains, Fairhaven was once at the center of a vibrant Humboldt Bay shipbuilding industry most known for its lumber schooners. These were designed with a shallow draft to allow the loaded vessel to cross coastal bars (such as at the notorious entrance to Humboldt Bay), uncluttered decks to facilitate loading, and capable of being sailed by small crews. Hans Ditler Bendixsen's shipyard (see the street named for him near the fire station at the north end of town) manufactured 93 of these ships between 1869 and 1901. Ultimately, the steamship rendered these sailing ships obsolete. A rather ordinary mile-long walk can be made from one end of town on Lindstrom Avenue and back on the parallel Lincoln Street.

⨳ Samoa

In 1889, conflict was brewing in the Samoan Island chain between Germany, Britain, and the United States over competing commercial and geopolitical interests. This standoff generated considerable patriotic fervor back home. So when a group of Eureka businessmen headed by David Page Cutten purchased land on the peninsula, they formed the Samoa Land and Improvement Company in the hopes that the name would help sell lots. The lumber town, initially developed by the Vance family after the original Vance Mill at First and G Streets burned down in 1892, retained the name Samoa. At the turn of the century, Andrew Hammond purchased the Vance holdings and aggressively expanded the operation. During this time, dozens of company houses were constructed including five huge bunkhouses for single men and the present day "Historic Samoa Cookhouse". For decades, Samoa was a bustling enterprise with its landmark, quarter-mile long Warehouse 14 (torn down in 1985) spanning the waterfront and 308 foot-tall smoke stack and adjacent electric power plant. In 1956, Georgia-Pacific Corporation bought the Hammond Lumber Company. By 1995, the sawmill operation in Samoa had been closed and by 2010 the remaining pulp mill on the peninsula was shuttered. The slowly decaying community of Samoa may yet rise from the ashes.

In 2000, the Samoa-Pacific Group, comprised of several local developers, purchased the town of Samoa and 75 adjacent acres. Their vision for the peninsula town includes almost 300 new homes, a business park, a major utility overhaul, retail shops and a town plaza. Although the massive project has slowly conquered some daunting hurdles, it has yet to get off the ground. ⨳

Region D:
Urban Corridor – Eureka (Indianola Road) South

Although Eureka is the largest coastal city between San Francisco and the Puget Sound, at less than 30,000 residents it only qualifies as 'urban' when compared with the rest of Humboldt County. Given Eureka's rich history as a seaport and commercial center some excellent walks re-trace some of the fishing, timber, and architectural legacy of the area. Several are identified here, however the possible walking combinations using public sidewalks and streets are almost infinite. And, from the covered bridges along Elk River and the old lumber town of Falk to Fay and Freshwater Sloughs, a variety of nearby destinations await as well.

With the Waterfront Trail extensions underway, the 1,001-acre McKay Community Forest coming on-line, and the Bay Trail plans unfolding, the prospect for some additional spectacular walking opportunities are very exciting.

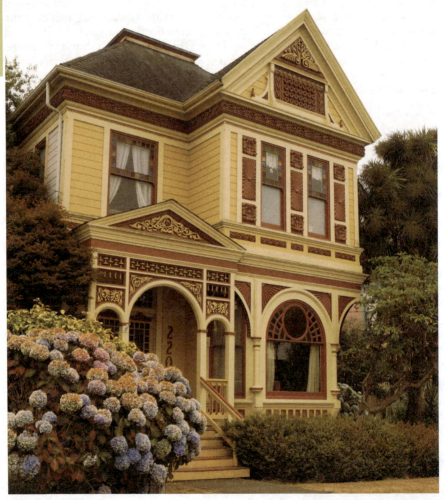

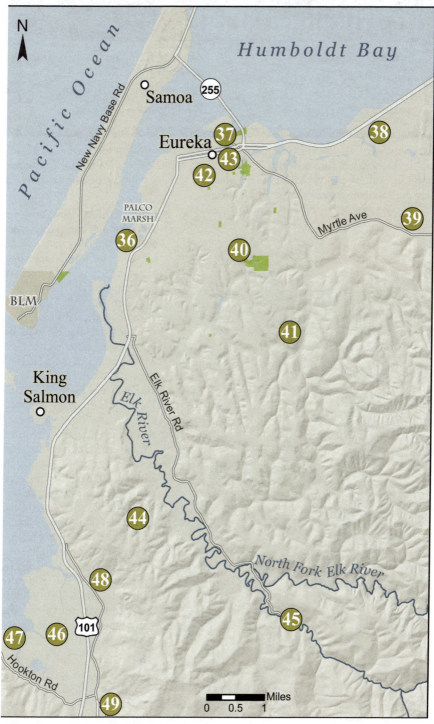

Region D: **Eureka South**

36 ·Hikshari' Trail

Length: 3.1 miles
Total ascent: flat
Elevations: sea level
Type: out and back

Access: flat, paved, wheelchair accessible
Dogs: leashed
Restrooms: yes

Description: This beautiful, multi-modal paved trail follows the edge of Humboldt Bay south before turning southeast along the Elk River. With four trailheads and tables along the way, this is a very pleasant walk or picnic spot along tidal mud flats, salt marsh, coastal prairie and scrub.

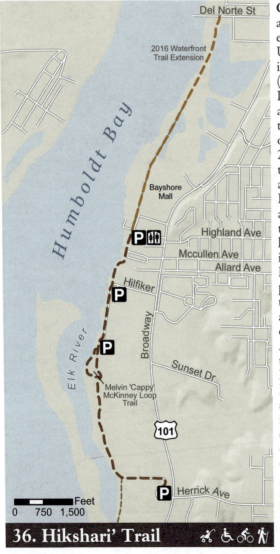

Getting there: There are four access points and parking areas for the Hikshari'. Take US 101 south 2.6 miles turning right on Truesdale Street (just past the Bayshore Mall). In 0.2 mile, as the road ends at the Bay, the Truesdale Vista Point parking lot will be on the left. Alternatively, go 2.9 miles south on US 101, turn right on Hilfiker Lane and proceed west 0.2 mile. Parking (unpaved) is available on the right just prior to Hilfiker Lane's sharp turn left (south). The third option involves continuing south on Hilfiker 0.3 mile to a paved parking area. The fourth option, the Pound Road Park and Ride, is 3.8 miles south on US 101 to the Herrick Avenue exit. Turn right into the signed Park and Ride. From the Park and Ride the Hikshari' Trail begins after a short walk north on the frontage road. Approximate driving time, 10 minutes.

The route: The Hikshari' Trail has excellent directional and natural history signage. From the Truesdale Vista Point trailhead, the southbound trail passes the Elk River Wildlife Sanctuary

Trail Access parking lot (0.6) and the junction with the Melvin "Cappy" McKinney Loop Trail, a short gravel path that is routed a little closer to the Elk River. The Loop Trail rejoins the main paved trail (0.8), which then crosses the railroad tracks (1.3), and reaches the Pound Road Park and Ride (1.5).

Extras. *Volume 1* outlines the walk on to King Salmon along the railroad tracks and the shoreline west of the PG & E power plant. It is also possible to cross the railroad bridge (over the Elk River) and turn west following any of a variety of social trails to the Elk River beach, and as of late 2016, consider walking the 1.3 mile paved waterfront Trail from Tuesdale north to Del Norte street.

37 · Eureka Waterfront Trail

Length: 4.0 miles
Total ascent: flat
Elevations: sea level
Type: partial loop or out and back
Access: flat, paved, wheelchair accessible
Dogs: yes
Restrooms: yes

Description: Written about by the likes of Raymond Carver, Eureka's waterfront was once a bustling combination of lumber mills, a robust fishing fleet and associated processing plants, and the vibrant but, at times, seedy, commercial district of a port town. Things are much quieter these days and many of the old warehouses have been razed. Nonetheless, the two-mile long waterfront is a pleasant walk. You may be as likely to see a curious harbor seal or rowers sculling down the channel as a fishing boat returning to offload its catch. (See also Walks #42 and #43.)

Getting there: It is possible to park any number of places along the route.

The route: Assuming that you park somewhere near 1st and 'F' Street, the length of the walk is about equidistant in either direction. If you start northeast first, you can stay on 1st Street. Even between 'H' and 'K' it is possible to walk on the unimproved, rough passage and continue on Waterfront Drive past the Humboldt Bay Aquatics Center, the Adorni Center, Halverson Park, and under the CA 255 bridge. As mentioned earlier, construction on an extension of this trail past Target, under US 101 to the Mrytletown area, is scheduled for 2017.

Arriving at 'T' Street (0.9), turn left and join a paved walkway that parallels a fence line to the Bay and turn left (1.0) to follow the Bay taking you back past the Eureka Boat Launch, Halverson Park, the Adorni Center, and the Humboldt Bay Aquatic Center. At the intersection of Waterfront Drive and 'L' Street (1.5 mile) turn left to 2nd Street. 2nd Street offers the opportunity to detour one block east to view the splendid Carson Mansion.

William Carson had this house designed and built by the Newsom Brothers between 1884-86 in the Victorian style (technically a larger classification that includes Gothic Revival, Italianate, French Second Empire, Eastlake, and Queen Anne styles). Across from the mansion is a second home, also designed by the Newsoms. It was built in 1887 as a gift from Carson to his son. It is an example of classic Queen Anne style with the corner tower, segmented windows, and a variety of patterned shingles. The structure housing the law offices on the northwest corner was built during the same period as the two houses and served as the headquarters for Carson's lumber empire (which once sprawled across the bay front along the now empty expanse of Halverson Park and beyond).

Continuing west on 2nd to the corner of 'G' is the Vance Hotel. Originally completed in 1871, the first electric lights in a non-industrial building in the county were installed here eight years later (powered by a generator at Vance's sawmill at the foot of 'G' Street). For decades this was the most prestigious lodging place on Humboldt Bay, but by the 1990s it stood empty until it was remodeled in 2000.

At 516 2nd Street is the Oberon Grill, the site of a saloon where, in July 1911, a legendary fistfight broke out between writer/adventurer/socialist Jack London and the future owner of The Pacific Lumber Company, 19-year-old A. Stanwood Murphy.

Take a right on 'F' Street (1.9) and follow it two blocks to the boardwalk that fronts the Bay between 'C' and 'G' Streets. Follow this promenade west to 'C' (2.1) and the Fisherman's Terminal, completed in 2011, where you can access the Madaket tours (last remaining of seven launches that once ferried people to a number of locations around the Bay) and admire several sculptures. Return to 1st Street by turning left; then turn right to continue southwest on 1st. Soon you will come to the Small Boat Basin (you can drop down and walk along the floating dock on west) and the Wharfinger Building (2.6). Follow the sidewalk on the Bay side of the Wharfinger Building and continue on south past decaying pilings indicative of a once substantial system of docks and views to the inactive skeletons of two pulp mills (only one still has much superstructure remaining) (2.9). In 2017, this route is scheduled to be improved between 'C' and Del Norte Street completing the Waterfront Trail. In late fall 2016, the 1.3 mile extension of the Waterfront Trail was opened between Del Norte and the north end of the Hikshari' Trail. This paved trail has surprisingly delightful views of the Eureka Marsh and the bay. See map for Hike #36.

On the return trip along 1st Street, a worthy detour is to turn right on 'C' Street

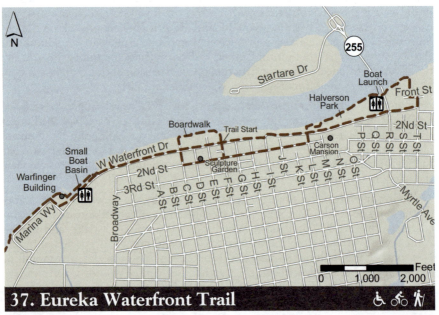

37. Eureka Waterfront Trail

and left on '2nd'. This takes you past the display honoring folk artist Romano Gabriel's sculpture garden (between 'D' and 'E'). Take a final left on 'F' Street to return to 1st Street (4.0). If you do choose to remain on 1st Street, you will pass one of the only remaining warehouses that once lined this street and Buhne's General Store (c1858), Eureka's oldest commercial building (between 'E' and 'F').

Much more historical and architectural richness in the area covered by this walk can be found in Jackson (1983), 'the Green Book' (Architectural Resources Group, 1987), and Brown (2013). The Humboldt County Historical Society (www.humboldthistory.org) has a number of resources.

38 · Fay Slough Wildlife Area

Length: 2.0 miles or longer
Total ascent: flat
Elevations: sea level
Type: out and back
Access: Closed from early February – March 31 to minimize disturbance to the geese. Hunting days are Saturdays, Sundays, and Wednesdays from mid-October to early February (hunting season).
Dogs: leashed
Restrooms: no

Description: On a sunny spring, summer, or autumn evening, this is a wonderful stroll into the heart of these wetlands. There most certainly will be a rich array of birds attracted by the fresh water, the salt water, and the fields. It does not take that long to leave the cacophony of US101 behind.

During the late summer as the ground dries, the California Department of Fish and Wildlife staff mows the north levee of Fay Slough which can make it possible to extend the walk along the levee to both the eastern and western boundaries of the Wildlife Area. I have also been able to follow a mowed path from the western boundary in a loop back to the entrance road.

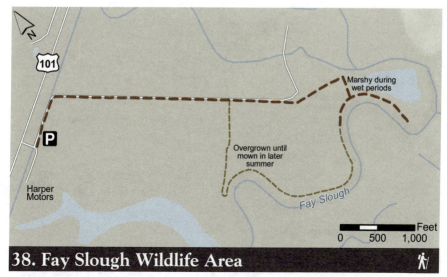

38. Fay Slough Wildlife Area

Getting there: Drive on US 101 north 2.6 miles. After passing Murray Field (airport) you will reach the Harper Motors complex on your right. Turn right at the entrance to Harper Motors. Park in the small parking area on the left (east) immediately after exiting US 101. Approximate driving time, 5 minutes.

The route: Proceed northeast from the parking lot along a graveled road (0.1) that soon turns southeast. This section of road is easy walking and would remain passable in most weather conditions (0.6). The road elevates slightly also marking a change in the roadbed and maintenance and, during certain times of the year can be somewhat overgrown (it is mown in the mid-summer which makes for easy walking). It crosses a seasonal wetland to the Fay Slough levee (1.0). Again, the levee can be overgrown in places (depending on when it has been mown) but can be followed in either direction (by going west on the levee it would be possible to loop back intersecting with the main entrance road; however on most of my visits the path along the levee is too overgrown). On a wet morning, gaiters or rain pants would be essential in the spring when the vegetation has grown high.

39 · Freshwater Farms Nature Reserve

Length: 1.6 miles
Total ascent: flat
Type: out and back
Access: currently available from roughly 8 – 5 every day; can be too wet at times during the rainy season.
Dogs: no
Restrooms: yes

Description: Located in an area historically dominated by tidal wetlands, the Freshwater Farms Nature Reserve property was originally converted to pasture in the early 1900s and historically functioned as a dairy farm. Under the more recent ownership of the Northcoast Regional Land Trust, this 74-acre property includes

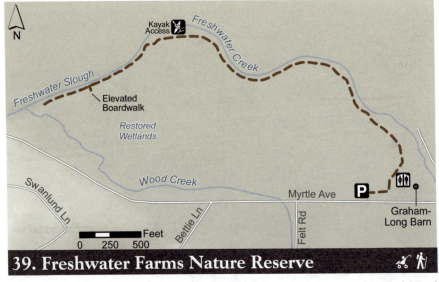

39. Freshwater Farms Nature Reserve

Freshwater Farms, photo by Mark Larson.

active bottomland pasture, wetland restoration of lower Wood Creek, and the former Freshwater Farms Nursery.

Getting there: Drive on US 101 north 0.5 mile. Turn right on Myrtle Avenue and continue for 4.2 miles. Approximate driving time, 10 minutes.

The route: The packed gravel trail begins from the east side of the parking area skirting the Farm Stand and barn. The trail turns left (0.1) and follows a dirt road, passing a copse of trees, and approaching Freshwater Slough. There is a kayak access (0.4) to the Slough that during moderate to high tides can be followed to Humboldt Bay. As road ends (0.6), the trail narrows and tightropes along the levee passing the access to the short elevated boardwalk and on to the end (0.8).

40 · Sequoia Park to Buhne Loop

Length: 2.6-3.7 miles	**Access:** open dawn to dusk
Total ascent: 360 feet	**Dogs:** leashed in park
Type: loop	**Restrooms:** yes

Description: This is an urban walk that includes Sequoia Park, a portion of a very popular walking route, and sidewalks through the 'hospital district' and pleasant neighborhoods. This route does cross busy Harris Street twice, once at an illuminated crosswalk but the other time at an unmarked crossing. Care is required.

Although accounts vary slightly, there is no question that the original acreage of Sequoia Park was transferred to the City of Eureka in 1894 by Bartlin and Henrietta Glatt. Initially called Forest Park, the parcel included the last large stand of virgin redwoods in Eureka, trees that still stand in the park gulch areas. The transformation of the land into a park is credited to Valentine Francis Harris (for whom Harris Street was subsequently named) who built the Duck Pond, road system, picnic grounds, and children's play area. Sequoia Park now totals 67 acres. It has two paved roadways that encircle much of the park with some packed earth trails through the middle.

Hiking Humboldt Volume 2

Getting there: Proceed north on US 101 for 0.5 mile before turning right onto Myrtle Avenue. Turn right on West Avenue in 0.4 mile. Head south on West Avenue for 0.6 mile continuing on 'S' Street for an additional 0.7 mile. Turn left on Harris Street and right on 'W' Street (0.2 mile). Follow 'W' Street past the Sequoia Park Zoo to Madrone Avenue (0.4 mile). Parking is available along Madrone Avenue on the south side of Sequoia Park. Approximate driving time, 8 minutes.

The route: Turn right (south) on 'W' Street, left on Hemlock (0.2), and left again on Dolbeer. Many locals walk the 'W' – Hemlock – Dolbeer – Chester mile-long loop that circles Washington School – ball fields – the National Guard Amory – and the City of Eureka reservoir. Our route continues north past Washington School and Chester Street to Harris (0.7) where there is a pedestrian activated safety system to warn on-coming cars. Continue on north to the St. Joseph Hospital complex (0.9). Cross the parking lot on the east side to Harrison Avenue. Turn left and continue north to Buhne Street (1.0). Turn left (west) and walk to 'P' Street (1.7). A continuous sidewalk lines the north side of Buhne. Turn left on 'P' Street. You will again cross Harris (2.0) but this time the crossing is unmarked and

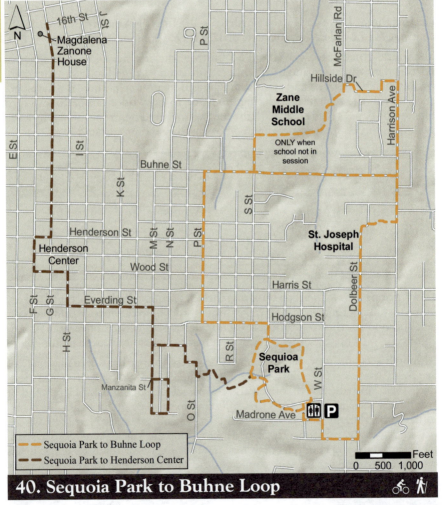

40. Sequoia Park to Buhne Loop

considerable care is necessary given the abundant traffic. Once across, continue on 'P' Street turning left on Hodgson Street (2.2). Continue east before turning south (right) again on 'T' Street (2.4). Watch for the entrance to Sequoia Park. The right fork descends to the Duck Pond and Sequoia Creek Trail before climbing steeply and returning to the Madrone Avenue parking area (2.6). The left fork stays at grade and bends around behind the Sequoia Park Zoo (2.7).

Possible Extension When Zane Middle School is NOT in Session: Instead of turning west on Buhne Street, continue north on Harrison Avenue to Hillside Drive (0.3). Turn left and follow Hillside as it bends to a junction with McFarlan Street (0.5). Turn left on a paved pedestrian walkway that continues for a short distance south before veering right across Zane Middle School playfields through the school parking area to its outlet on 'S' Street (1.0). Turn left on 'S' Street to the intersection with Buhne (1.1). Turn right on Buhne Street and resume the primary route. This option avoids the heavy traffic that sometimes travels on Buhne.

Extras. Sequoia Park to Henderson Center. Instead of south from Sequoia Park, this route leaves the west side of the park on the Sequoia Creek Trail to reach 'O' Street. Turn right on 'O' and proceed to Bryant Street, where you will turn left. In two blocks you will reach 'M' Street (0.9). Continuing south on 'M' Street takes you on a 0.5 mile diversion through a pleasant neighborhood. Turn left on Manzanita, right on 'N', right on Madrone and right again on 'M' Street which will return you to the Bryant Street intersection. 'M' Street will take you to Everding Street in two blocks (1.0). Turn left on Everding and proceed to 'H' Street where a right turn leads to a traffic light which facilitates crossing busy Harris Street (1.4 mile). After one more block on 'H' Street, turn left onto Wood Street. Continuing two blocks on Wood to 'F' Street places you in the middle of Henderson Center's commercial district, with a variety of eating and shopping opportunities (1.5). Take note of two Henderson Center Murals – Randy Spicer's tropical fish scene at 2931 'F' Street between Henderson and Harris and Duane Flatmo's old time gas station scene at 2737 'F' Street on Henderson and 'F' Street.

The route continues by going one block east and then turning left (north) on 'G' Street to 16th. Eureka civic beautification efforts have been particularly successful along 'G' Street with the addition of 'street trees' and many well-kept historic homes. Walk as far as you wish along 'G' Street perhaps as far as 1604 'G' Street, an excellent example of a Queen Anne style home. Retrace your steps.

41 ·McKay Community Forest

Length: 2.7 miles
Total ascent: 350 feet
Elevations: 140 – 350 feet
Type: partial loop

Access: only when Winship Middle School is not in session
Dogs: yes
Restrooms: no

Since the transfer of the 1,000-acre McKay Community Forest to the county in 2014, we have been anxiously awaiting the development of that parcel. Efforts are underway to develop a trail plan with consideration for sustainability and accommodating multi-use goals. The McKay Community Forest property did not come with perfect, "ready-to-go" access points. Access points need to have adequate parking and be compatible with adjacent properties, in addition to linking to trail segments. The county is exploring potential trailheads that include Harris Street, Redwood Acres, the new Hospice of Humboldt facility, Manzanita Avenue, Redwood Fields, and Northridge Drive. The main logging road through the McKay Tract (the R-Line) is not part of the community forest and remains under Green Diamond's ownership. As of 2017, there is no signage or trail maintenance, and minimal monitoring of the space..

It is possible to walk along the old existing logging roads and social trails. As you wait for the county staff and community volunteers to begin building trails, here is an option for the more intrepid explorer.

Description: This walk is along an old logging road, chewed up by mountain bikes and neglect. The route remains in the riparian corridor to a crossing of Ryan Creek that leads to the R-Line on Green Diamond land. Retrace your steps or cautiously climb a steep mountain bike trail return. Given the absence of signage, it is important to be comfortable with way finding.

Getting there: Go south on H Street for 2.6 miles to Fern Drive. Continue for 0.4 mile to Excelsior Road. Turn right for 0.4 mile and left on Holly Street for 0.2 mile. Turn left on Walnut Street for 0.2 mile and right on Cypress Avenue. Approximate driving time, 11 minutes.

The route: Follow the unpaved road on the left side of Winship Middle School and enter the forest passing a gate (0.3). Under power lines (0.5) continue straight leaving the dirt access road. The trail splits (0.7) and take the right fork. The trail continues along this old logging road to Ryan Creek (1.4). A step-across stream much of the summer and fall, the short trail on the opposite side leads to the R-Line which is on Green Diamond land. I suggest returning the way you came or climb the steep bike trail (1.7). Once on the top, continue to follow the mountain bike trails that stay on the ridge as you return to the access road (2.2) and Winship Middle School (2.7).

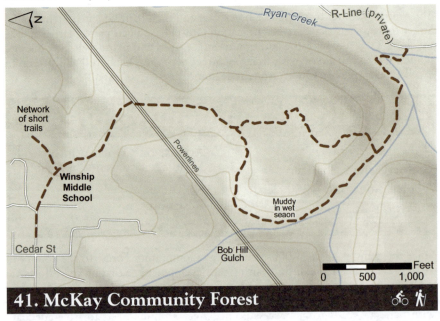

41. McKay Community Forest

42 · Eureka Architecture Walk

Length: 2.8 miles
Total ascent: flat
Elevations: 10 – 50 feet
Type: partial loop

Access: most of this route is on public sidewalks.
Dogs: yes
Restrooms: yes

Description: Eureka dates from May, 1850 when it was established to supply the gold miners seeking their fortunes inland. By 1865, the local economy began to shift as demand for lumber increased in the more populated areas farther south. Prominent Eurekans who prospered from commerce and the fishing and timber industries, could easily purchase lumber and employed talented craftsmen to build the Victorian-era homes that still exist today. This walk is routed by a sample of remaining homes, many in excellent condition. This walk and its companion walk through Old Town provide a glimpse into this architectural past.

Getting there: It is generally possible to find 2-hour street parking on 'F' Street between 6th and 7th or nearby. This should be plenty of time to complete this walk. On the south side of 7th, there are no time restrictions. Start at or near the Eureka Theatre and the Morris Graves Museum of Art (the former Carnegie Library, 1902). This is just three blocks west and two blocks south of the Humboldt County Courthouse.

The route:

Proceed east on 7th Street past the Eureka Inn taking a right on 'H' Street.

The Eureka Inn (1922). This 150-room (104 guest rooms) structure is listed on the National Register of Historic Places. It was built in the half-timbered Tudor style and worth a trip inside.

730 'H' Street – The Thomas F. Ricks house, built (c. 1885) in the Eastlake style, is on the National Register of Historic Places.

In two blocks turn right on 9th Street and left on 'G' Street.

904 'G' Street - The Simpson-Vance House is also on the National Register of

∞ Brief Overview of Victorian Style

Although this walk can be enjoyed at a number of levels, the experience is definitely enhanced by a basic understanding of the features of Victorian architecture. What is labeled as Victorian can be broken down into a number of styles common during the Victorian era (roughly 1850 – 1900). On this walk, many of the highlighted homes have been built in the Stick or Eastlake style and the Queen Anne Revival style. Stick or Eastlake houses will have square bays and square towers, are always made of wood, often have small, rectangular carved panels under the windows and eaves, may use spindles and knobs and other borrowings from furniture. Houses built in the Queen Anne style generally have projecting gables with a round or octagonal tower at the corner with an onion or witch's hat on top. The Queen Anne style draws extensively from earlier styles with its use of patterned shingles, colonnaded single-story wraparound porches, and steeply pitched roofs. Watch for the distinctive Palladian windows (a three-part window in which the center window is arched and taller and wider than the flanking, square-headed windows). ∞

Hiking Humboldt Volume 2

Historic Places. The Redwood Community Action Agency occupies this grand Queen Anne style house built in 1892.

In two blocks turn left on 11th and right on 'H' Street. Continue to 17th Street and turn right and right again on 'G' Street. Walk on 'G' Street to 9th Street. Turn left and left again on 'F' Street.

1125 'H' Street – Cornelius Daly Inn and Bed and Breakfast. This Colonial Revival, built in 1905, takes its influence from the early colonial styles of the Atlantic Seaboard.

1134 'H' Street – Queen Anne style (1900)

1230 'H' Street - 8,500 square foot Charles Wright House

1411 'H' Street – Stick/Eastlake house (1890)

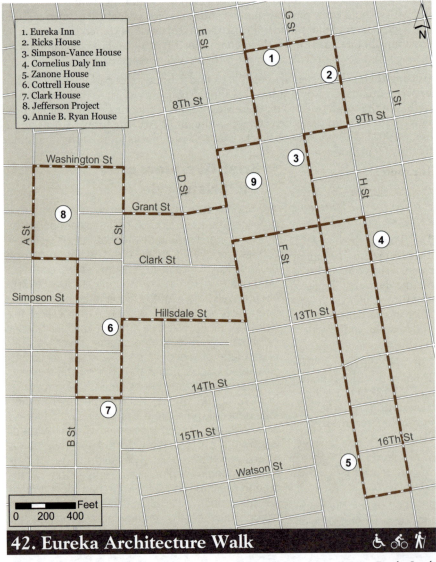

1. Eureka Inn
2. Ricks House
3. Simpson-Vance House
4. Cornelius Daly Inn
5. Zanone House
6. Cottrell House
7. Clark House
8. Jefferson Project
9. Annie B. Ryan House

42. Eureka Architecture Walk

1603 'H' Street – Colonial Revival style house (1904)

1604 'H' Street – This cottage features an intricately carved Eastlake porch (1887)

On reaching 17th Street, turn right, proceed one block, turn right again on 'G' Street

1604 'G' Street – Eastlake style cottage (1887) This house, the Magdalena Zanone House, is on the National Register of Historic Places.

1501 – 1503 'G' Street – Queen Anne style house (1888)

1226 'G' Street – Stick/Eastlake style house (1888)

1103 – 1109 'G' Street – Queen Anne style house (1902)

Turn left on 11th Street and left on 'E' Street.

1302 'E' Street – Queen Anne/Colonial Revival style house (1893)

1304 'E' Street - Queen Anne/Eastlake style cottage (1893)

Turn right on Hillsdale and left on 'C' Street in two blocks.

Hillsdale Avenue – although only two blocks long, this offers a glimpse of late 19th Century architecture at its peak.

1228 'C' Street – The Cottrell House (1902). This house blends Eastlake and Queen Anne features. It is on the National Register of Historic Places.

1406 'C' Street – The William S. Clark house (1886) was one of Eureka's nicest homes. It is an Eastlake style with some Queen Anne flourishes. It is on the National Register of Historic Places and operates as a bed and breakfast

Turn right on 14th and right again on 'B' Street. Turn left on Clark and right on 'A' Street. Turn right on Washington Street and right again on 'C' Street. Turn left on Grant and left on 'E' Street. Turn right on 9th Street and left on 'F' Street returning to the beginning of the route.

1103 'B' Street – Built in 1871 (major alterations in 1902) with some Queen Anne details

Jefferson Project – formerly the Jefferson Elementary School, this space has been transformed by community volunteers of Eureka's Westside Community Improvement Association.

10 W. Clark – Craftsman bungalow (1912)

'E' Street had a horse drawn railway system on it from 1892 – 1897

1000 'F' Street – Annie B. Ryan House (1892). This Queen Anne cottage is being restored by classes from the College of the Redwoods with the gardens (accessible from 'E' Street) being developed by local volunteers.

917 – 919 'E' Street – House in the Queen Anne/Classical Revival style with a corner tower and classically detailed roof pediment (the triangular gable end of a roof)

NW Corner of 9th and 'G' – California bungalow, now mostly hidden by a fence.

More historical and architectural richness exists in the area covered by this walk than can be recounted in the space available here. See Jackson (1983) and the Architectural Resources Group (1987) for wonderful detail.

43 · Eureka Old Town Mural & Historical Walk

Length: 3.4 miles	**Type:** loop
Total ascent: flat	**Dogs:** yes
Elevations: 20 – 35 feet	**Restrooms:** yes

Description: Some of the most interesting walks have turned out to be incredibly close to home. Case in point is this meandering journey through Eureka's commercial district and Old Town (an 11-block long, three-block wide district of Late Victorian, Greek Revival, Classical Revival storefronts and residences recognized on the National Register of Historic Places) designed to pass nearly two dozen murals and, in the process, get a taste of the historic architecture. There may be a few cars to dodge but no streams to ford. And unless you get really lost, you won't come home with your shoes muddy.

Alley Cats by Duane Flatmo and the Rural Burl Mural Bureau

Local artist Duane Flatmo and the Rural Burl Mural Bureau are largely responsible for the proliferation of murals. Flatmo's mural career began with the Bucksport Mural on South Broadway in 1984 and expanded a decade later with the creation of the Mural Burl, a program involving area youth in mural projects. He has been involved in more than 50 murals over the past three decades.

This walk visits 22 murals including high profile murals like those visible from the entrance to the Arkley Center for the Performing Arts or on the south side of the Eureka Co-op. Less grand but no less interesting are images of wild plants, majestic egrets, and surreal street scenes. There is a massive whale and its calf on 'A' Street and a winged grizzly (Eureka's greatest animal thespian "Bearymore") adorning the north side of Redwood Curtain Theatre. There are horse drawn fire wagons next to the public library and a rendition of Murray Field circa 1930 visible from 4th Street. Some will find the most intriguing mural the one that you can't see. Almost totally obscured by the construction of the George Petersen Insurance Building, a slim 3-inch gap on the west side of the building offers a glimpse of the mural between 'D' and 'E' on 4th Street. "Earthquake Aftermath", which Flatmo said took the Mural Bureau some six months to complete, hadn't been up much more than a year before construction of the adjacent building almost obscured the scene.

Admittedly, the murals run the gamut in terms of quality. But, considered as a whole, they make for an intriguing, whimsical quest as you weave around buildings that often date back a century and a half.

Getting there: Begin at any number of places along the suggested route.

The route: The details of this walk are extensive, so we have put them on our website: v2.hikinghumboldt.com

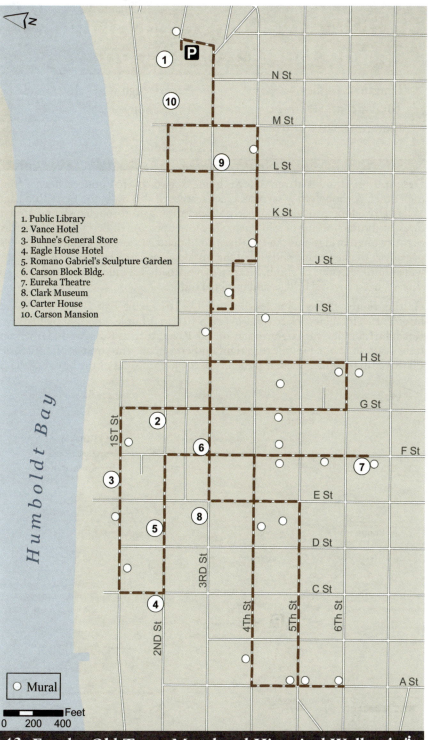

44 · Elk River Covered Bridges and Berta Road Loop

Length: 2.7 miles
Total ascent: 800 feet
Elevations: 20 – 700 feet

Access: high water closes roads
Type: loop
Dogs: yes
Restrooms: no

Description: The Elk River Valley is home to two covered bridges, not far from each other. Although they serve as a nice feature of this walk, the Berta Road and Valley Drive loop provides some aerobic elevation gain through a second growth forest and rural housing development. The lower portion of Berta Road that crosses the covered bridge and the Elk River flood plain carries considerable traffic (especially at the beginning and end of the work day) as a one-lane road and does not widen until it begins to climb. Nearby Zanes Road (1.2 mile round trip) is much shorter, has a covered bridge, and minimal traffic.

Getting there: Drive 3.5 miles south on US 101 taking Exit 702 (Herrick Avenue). Turn left on Herrick crossing over US 101. In 0.1 mile turn right on Elk River Road. In 1.5 miles, turn right to stay on Elk River Road as Ridgewood Drive continues east. In about 1.0 mile turn right on Berta Road. The covered bridge crosses Elk River in 0.1 mile. There is pull out space on both sides of the bridge which is

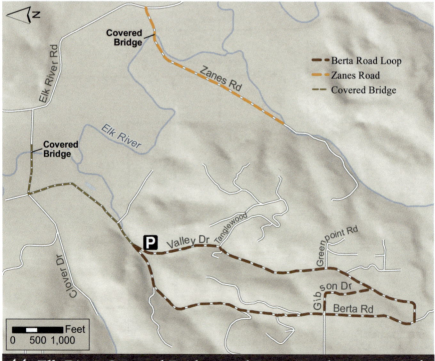

◦ Why Covered Bridges?

For many centuries, wood was a preferred material for building bridges in forested regions of the world. It was strong, abundant, relatively lightweight, and easy to work with. However, when exposed to the elements, the wooden trusses tended to deteriorate rapidly. Covered, they could last for centuries. By the 1870s, there were well over 10,000 covered bridges in the United States. As iron began to supplant wood in bridge construction, the numbers diminished to fewer than 700 of these historic structures. The Berta Road bridge was built in 1936 and its Zanes Road neighbor a year later. ◦◦

not intended for parking. Parking can be found 0.7 mile further at the junction of Berta Road and Valley Drive and on the right side of Valley Drive as it proceeds up hill. Approximate driving time, 20 minutes.

The route: Berta Road veers to the right and Valley Drive to the left. Valley Drive offers a somewhat more gradual climb and less opportunity for route confusion. Walking up Valley Drive you will pass Tanglewood and Greenpoint Roads. Stay to the right as you climb through this second growth spruce forest. The road changes from paved to hard packed gravel shortly after passing Greenpoint. Eventually the road intersects with Berta (1.4). Turn right before dropping down (2.7) to rejoin Valley (and your vehicle). Be aware that much of Valley Road is a private thoroughfare although it provides access to a large number of homes. If you choose to venture from your parking spot to the covered bridge (1.4 mile round trip), walk alertly along this narrow, one-lane road through the grazing land in the Elk River flood plain. Fortunately, the rough road prevents cars from driving too quickly.

Berta Road covered bridge.

Hiking Humboldt Volume 2

45 · Elk River Trail to Falk

Length: 2.2 miles
Total ascent: 150 feet
Elevations: 130 – 170 feet

Access: sunrise to sunset
Type: out and back
Dogs: leashed
Restrooms: yes

Description: Although the longer version of the hike into the Headwaters Forest via the Elk River Trail is included in *Volume 1*, the first mile to the historic logging community of Falk has been included here because it is paved and accessible. The trail is sprinkled with informational signs, benches, and picnic tables along this first mile. The trail to Falk is never far from the Elk River.

Falk Mill in 1907 from the Swanlund-Baker Collection, Humboldt State University Library.

Getting there: Drive south on US 101 for 3.8 miles taking Exit 702 (Herrick Avenue). Turn left on Herrick Avenue crossing over US 101. Turn right on Elk River Road (0.1 mile) and drive almost 6 miles, staying right at the two forks. Elk River Road ends in the trailhead. Approximate driving time, 25 minutes.

The route: From the parking lot walk southeast along the paved trail. A short alternative unpaved trail takes off to the right (0.3) and parallels the river rejoining the main trail in 0.2 mile. The main trail passes the Educational Center (0.6), created from a restored lumber train barn abandoned when the mill shut down in 1937. All along the way to the old townsite of Falk, now long disappeared, are information signs about the natural and logging history of this area. The pavement ends at the site of Falk (1.1). Return the way you came.

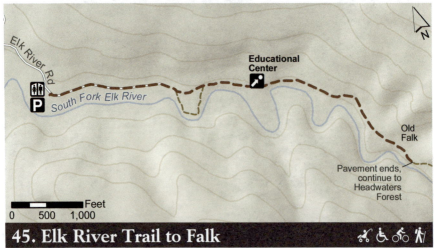

46 · Humboldt Bay Wildlife Refuge – Shorebird Loop

Length: 1.75 miles
Total ascent: flat
Elevations: sea level
Access: 8:00-5:00 daily
Type: partial loop
Dogs: no
Restrooms: yes

Description: This short walk through the estuary created by Salmon Creek and the southern part of Humboldt Bay provides a glimpse into the extensive wetland and saltmarsh restoration efforts. This is a level, gravel trail with an observation kiosk, interpretive panels, and a viewing platform. The trail winds its way past freshwater wetlands and a brackish pond until it bends back at Hookton Slough. This area is quite exposed and can often be buffeted by strong winds off the ocean. Early in the day minimizes the chance of windy conditions.

Getting there: Drive south about 10.4 miles on US 101 to Exit 696 (Hookton Road). Turn right on Eel River Drive and almost immediately left onto the Humboldt Bay National Wildlife Refuge access road. Follow that road for 1.6 miles to the Visitor Center parking lot. Approximate driving time, 20 minutes.

The route: This signed route leaves from the south side of the Visitor Center. All potential wrong turns are well marked. Benches, interpretative panels, and other features are spaced out along the trail.

∞ Aleutian Cackling Geese

The recovery of the Aleutian cackling geese (which are differentiated from Canada geese) from no more than a few hundred birds in the late 1960s to well over 140,000 birds is a conservation success story. Once widespread along the Pacific Flyway, their numbers began declining because of the introduction of Arctic foxes to the Aleutian Islands by fur traders. These fox preyed on vulnerable goose rookeries and nearly wiped out the subspecies. After Aleutian cackling geese were declared endangered (1967), an arduous process of eliminating the foxes on four key islands was initiated. Local biologist, Paul Springer, was the primary architect of this recovery. The rebound began almost immediately resulting in the removal of the Aleutian cackling goose from the threatened (1990) and endangered species lists (2001). These days the dawn fly-off can be a special sight as thousands of geese take off to forage in area grasslands. Populations peak at the Refuge in the spring until they depart for the Aleutians in mid-April. ∞

Photo by Mike Peters.

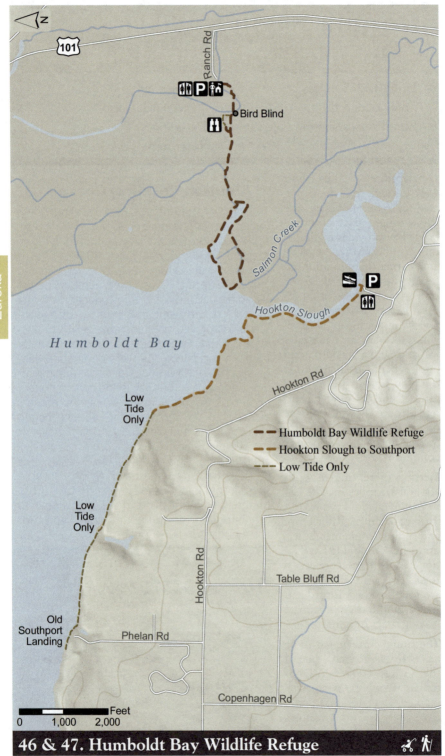

46 & 47. Humboldt Bay Wildlife Refuge

47 · Humboldt Bay Wildlife Refuge – Hookton Slough

Length: 3.0 miles
Total ascent: flat
Access: sunrise to sunset
Type: out and back
Dogs: no
Restrooms: yes

Description: This walk follows the west levee of Hookton Slough as it meanders northwest to join Humboldt Bay. This is a level, grassy trail with a gravel base and interpretative panels along the way. With the slough on one side and wetlands on the other, this is an excellent avian viewing area. I have seen river otters in this area as well. This area is quite exposed and can often be buffeted by strong winds. Morning walks maximize the chance of less windy conditions.

Getting there: Drive south about 10.4 miles on US 101 to Exit 696 (Hookton Road). Continue on Hookton Road for 1.4 miles. Turn right onto the Hookton Slough Trail Access Road and proceed into the parking lot (0.1 mile). Approximate driving time, 20 minutes.

The route: This signed route leaves from the west side of the parking lot and follows the levee out and back (1.5 miles each way).

Extras. In low tide conditions, it is possible to walk on the sandy shoreline on west from the end of the formal trail for another 1.0 mile to the remnants of Southport Landing. This is a rare area of Humboldt Bay were the shoreline is not mud. It is important to accurately gauge the tidal movement as the shoreline, with a few exceptions, is an impenetrable mass of vegetation that would make an unplanned exit difficult.

∞ Hookton Slough and Southport Landing

The sleepy south end of Humboldt Bay was not always so. Before the railroad and highway, shallow draft ships using the Hookton Channel and the Southport Channel were the preferred way of transporting goods out from the Eel River valley. Since the trail around the Bay was virtually impassable during the rainy months, the first wharf along Hookton Slough was constructed in 1856. At that time, Wiyot villages and camps occupied the perimeter of the marshy mouth of Salmon Creek.

A second wharf was erected in the 1870s at Southport Landing, which lies several miles to the west. Southport Landing amenities included a half-mile long wharf, a warehouse that remained until 2007, Charles Heney's stately home (built in 1888) that still stands a hundred yards south of the bay, and a 5-mile long railroad (see Loleta Tunnel sidebar).

Since then, mills have come and gone. The little community of Beatrice, near the east end of Hookton Slough, is survived only by the Salmon Creek School (now the Swiss Hall). Two decades have passed since a train rumbled by and far longer since a ship laden with freight plied these waters. Traffic now races by on US 101, unaware of this rich history. ∞

48 · College Of The Redwoods Campus

Length: up to 2.0 miles	**Type:** loop
Total ascent: 180 feet	**Dogs:** no
Elevations: 115 – 345 feet	**Restrooms:** yes
Access: busy when school is in session	**Fee:** $2 parking except weekends.

Description: The basic route meanders around the beautiful College of the Redwoods campus. In addition to the academic buildings the campus is nicely landscaped and includes two small lakes, the massive Shelter Cove Fog Bell, and some public art. This walk can easily be combined with a walk through the nearby Humboldt Botanical Gardens.

Getting there: Drive south about 7.6 miles on US 101 to Exit 698 (Tompkins Hill Road). Follow the exit .5 mile as it winds back underneath US 101 turning right on Tompkins Hill Road. In about .8 mile turn left into the signed main entrance and the expansive parking lot for the College of the Redwoods. A parking permit is required for most hours Monday – Friday. Approximate driving time, 15 minutes.

The route: Exit the southeast side of the parking lot, veering right on the pathway leading between the Child Development Center and Community Stadium. Turn left at the softball field and proceed north past the east side of the fieldhouse and the Physical Education Building. Stay east of the new Administration/Student Services building and continue walking north through the parking lot for the residence halls. Turn left proceeding along the south side of the first small lake. Continue on the road (or as you descend, passing the second lake you can move to the sidewalk on the left side of the road) down the hill and back up to the Creative Arts building. The Humboldt Botanical Gardens are just beyond this turnaround point. Take a brief detour through the covered passage in the middle of the building. Return to the main campus but this time, as you climb the hill, move closer to the buildings. Pass the former Physical Science/Math building and the former Life Science building, both of which are no longer in use. Pass between the Redwood Business complex (on your right) and the new Science and Math and Humanities

∞ College of the Redwoods

Ground was broken at the current location of the College of the Redwoods in September, 1965 and first used for classes three years later. Seven sites were seriously considered (from McKinleyville to Fortuna) and after a contentious process, the 160-acre Bartlett ranch five and a half miles south of Eureka was selected. An additional 113 acres of adjacent ranch lands were added to the original parcel. It is a spacious and picturesque setting.

The main campus was built for a cost of $3.1 million. In 2006, voters passed a $40 million bond measure that has made possible a series of renovations and new buildings now complete.

In 1975, residents of coastal Mendocino County voted to join the Community College District as did Del Norte County three years later. Recent enrollments at the main and branch campuses have hovered around 8,000 students. ∞

facilities (on your left). You can finish your walk by either passing the Learning Resource Center on the left or right. If you pass on the right, veer down toward the parking lot where you will pass the Shelter Cove Fog Bell. If you pass on the left, turn right on the east side of the building. Pass the bus stop and proceed toward the parking lot (the bell will be on your right).

The central portion of the main campus complex is relatively flat and linked by wheelchair accessible routes.

48a · Humboldt Botanical Gardens

Length: up to 2.5 miles
Total ascent: 180 feet
Access: $8, confirm open hours at www.hbgf.org, some ADA accessible
Type: loop
Dogs: no
Restrooms: yes

Description: Despite only being 44 acres, the garden has a network of roads, walkways, paths, and cruder walking options that cover the extensive and picturesque grounds. The stunning Dedekam Ornamental Terrace Garden (ADA accessible) near the Botanical Garden Enterance and the Moss Family Temperate Woodland Garden located about .25 mile east on the main pathway/road offer walkways designed more to appreciate the flora than a walk for exercise. Those areas should be enjoyed at a slow pace. In contrast, the central road and the paths above and below that main road offer two miles of aerobic options with minimal backtracking. The grounds offer a plethora of benches, vista points, informational signage, and even an Earth Sculpture that combines features of a labyrinth and a ziggurat (you

can walk a half mile on its 100-foot diameter earth mound).

Getting there: Follow the directions to Hike #48. Once you turn on Tompkins Hill Road, turn left in 0.3 mile into the signed North Entrance for the College of the Redwoods. A Humboldt Botanical Garden sign marks the turn as well.

Ziggurat in upper gardens.

The route (shown on Hike #48 map): It is difficult to get lost on the Botanical Garden grounds. For that reason, exploring the main road and the many side trails would be a reasonable strategy when walking the Botanical Garden.

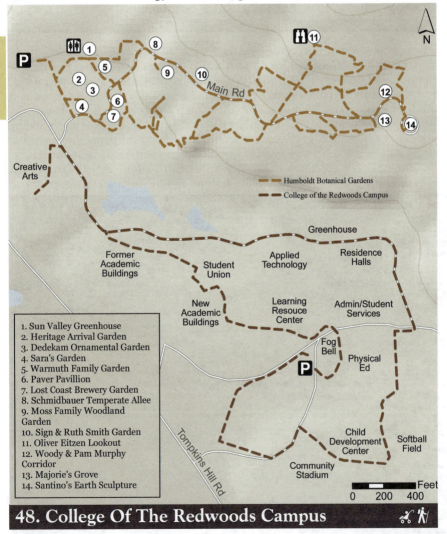

1. Sun Valley Greenhouse
2. Heritage Arrival Garden
3. Dedekam Ornamental Garden
4. Sara's Garden
5. Warmuth Family Garden
6. Paver Pavillion
7. Lost Coast Brewery Garden
8. Schmidbauer Temperate Allee
9. Moss Family Woodland Garden
10. Sign & Ruth Smith Garden
11. Oliver Eitzen Lookout
12. Woody & Pam Murphy Corridor
13. Majorie's Grove
14. Santino's Earth Sculpture

48. College Of The Redwoods Campus

49 · Tompkins Hill Road

Length: 5.6 miles
Total ascent: 580 feet
Elevations: 40 – 470 feet
Type: out and back
Dogs: yes
Restrooms: no

Description: Tompkins Hill Road between Hookton Road and Palmer Creek Road is 5.3 miles in length. The southern half, while picturesque, has too much traffic and is too narrow to be a pleasant walk. The north 2.6 miles, however, has far less traffic and provides a pleasant bucolic experience and during the final half-mile rises sufficiently high to provide views back over the Salmon Creek estuary and the South Bay. On a beautiful winter weekday afternoon, I encountered 15 cars while walking this stretch of the road.

Getting there: Drive south 10.4 miles on US 101 to Exit 696 (Hookton Road). Turn right on Eel River Drive as it circles back over US 101 to an intersection with Hookton Road (0.4 mile). Turn left on Hookton Road. After 0.1 mile, turn left on Tompkins Hill Road and continue 0.1 mile to the Swiss Hall. There is parking along the east side of the road and to the south of the Hall. The 0.2 mile south to the intersection with Tompkins Hill Road is very busy and special care must be taken to safely navigate this short initial walk. A second option is to turn right on Tompkins Hill Road from Hookton Road and drive 2.5 miles and park at the south end of the walk. Ample room for cars exists on the west side of the road for the final 0.1 mile with the best being where the road levels out and bends east of the ridge into the trees. Approximate driving time, 16 minutes.

The route (no map): From the Swiss Hall, Tompkins Hill and Hookton Roads diverge a short distance south (0.2). From the intersection Tompkins Hill Road splits the Holgeson Dairy passing next to barns and holding pens (0.3). To the left a nondescript road rises to the estate of renowned artist Morris Graves (not accessible). To the right, through a gate belonging to the dairy, the vestige of Singley Lane crosses the valley eventually climbing Table Bluff just east of the moribund Northwest Pacific Railroad prism (that soon reaches the Loleta Tunnel – see the separate entry). Tompkins Hill Road continues south passing a road that provides access to timberlands to the east (1.1). During certain times of the year there can be logging truck traffic emerging from this road. The road soon crosses a fork of the Salmon Creek (1.2) and a second fork (1.8) as the road passes a roadside farm. Eventually the road starts its steady climb up Tompkins Hill (2.3). It makes a sharp and steep turn (special care required here) and emerges onto the exposed hillside as it continues to climb (2.8). Where the road turns to the left side of the ridge and re-enters trees (also marked by a few mailboxes) makes a good place to turn around. Enjoy the view from this vantage point out over the Salmon River estuary and South Bay as you retrace your steps.

View from Tompkins Hill

Region E:
Fortuna - Ferndale - Rio Del

The broad, flat and fertile Eel River delta dominates the landscape in this region. In summer and fall, when the flow of the Van Duzen and the mighty Eel diminish to a trickle, it is difficult to imagine that the Eel could ever create such a grand landform. But, come winter rains, the Eel River can quickly change personalities. During these times of indiscriminate fury, the river carries the highest suspended sediment load of any river of its size in the United States.

This section includes a number of road walks across this agricultural bottomland and around the communities of Loleta, Ferndale, and Fortuna. In addition, there are walks on the major ridges serving as the northern (Table Bluff) and southern boundaries (Bear River Ridge) of the Eel River delta, several walks along the sandy beaches and dramatic headlands in this region, and even a walk into Headwaters Forest.

Nancy Spruance

Region E: **Fortuna - Ferndale - Rio Dell**

50 · Singley Road/Table Bluff Cemetery

Length: 3.6 miles
Total ascent: 300 feet
Elevations: 80 – 360 feet
Type: out and back
Dogs: yes
Restrooms: no

Description: Once a bustling community, downtown Loleta is now dominated by the moribund railroad and the large but defunct creamery building that remind visitors of better times. The route follows Loleta Drive as it climbs up Table Bluff to the east crossing over US 101, where it magically becomes Singley Lane. This road takes a right-hand bend to become Singley Hill Road, offers access to the Table Bluff Cemetery down a dead end (pun intended) west spur (amputated years ago by 101) and Bear River Casino in the other direction. The views from the ridge of the Eel River Valley and north into the Salmon Creek and Tompkins Hill area are very rewarding.

Consider combining this walk with a ride on the Timber Heritage Association's infrequent "speeder" rides from downtown Loleta to the Table Bluff tunnel. A stop at the Loleta Cheese Factory (and its very pleasant garden oasis complete with picnic table) is also a worthy diversion.

Getting there: Drive south about 12.5 miles on US 101 to Exit 694 (Loleta Drive). Turn right and continue on Loleta Drive for 0.9 miles. Turn left on Main Street. There is ample parking in this area although be careful to observe the 15-minute parking restrictions in some areas. Approximate driving time, 20 minutes.

The route: There are several ways, in addition to the direct walk up Loleta Drive, to pass through Loleta. After passing the Loleta Cheese Factory and the carcass of the massive Golden State Milk condensed milk plant (which most recently served as a location in the movie *Halloween III*), a short detour left on Scenic Drive and right on Park Street will soon rejoin Loleta Drive. Follow Loleta Drive as it crosses over the top of US 101 (0.9). Of course, this requires some care but this road tends to receive limited use. The route continues as Singley Lane until it intersects with Singley Hill Road (1.3). Turn left to reach the Table Bluff Cemetery (est. 1887) with grave markers dating from the late 1800s (1.8).

Just a short distance from the Cemetery's main gate, frontiersman and early settler, saloonkeeper, and Indian agent Seth Kinman is buried along with his mother (Ellen), daughter (Ellen), son (Carlin), and various family members (see Hike #60 sidebar). Below the marble and granite monuments to the east are the simple markers in the Wiyot section of the cemetery with dates that reflect the limited life expectancy of a marginalized people.

Other graves of note include descendents of the Perrott clan including Lynn and Vera (Perrott) Vietor whose generosity began the Humboldt Area Foundation and Laura Perrott Mahan, who (along with her husband) played a huge role in the protection of the virgin redwoods of Dyerville Flat (aka Founders Grove area). The Perrott family's summer home "Forest Lodge" was incorporated into Humboldt Redwoods State Park and their 640-acre land grant is the site of Loleta.

Extras. Turning right from Singley Lane and proceeding along Singley Hill Road for 1.2 miles leads to Bear River Casino, which can be an alternate trailhead.

50a · Loleta Tunnel

Length: 2.8 miles
Total ascent: flat
Elevations: 40 – 60 feet
Access constraints: This walk involves trespassing on NCRA right-of-way. Bring flashlight.
Type: out and back
Dogs: yes
Restrooms: no

Description: The tunnel NWP #40 burrows for nearly 0.4 mile underneath Table Bluff just north of Loleta. It involves an easy walk along the tracks and with a flashlight or headlamp the tunnel can be quite safely navigated. The walk does involve walking on railroad ties.

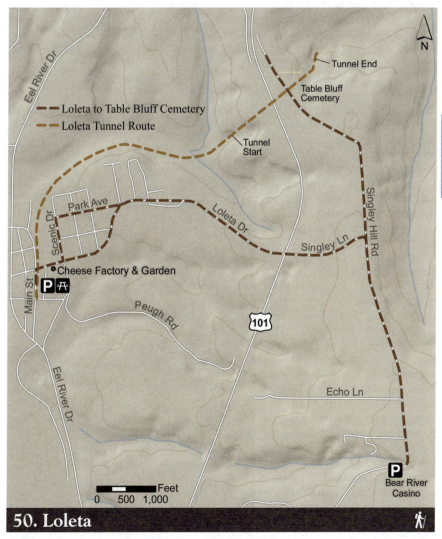

∞ Loleta Tunnel History

When the lumbermen of the 1870s and 1880s wanted to transport logs and lumber from the Eel River Valley to Humboldt Bay for milling or shipping, Table Bluff presented a formidable obstacle. Initial efforts, lead by local entrepreneur Charles Heney, involved construction of a five-mile wooden-track railroad around the western end of Table Bluff to Southport Landing (just beyond the western terminus of the Hookton Slough walk). This solution was destroyed by a storm in the winter of 1878. However, as Barry Evans noted (*North Coast Journal*, February 14, 2013), roads over Table Bluff were a barely viable alternative. A report in the *Humboldt Times* (April 15, 1876) observed, "...surely we never before saw a highway in such deplorable condition. Great ruts and mudholes, into which the horse sank over knee deep and it is a mystery to us how the Rohnerville stages succeed in pulling through them."

In 1882, several lumber barons (including William Carson, John Vance, and Captain Henry Buhne) established the Eel River and Eureka Railroad and worked to solve the Eel to the Bay transportation problem. The tunnel was completed in the summer of 1884. In 1907, many local railroads were reorganized as the Northwestern Pacific Railroad that continues to exist today. However, the last train used these tracks in the late 1990s. ∞

Getting there: Same as Singley Road/Table Bluff Cemetery above.

The route: The parking is adjacent to the railroad tracks. Picnic tables on the nearby grassy strip make for a pleasant lunch spot before or after the walk. A large "Hiking Trail" sign has been erected on the north side of Loleta Drive pointing you in the general direction. Walk north along the railroad tracks bending around the northern boundary of Loleta, largely obscured by hillside and vegetation. Thanks to the efforts of the Timber Heritage Association, that periodically offers 'speeder' rides along this short stretch of track [http://timber-heritage.org/ride-the-rails-on-a-historic-speeder-crew/], the brush is largely kept at bay. Despite nearly two decades of non-use the tunnel remains in good shape requiring only a light to navigate (1.0). The north end emerges into a tangle of undergrowth as nature reclaims the right-of-way (1.4). During wet times of the year, there can be some water accumulation at both ends of the tunnel although the south end is generally passable. Return the way you came.

51 · Table Bluff Loop

Length: 2.7 miles
Total ascent: 230 feet
Access: closed February-March
Type: loop
Dogs: leashed
Restrooms: no

Description: This walk offers outstanding views of two of the most distinctive features of the Humboldt County coastline – the Eel River valley and estuary and Humboldt Bay – from the vantage point of Table Bluff.

Getting there: Drive south about 10.4 miles on US 101 to Exit 696 (Hookton Road). Continue on Hookton Road for 3.1 miles where you go straight at the junction with Table Bluff Road. You are now on Table Bluff Road. Proceed west for 1.6 miles until you see a sign and entry for the California Department of Fish and Game's Ocean Ranch Unit. Approximate driving time, 30 minutes.

∞ Lighthouse Ranch

In the early years of regular ship traffic in and out of Humboldt Bay, sailors were guided by the north spit's Humboldt Harbor Light Station. Despite being too low to be effective, it took nearly a quarter century to relocate to the more visible 150-foot crest of Table Bluff. For 83 years the Table Bluff facility provided navigational support to vessels between the mouth of the Eel and Humboldt Bay. During WWII, the compound was expanded to include a lookout station charged with monitoring the coast. Accommodation for both single men and married personnel was constructed. In 1953 the lighthouse was automated until being decommissioned in 1975.

Things got much more interesting in the early 1970s when 'hippies' occupied the station's empty buildings. By the time I moved to Humboldt County in the mid-1980s, it had been converted into a Christian center known as Lighthouse Ranch. Owned by several different evangelists spanning nearly four decades, the property attracted young travelers looking for spiritual direction. Some passed through, others engaged in the back-to-the-land culture of the Ranch. Residents also experimented with alternative dwellings.

The two-story lighthouse tower was moved to the Woodley Island Marina in 1987 and the Ranch was purchased by the Wildlife Conservation Board and the Coastal Conservancy in 2005 (and subsequently transferred to BLM). In 2012, all the remaining structures were demolished. ∞

The route: This route is easiest to follow when done in a clockwise fashion. Proceed from the parking lot south past the gate and along the road (0.4). Turn right (west) past old ranch facilities and veer right when the road forks (0.5). [if you veer left instead, this road follows the levee 0.7 mile to an arm of McNulty Slough.] The route intersects a dirt track that parallels the ocean and is used by vehicles that enter from the County Park (0.7). From here, make your way over to the beach. There is no established trail. Follow the beach north to the obvious bathroom and parking area for the County Park (1.5). This area is particularly popular among hang gliders who launch from the top of the bluff. From the base of the bluff the route follows the road to the top and proceeds south through the grounds of the old Light-

Hiking Humboldt Volume 2

house Ranch/Table Bluff Lighthouse, where BLM has installed restrooms and picnic facilities. Continue south along any of the pathways though the old lighthouse complex to Table Bluff Road and on to the Ocean Ranch Unit parking lot (2.7).

Note: We have walked the first half-mile south from the Ocean Ranch parking lot in the early summer before the route has been mowed. The grasses can feel like they are going to swallow you but push through and the path clears as you cross the dam to the small pond.

Table Bluff Lighthouse, Palmquist Collection, Humboldt State University Library.

Extras. Of course, this hike can easily be extended by walking additionally south or north along the beach. To the south is the mouth of the Eel River (Hike #22 in *Volume 1*) and to the north is the South Jetty. Both are lengthy walks.

South Spit and Jetty. The 4.5 mile long South Spit offers a variety of walking options: walking the South Jetty Road, walking the beach along the South Spit, parking at any of the six designated parking areas spaced out along the length of the Spit and walking to the beach or creating a loop walk, enjoying the South Jetty area. The downside of walking anywhere on the South Spit is that it can be windy, the beach tends to be soft-packed (versus the firmer beaches along the Samoa Peninsula, Clam and Moonstone and Luffenholtz Beaches, and Centerville Beach south to Fleener Creek), and from mid-September through February driving is permitted on the beach. The upside is that the South Spit is not heavily used, it is a beautiful setting and offers a different perspective on Humboldt Bay, and the Bar and Jetty can be quite dramatic. Take good care to stay clear of the breakwater as the sea regularly washes in unsuspecting people.

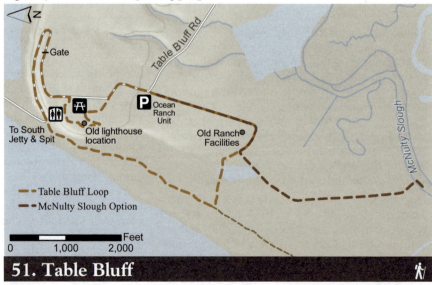

51. Table Bluff

52 Cannibal Island – Crab Park – Cock Robin Island

Length: up to 5.0 miles
Total ascent: flat
Access: subject to flooding
Type: out and back
Dogs: yes
Restrooms: no

Description: The Eel River delta stretches from Table Bluff to the hills south of Ferndale and inland to Loleta and, you could argue, to Fortuna. It is a massive area of rich alluvial soil that has made this highly productive dairy land. The estuary, with its extensive network of sloughs and wetlands that braid the delta, is fantastic wildlife habitat. This delta ecosystem can be experienced quite fully on this walk.

Once again there are many possible permutations in walking and exploring this area. Park at Crab Park and walk nearby beaches across from the mouth of the Eel River before road walking east along Cannibal Island Road to Cock Robin Island. If conditions are adequately dry, walk the California Fish and Wildlife land to the abandoned homestead (see Extras).

Getting there: Drive south on US 101 10.4 miles to Exit 696 (Hookton Road). Turn left and follow Eel River Drive 2.5 miles toward Loleta. Turn right (west) on Cannibal Island Road and drive 4.1 miles to Crab Park and a small, gravel parking lot not sufficient for trailers to turn around but adequate for cars and trucks. Approximate driving time, 30 minutes.

The route: The beach and shoreline on the estuary just west of the Crab Park parking lot is walkable both north (to Mosley Slough) and south for about 0.3 mile. The walk south offers nice views across the estuary and out to the mouth of the river. Once you have completed your exploration of the Crab Park area, walk east on Cannibal Island Road to Cock Robin Island Road (1.2). Turn right (south) on Cock Robin Island Road. The route reaches the Pedrazzini Boat Launching Facility and the bridge to Cock Robin Island (1.6). Continue across the bridge (1.8) and along a tree-lined gravel road to its end (2.5). A walking path continues to the Eel River but this can be very wet and muddy much of the year (this has been used as an obstacle, including an Eel River crossing, in past Kinetic Sculpture races).

Cannibal Island was named for a combative collection of people who lived together there who, it was said, "fought like cannibals" (Turner and Turner, 2010). While fighting never has been the characteristic most associated with cannibals,

Cannibal Island homestead.

Hiking Humboldt Volume 2

apparently the name stuck. Interestingly, Cannibal Island Road does not actually go to Cannibal Island but instead ends on Mosley Island.

Extras. Just east of the bridge to Mosley Island and Crab Park is a little used road that goes north past a broken gate. This once serviced an isolated homestead to the north in the midst of a swirl of sloughs and tidal channels. During dry times it is possible to walk for 1.0 mile (one-way) north to an old homestead along the now abandoned line of power poles crossing a small arm of McNulty Slough just before reaching the ruins of the old homestead. Although this land is under the control of the California Fish and Wildlife Department, it is leased as pasture land and there may be cattle grazing.

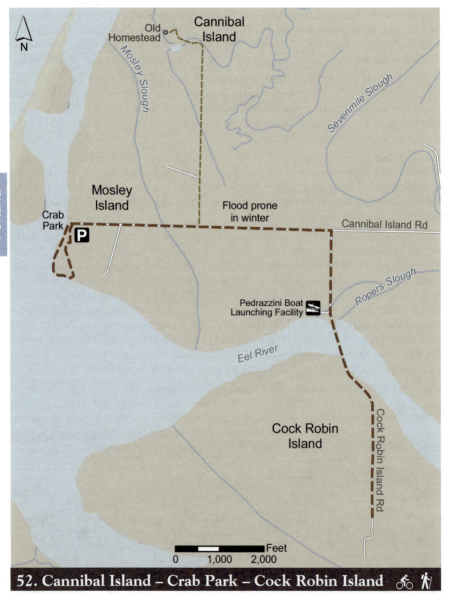

52. Cannibal Island – Crab Park – Cock Robin Island

53 · Centerville Beach South and Fleener Creek Loop

Length: 2.8 miles
Total ascent: 600 feet
Elevations: sea level – 300 feet
Access: impassable at medium to high tides
Type: loop
Dogs: yes
Restrooms: no

Description: Despite its relatively short length, this hike offers a variety of features. It also can be recombined in a number of ways to suit the interests and abilities of the hikers. The Centerville County Park offers off-road parking (but not much more) and a good starting point for the loop because of the prevailing northwesterly winds. As you proceed south, dramatic fossil-laden bluffs loom above that were, in geological terms, sea floor not that long ago. At Fleener Creek the route turns east following the trail as it switchbacks steeply to the parking lot. To complete the loop, the route continues north on the lightly used Centerville Road. The road passes the site of the now dismantled Naval facility, which was used for oceanographic research and undersea surveillance from 1958 - 1993. As of August, 2016, the BLM has plans to construct the Centerville Bluffs East Picnic Area here. The route can also begin at the Fleener Creek parking lot. It can be shortened to just the beach walk or Fleener Creek.

Getting there: Proceed south on US 101 14.3 miles to Exit 692 (Fernbridge/Ferndale). At the end of the exit ramp turn right on Singley Road/Fernbridge Drive. In 0.5 mile turn right on CA 211, which crosses the Eel River on Fernbridge. Continue 4.1 miles toward Ferndale turning right on Arlington Avenue and in 0.3 mile left on 5th. Proceed 0.4 mile to Shaw Avenue. Turn right on Shaw Avenue and

∞ Centerville Beach Road

Until the 1891 completion of the Wildcat Road through rugged inland terrain, the four miles of broad, firm sand beach south of Centerville was a preferred portion of the stage and wagon route between Petrolia and the Eel River Valley. Even though there was an inland alternative as early as 1875, the smooth surface of the beach was often irresistible. As a result there were many tales of travelers who unwisely chose to chance the beach only to have their stage or wagon snatched by the hungry ocean. Rohde (2014) documents the perilous nature of the journey citing a number of examples including the December 1878 wreck of the Mattole stage: "the driver managed to save himself and the horses but the mail and freight were washed out to sea and lost. This was the second such accident in less than three weeks' time. Three months later, near the southern end of the beach run, another stage was caught in the surf. It overturned, spilling two passengers into the water and trapping two more inside . . ."

Today, the Centerville beach to the south would rarely accommodate a stage or wagon except in the lowest of tides. Beach erosion, landslides, and perhaps, sea level rise have limited passage to pedestrian and equestrian traffic and still, you must keep a careful watch on the tide tables and the temperamental ocean. ∞

Fleener Creek

again right on Centerville Road (0.2 mile). Proceed west on Centerville Road 4.5 miles to the County Park or 5.5 miles to the Fleener Creek trailhead parking area. Approximate driving time, 40 minutes.

The route: From the Centerville Beach parking lot, walk south. The initial soft sand near the parking lot gives way to firmer sand as the beach becomes bounded on the landside by sheer cliffs. These impressive formations offer few outlets if you misjudge the tide and care should be taken in timing this section of the walk. The grey layer of unconsolidated mud that forms the bluffs (0.6) is rich with fossils of scallops, cockles, snails, and clams. (Anderson, 2011) The fossil-bearing mud layer continues almost to Fleener Creek where the beach broadens and the bluffs briefly flatten (1.2). Even though the creek may disappear during the dry months, the inviting valley opens to the east and provides the way to the Fleener Creek Overlook. A narrow fenced opening on the north side of the Creek provides access to the trail to the Overlook and Centerville Road (1.7). From the Overlook, turn left and follow the road that passes the location of the former Naval facility (2.0) and continues its descent back to the County Park (2.7).

Extras. In tides of -1.0 or lower it may be possible to safely reach Guthrie Creek 1.2 miles further south. It is important to be very cautious as the high cliffs offer little respite if you misjudge.

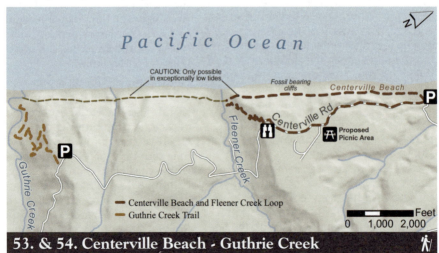

53. & 54. Centerville Beach - Guthrie Creek

54 · Guthrie Creek Trail

Length: 2.0 miles
Total ascent: 470 feet
Elevations: sea level – 470 feet
Access constraints: steep trail to beach.
Type: out and back
Dogs: yes
Restrooms: yes

Description: Guthrie Creek and Fleener Creek overlooks and trails are part of the 463-acre Lost Coast Headland property managed by the BLM. The dramatic coastline south of the Eel River estuary and flood plain is a sample of the wild coastal landscape that continues southward for many miles. The most convenient access to this remote area is the Lost Coast Headlands. Yet, you will often have Guthrie Creek to yourself. The BLM estimates that 90 percent of visitors get no farther than the Fleener Creek Overlook. This trail follows an old road grade that makes long switchbacks to drop the 400 feet to Guthrie Creek. (In summer 2017, the landowner re-established the road.) Eventually the trail makes a final steep descent to the beach. During times of low flow Guthrie Creek almost disappears but during high water it can shrink the available pocket beach. Additional short walks are possible north and south along the beach.

Getting there: Follow the same directions for Hike #53 but drive two miles beyond Fleener Creek Overlook to the Guthrie Creek trailhead parking area. This is just a short distance from the end of the Centerville Road. Approximate driving time, 50 minutes.

The route: The trail begins from the west end of the Guthrie Creek Overlook and trailhead and is well signed. The trail is gently graded until the final, previously mentioned descent to the beach (1.0). In tides of -1.0 or lower it may be possible to walk the beach north to Fleener Creek and on to Centerville Beach County Park.

55 · Poole Road

Length: 4.6 miles
Total ascent: 800 feet
Elevations: 30 – 750 feet
Access constraints: stay on road!
Type: out and back
Dogs: leashed (open range)
Restrooms: no

NOTE: Near the beginning of Poole Road, an imposing sign strongly underscores the intent of local landowners to prosecute anyone straying from the county road. Re-read my advice on page 10.

Description: This rural gravel road rises quickly through quiet hilltop pastures to provide views north across the Eel River estuary and west over the ocean. Your primary company may well be cattle grazing nearby or raptors riding the winds.

Getting there: Proceed south on US 101 14.3 miles to Exit 692 (Fernbridge/Ferndale). At the end of the exit ramp, turn right on Singley Road/Fernbridge

Drive. In 0.5 mile turn right on CA 211, which crosses the Eel River on Fernbridge. Continue 4.1 miles toward Ferndale turning right on Arlington Avenue and in 0.3 mile left on 5th. Proceed 0.4 mile to Shaw Avenue. Turn right on Shaw Avenue and again right on Centerville Road (0.2 mile). Proceed west on Centerville Road 3.7 miles. Poole Road exits from Centerville Road on the left, rising steeply as a single-lane road. There is limited parking at the base of Poole Road and again 0.2 mile up Poole Road on the left (just before the intimidating aforementioned sign). Approximate driving time, 35 minutes.

The route: The route is very simple. Follow Poole Road. The first 0.2 mile is paved with the remainder being gravel. As the gravel begins you will pass the warning sign and continue to climb steadily through pastureland with some roadside stands of conifers. The road shifts to the east side of the ridge (1.2) dropping down and then back up an even higher ridge that offers commanding views out over the ocean. The road crests (2.1) and soon reaches a cattle guard signed 'private property' and 'no trespassing' (2.3). I used this as a turnaround. This is a walk where the return trip has you facing the view and can feel like a very different experience from the walk in.

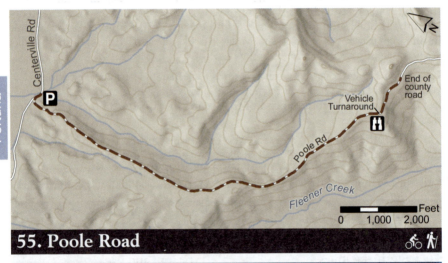

55. Poole Road

56 · Russ Park

Length: 2.5 miles	Type: loop
Total ascent: 940 feet	Dogs: yes
Elevations: 100 – 620 feet	Restrooms: yes

Description: This 110-acre park is surprisingly wild, the trails aerobic, and the views down to Francis Creek or out across the Ferndale Bottoms impressive. Although generally well maintained, the trails are often narrow and/or steep with enough roots that care must be exercised. Several choices of routes beyond my suggestion, including a longer hike in *Volume 1* (Hike #25), can be found here. The park is home to robust stands of Sitka spruce.

View from Russ Park by Nancy Spruance

The park was donated to the City of Ferndale by Zipporah Patrick Russ in 1920. Zipporah Pond lies in a small hollow near the top of the park.

Getting there: Proceed south on US 101 14.3 miles to Exit 692 (Fernbridge/Ferndale). At the end of the exit ramp, turn right on Singley Road/Fernbridge Drive. In 0.5 mile turn right on CA 211, which crosses the Eel River on Fernbridge. Continue 4.1 miles toward Ferndale turning left at the Victorian Inn on Bluff Street/Ocean Avenue. Follow Bluff Street for 0.6 mile to the Russ Park Trailhead parking area on your right. Approximate driving time, 35 minutes.

The route: From the main trailhead off Bluff Street, the trail departs from the south side of the parking lot to a signed trail junction in less than 100 yards. To the left climbs the 'Main Trail' and to the right contours the Bluff Street Trail. The suggested route (left) gains 400 feet in elevation as it switchbacks up to a signed junction with the Maple Leaf Loop Trail (0.5). Follow the Maple Leaf Loop Trail as it continues the climb to the Eagle Point Spur (0.7). This short spur (0.1 each way) ends at a bench with a view across the deep Francis Creek Valley to forested Sugarloaf Mountain (no higher than the view point). The Maple Leaf Loop Trail drops steeply losing much hard-earned elevation to the Eugene Street Trail junction (1.3). The Eugene Street Trail descends to Eugene Street and can be walked

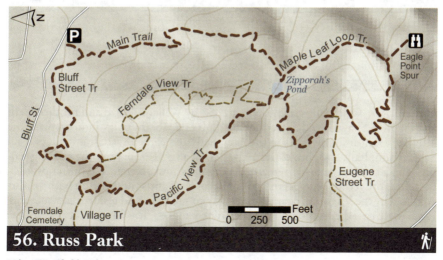

56. Russ Park

back into Ferndale past the Ferndale Cemetery. The Maple Leaf Loop Trail climbs back to the ridge top at a junction with the Pacific View Trail (1.5). From here, it is easy to return to the parking lot via the 'Main Trail' (2.0), take the short loop around Zapporah's Pond, or continue the larger loop around the Park on the Pacific View Trail or the Ferndale View Trail (which departs from the Pond Loop and descends to the Bluff Street Trail). The Pacific View Trail follows the ridge to the northwest as it drops, at times steeply, to a junction with the Village Trail (emerging onto the upper portion of the Ferndale Cemetery; 2.0). There are a number of opportunities to look down into the Francis Creek valley and out to the Ferndale Bottoms along this section of trail. From the junction with the Village Trail, the route contours back east to a trail junction near the parking lot (2.5). Along the way the trail intersects with the Ferndale View Trail and merges with the Bluff Street Trail. The section between the Village Trail and Ferndale View Trail has experienced erosion that requires extra care., especially in wet conditions.

Zipporah's Pond - Nancy Spruance

57 · Ferndale Architectural and Historical Walk

Length: 3.1 miles	**Type:** loop
Total ascent: flat	**Dogs:** yes
Elevations: 40 – 70 feet	**Restrooms:** yes

Description: Originally established in 1852 by Willard Allard and brothers Seth and Stephen Shaw, Ferndale became the hub of a vibrant dairy industry with the influx of Danish immigrants in the late 1860s and early 1870s. Immigrants from Switzerland, Italy, and the Azores arrived soon after. Throughout the ensuing century and a half, the area has remained a center of milk, cream, and butter production. In more recent years, Ferndale has become a tourist destination with visitors attracted by the Victorian character of many commercial and residential structures. From these two themes come Ferndale's nicknames – "The Cream City" and "The Victorian Village". This walk, in the shape of a figure 8, includes the central business district, Ferndale Cemetery, several residential streets, and the fairgrounds.

The route passes several buildings on the National Register of Historic Places.

Getting there: Take US 101 south 14.2 miles taking Exit 692. At the end of the exit ramp, turn right on Singley Road/Fernbridge Drive. Again, turn right on CA 211 (0.5 mile), crossing Fernbridge and staying on CA 211 for 4.5 miles to the somewhat arbitrary starting point of the Shaw House Inn, 703 Main Street. There is ample on-street parking along Main Street. Driving time, 30 minutes.

The route: It seems fitting to begin with the Shaw House Inn, which is on the National Register of Historic Places and originally the home of one of Ferndale's founding fathers, Seth Shaw. The route continues south along Main Street (through the Main Street Historical District also on the National Register of His-

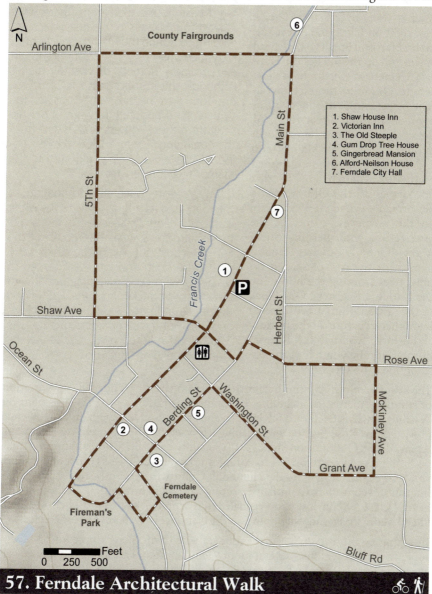

57. Ferndale Architectural Walk

toric Places). Take special note of two Eastlake/Stick style commercial buildings, one at 475 Main (also on the National Register) and the Victorian Inn at the corner of Main Street and Ocean Avenue (1891).

Just before the end of Main Street, turn left (east) on Berding Street (0.5), which bends to the left as it transits through Fireman's Park. After crossing over Francis Creek, turn right on Cleveland Street and left on Harrison Street (0.6). Ahead of you and up the hill lies the Ferndale Cemetery, worthy of a short detour. Our route turns left on Eugene Street and in one block turns right on Berding Street (0.7). At the corner of Ocean (also known as Bluff Street east of Main Street) and Berding is the refurbished Methodist Church (1871) that now serves as The Old Steeple, a performance venue. At 455 Ocean, on the northwest corner of the intersection with Berding Street is the "Gum Drop Tree House" named for the row of shaped cypress trees fronting the house (on the National Register). One block to the east on Bluff Street (Ocean) is another structure on the National Historic Register, the Rectory of the Catholic Church of the Assumption (563 Ocean).

> ## ∞ Camp Weeott
>
> These days, the Camp Weott Road (contemporary name is Weott, the old camp is Weeott) ends inconspicuously at a narrow remnant of Morgan Slough. There is sadness here when you consider the history of this area.
>
> Prior to the arrival of white settlers in the 1850s, the Eel River delta was home to the Wiyot people. Because the estuary offered easy access to salmon, there were at least four villages in the area, which according to Rohde (2014) included Tolotpilik, which "had very many houses with an extraordinary number of wealthy men." Although the horrific massacre of February, 1860 was the most egregious act, the Wiyots' land and culture were under assault from these aggressive outsiders from the beginning. Later in 1860, the remaining Wiyots were forcibly relocated to the Klamath River reservation.
>
> Camp Weeott, once the destination of the road, had its origin in the 1920s when Humboldt County acquired a few acres for fishing access near the mouth of the Eel. A water supply, outbuildings, and road were built, and lots were rented to residents who constructed seasonal cabins. According to Rohde, the 1955 flood destroyed at least 17 cabins, boat docks, and much of the camp infrastructure. The 1964 flood washed away the remaining land and buildings. ∞

The next two blocks continuing north on Berding have a wonderful concentration of stunning Victorians including the Gingerbread Mansion (0.9). Turn right on Washington Street, left on McKinley Avenue (1.2), and left again on Rose Avenue (1.4). Follow Rose Avenue until turning left briefly on Berding and right on Shaw Avenue (1.7). Continue on Shaw (2.0), crossing over Main Street and turning right on 5th. Proceed north on 5th to Arlington Avenue (2.4) This corner and just beyond serve as an entrance to the Humboldt County Fairgrounds. Turn right on Arlington and continue east until intersecting with Main Street (2.7). A short detour north (left) on Main, just past Ferndale High School, is the Alford-Nielson House (1299 Main Street), another home on the National Register of Historic Places.

By taking a right turn on Main, the route returns to the Shaw House Inn (3.1). En route to the Shaw House, several more Victorian homes are along the way as well as are the Ferndale Public Library (also on the National Historic Register) and the Ferndale City Hall.

58 · Ferndale Bottoms Walk

Length: variable
Total ascent: flat
Elevations: 0 – 20 feet
Type: variable
Dogs: yes
Restrooms: none

Description: On the south side of the Eel River, lies flat fecund dairy country, crisscrossed by roads with little traffic, and steeped in history. Like the Arcata Bottoms, it is easy to design your own route selecting from the variety of interlacing roads. The views are distinctly bucolic framed by higher country in three directions. At times the Bottoms are buffeted by cool ocean winds.

Getting there: Proceed south on US 101 14.3 miles to Exit 692 (Fernbridge/Ferndale). At the end of the exit ramp, turn right on Singley Road/Fernbridge Drive. In 0.5 mile turn right on CA 211, which crosses the Eel River on Fernbridge. The entrance to Goble Lane is on the right 1.3 miles southwest on CA 211. At 3.2 miles from Fernbridge on CA 211, turn right on Port Kenyon Road. From here, Fulmor Road is 0.1 mile west and Dillon Road is an additional 1.4 miles west on Port Kenyon Road. Approximate travel time, 25 minutes.

The route: GOBLE LANE – This east-west road stretches from CA 211 to Dillon Road (3.6). The first 0.9 mile is gravel and the remainder paved with parking at the intersection with CA 211. The eastern 1.2 miles are particularly quiet. The road is crossed by Fulmor and Dillon Roads and is some distance from the Eel River.

FULMOR ROAD – This north-south road extends from Port Kenyon Road to the Eel River and is bisected by Goble Lane. North of Goble Lane, Fulmor passes two dairy operations (0.7) before turning west and paralleling the Eel River to a dead end (1.1). A couple possible parking pull-outs exist on this final stretch. The views out over the Eel River are excellent. South of Goble Lane the road reaches Port Kenyon Road (0.9). There are some off-road options for parking on Port Kenyon Road just west of the intersection with Fulmor Road.

DILLON ROAD – From the intersection with Goble Lane, Dillon Road connects with Camp Weott Road (0.5) to the north and with Port Kenyon Road to the south (0.8). Like the other roads in this area, it is through flat, agricultural countryside.

CAMP WEOTT ROAD – This quiet road extends west to a turnaround (1.8), small parking area, and a boat launch (into a slough). The final 0.2-mile of this road is gravel. The road parallels Morgan Slough for much of its length so there is more bird habitat.

PORT KENYON ROAD WEST OF DILLON ROAD – This road extends west of Dillon Road (1.8). For the first half mile (to Meridian Road), the road is lined by a number of houses and sees more

Ferndale Bottoms - Nancy Spruance

car traffic. West of Meridian, there is little traffic. Parking is available around the intersection of Meridian and Port Kenyon Roads and at the west end of Port Kenyon Road. This section of road parallels the Salt River, the subject of considerable restoration work.

Until 1908, ships entered the Eel River and traveled up the Salt River (then 11 feet deep at low tide) to the wharves of Port Kenyon. They carried passengers as well as lumber, salmon, and agricultural products like butter, eggs, apples, potatoes, oats, and wool. Logging and agricultural practices caused so much siltation that a massive, long-term restoration effort has been undertaken to improve the hydrological and ecological health of the watershed.

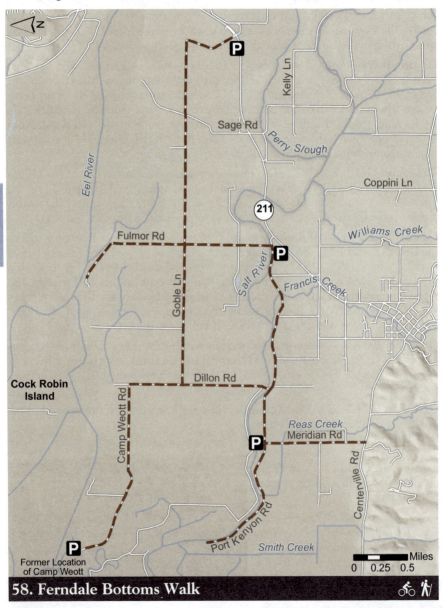

58. Ferndale Bottoms Walk

59 · Williams Creek Road

Length: 5.2
Total ascent: 500 feet
Elevations: 80 – 380 feet
Type: out and back
Dogs: yes
Restrooms: none

Description: This pleasant walk begins just outside Ferndale and follows a narrow but lightly used county road to the end of county maintenance. Forests blanket the hills that rise on both sides but the valley floor is home to a string of working ranches, pastures, and residences. The road crosses Williams Creek twice and benefits often from the character the small stream adds to the setting.

Getting there: Drive south about 14 miles on US 101 to Exit 692 (Fernbridge/Ferndale). At the end of the exit ramp, turn right on Singley Road/Fernbridge Drive. In 0.5 mile, turn right on CA 211 which crosses the Eel River on Fernbridge. Proceed 4.8 miles and turn left on and follow Bluff Street/Ocean Avenue for 0.8 mile merging with Grizzly Bluff Road. Turn right on Williams Creek Road (0.1 mile). Proceed just past the new bridge over Williams Creek for the best parking (0.2 mile). Approximate driving time, 40 minutes.

The route: This is a straightforward road walk. There are no confusing intersections, baffling twists or turns, and no threatening signs until you reach the end of the county road (2.6 miles) where you turn around.

59. Williams Creek Road

Bear River Ridge

This quiet one-lane gravel road through open ridge-top pastureland with magnificent views is one of the most spectacular road walks in Humboldt County. Bear River Ridge Road stretches for almost ten one-way miles. Unless you plant a car at each end, it is more realistic to consider each half of the road its own day walk. The highpoint of the ridge lies near the middle.

At different times of the year, the pastures may be green and abundant with flowers and livestock, brown and dry, or even snow-covered. And, be forewarned, there was good reason that this area was once considered as the site for a wind farm.

60a Bear River Ridge Road – Southeast End

Length: up to 8.8 miles
Total ascent: 1150 feet
Access: all land along road is private.
Elevations: 1950–2600 feet
Type: out and back
Dogs: yes
Restrooms: none

Description: From the southeast end, the views begin from the parking area at the intersection with Monument Road perched nearly 2,000 feet above Scotia. Panoramas include the Lassics and South Fork Mountain far to the east. Later, the ridge looks north up the Eel River Valley to Fortuna and Humboldt Bay, west to the ocean, and south along the Bear River drainage.

Getting there: Take US 101 south for 25 miles. Take Exit 681 (Rio Dell) and at the end of the exit ramp, turn right on Wildwood Avenue. In 0.5 mile turn right on West Davis Street and one block later, turn left on Pacific Avenue. In 0.4 mile Pacific Avenue becomes Monument Road. In 4.6 miles Monument Road veers left behind a very heavy-duty metal gate and Bear River Ridge Road veers right. At this intersection, there is space for several cars. Take care not to block the gate. Approximate driving time, 45 minutes.

The route: From the parking area the road climbs to reach the ridge top. For the next four miles the road follows the crest of Bear River Ridge. Generally cattle and sometimes sheep graze in the open range along the road. To the south, the road overlooks the Howe Creek valley. A large barn lies off to the north (1.6) and Kinman Pond on the left side of the road (4.0) before a final climb to a rather non-descript high point (4.4). Several private dirt roads are spaced along the route diverging left and dropping off the ridge. This area was once home to Seth Kinman.

60b Bear River Ridge Road – Northwest End

Length: up to 7.0 miles
Total ascent: 1000 feet
Access: all land along road is private.
Elevations: 2050–2600 feet
Type: out and back
Dogs: yes
Restrooms: none

Description: From the north end, the walk could begin at the intersection with the Ferndale-Petrolia Road (the 'Wildcat') but better is at the Bear River Road junction. From this direction, the best views are to the west down the Bear River valley to the ocean and, periodically, to the north over the Eel River estuary, diminutive Table Bluff, and Humboldt Bay. From the high point of the road, views to the east become more impressive.

Getting there: Take US 101 south for 14.2 miles. Take Exit 692 (Fernbridge/Ferndale). At the end of the exit ramp, turn right onto Singley Road/Fernbridge Avenue. In one-half mile turn right on CA Route 211, crossing over the Eel River on Fernbridge. In 4.8 miles (which takes you to the Victorian Inn on Main Street), turn right on Bluff Street/Ocean Avenue. In less than 0.1 mile turn left on Wildcat

∽ Seth Kinman

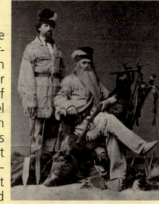

Few figures in Humboldt County history are more colorful and, at times, more controversial than Seth Kinman. A charismatic mountain man, Kinman built a cabin high on Bear River Ridge in the 1850s. He explored the jumble of steep ridges and pristine rivers south of the Eel River Valley and reported them to be rife with game. Kinman claimed that he and his partners once counted 40 grizzlies from one viewpoint above the Mattole Valley. According to historian Lynwood Carranco, Kinman contends that over 800 grizzly bears and countless elk died at his hands. So overwhelmed with elk antlers was Kinman that he created a fence with them and subsequently fashioned elk-horn chairs that would make him famous. In 1857, Kinman crafted a highly polished elk-horn chair for President James Buchanan.

From the Palmquist Collection, Humboldt State University Library.

With the chair in a beautiful redwood box, Kinman made the long trip by sea crossing the isthmus of Panama overland and sailing on to New York where his picturesque hunter's dress made him the talk of the town. Kinman later delivered similar chairs to Abraham Lincoln and Rutherford Hayes and an amazing grizzly bear chair for Andrew Johnson.

At various times, Kinman served as an official government agent with local Indians. Carranco summarizes Kinman's feelings toward Native Americans as mixed, "Sometimes he regarded them as human beings, and at other times they were only predatory animals to shoot at." In general, the predominant attitudes of the time led to horrendous atrocities that will live in infamy.

In his later years, Kinman operated a hotel and saloon (or "thirst parlor") in the community of Table Bluff where many of his curios were on display. He died in 1888 and is buried in Table Bluff Cemetery along with his mother (Ellen), daughter (Ellen), son (Carlin), and various family members. ∽

Avenue towards Petrolia and follow it as it winds its way steeply uphill for the next 6 miles. After 6 miles, turn left onto Bear River Ridge Road. Limited parking exists near the intersection on the east side of Bear River Ridge Road, near a small quarry (0.3 mile up the Bear River Ridge Road), or 0.9 mile from the intersection (past the ranch houses), but I recommend beginning at the junction with Bear River Road (1.7 miles). Approximate driving time, 55 minutes.

The route: The road from the northwest end also follows the undulating Bear River Ridge. Several unmarked intersections could confuse the route. In most cases, it is obvious which is the main road. In general, favor the option that follows the ridgeline. The road crests at about 2,600 feet before beginning to lose elevation (3.5). This is the same high point that serves as the arbitrary turn around point for the walk from the south end. It is easy to select a different section or length of road for your walk.

60. & 61. Bear River Ridge

61 · Upper Bear River Road

Length: up to 4.8 miles	**Elevations:** 300–1995 feet
Total ascent: 650 feet	**Type:** out and back
Access Constraints: all land along road is private. Can be windy.	**Dogs:** leashed (open range)
	Restrooms: none

Description: This paved road walk starts at the top of Bear River Ridge with its stunning views west to the ocean. The road drops about 500 feet in the first 2.4 miles with a few gentle inclines in between to break the downhill plunge. For the second half of the walk, the road descends even more precipitously. The route includes a number of steep switchbacks entering trees for only the final 0.3 mile. (The road continues west from the river crossing becoming gravel about 0.3 mile past the bridge.) The reverse walk is as unrelentingly up as the down walk was down and best for those interested in a serious aerobic workout. The recommended combination for an out-and-back hike is to walk only the first 2.4 miles down before making the trudge back uphill.

Getting there: Take US 101 south for 14.2 miles. Take Exit 692. At the end of the exit ramp, turn right onto Singley Road/Fernbridge Drive. In one-half mile turn right on CA Route 211, crossing over the Eel River on Fernbridge. In 4.8 miles, turn right on Bluff Street/Ocean Avenue. In less than 0.1 mile turn left on Wildcat Avenue towards Petrolia and follow it as it winds its way steeply uphill for the next 6 miles, then turn left onto Bear River Ridge Road. In 1.7 miles, Bear River Road veers to the right and down from the ridgeline. There is adequate parking for several cars at this intersection. If you are utilizing a car shuttle, leave one car near the bottom, about 0.1 mile east of the bridge over Bear River (at an intersection with a side road) where there is limited roadside parking. Approximate driving time, 1 hour and 5 minutes.

The route: This is a straightforward road walk. The first half of the walk descends steadily through a bucolic landscape with superb views (2.4). If you have not arranged a car shuttle, this is a good place to turn around before the descent steepens and switchbacks toward the valley floor. If you are continuing, the views west down the Bear River valley remain glorious. The road enters trees (4.4), passes some seasonal cabins, and soon flattens out, eventually crossing the Bear River. Care must be taken as there is generally livestock grazing in the open range along the road.

The road does continue west from the bridge becoming graveled after a second bridge (4.3). It is possible to walk further although I understand there is no public access to the Petrolia – Ferndale road.

62 ˙Headwaters Forest – Salmon Pass Trail

Length: 2.8 miles	**Elevations**: 1300–1995 feet
Total ascent: 650 feet	**Type**: partial loop
Access: hikes must be guided and can be scheduled between May 15 and November 15.	**Dogs**: no
	Restrooms: yes

Salmon Pass Trail hikes must be guided. To make arrangements contact the BLM at (707) 825-2300 or use the online calendar system.

Description: The area now known as the Headwaters Forest Reserve was the site of widespread public protests from 1986 through 1999 in response to logging practices by Pacific Lumber Company (under the controversial ownership of Maxxam, Inc.) that threatened the largest remaining stands of old growth redwood under private ownership. These efforts culminated in the acquisition by the federal government and the State of California of 7,472 acres in 1999. Of this total just over 3,000 acres of old growth forest was protected. The remaining acreage consists of previously harvested timberlands designed to protect the watershed and preserve wildlife habitat. This land is now the Headwaters Forest Reserve.

The old growth loop accessible from the Elk River trailhead is included in *Volume 1*. The Salmon Pass trail visits a small island of old growth that can be reached from Fortuna. The trail meanders through second growth woodlands before looping through the old growth forest. The trail offers some limited territorial views.

Getting there: Take US 101 south 18.1 miles taking Exit 688 (12th Street). At the end of the exit ramp, follow the signs for 12th street by turning right on Riverwalk Drive (0.1 mile), crossing over the freeway. In 0.1 mile, immediately after the disused railroad tracks, turn right on Newburg Road. In 1.1 miles, after crossing both Main Street and later Rohnerville Road look for the entrance to Newburg Park on your right. A Headwaters kiosk is in the parking lot where you will meet your guide. From Newburg Park, the trailhead is 0.9 mile east on Newburg Road and an additional 3.5 miles on a gravel road behind a locked gate. Approximate driving time, 45 minutes.

The route: From the trailhead for Salmon Pass Trail, the well-constructed trail proceeds through a young second growth forest (0.7). The overarching growth of alders is surprisingly pleasant. Stay right as the trail enters the old growth stand and climbs steadily to a ridge above Salmon Creek (1.3). The trail

Headwaters Forest

follows decommissioned logging roads along the ridge crest (1.5) before returning to the old growth and dropping down to and crossing an intermittent tributary of Salmon Creek completing the loop (2.1). Turn right unless you intend to walk a second lap as this offers the way back to the parking lot (2.8).

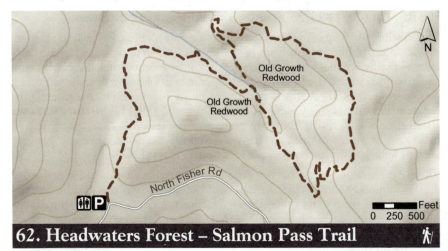

62. Headwaters Forest – Salmon Pass Trail

63 · Fortuna Riverwalk

Length: up to 6.0 miles
Total ascent: flat
Access: much of the walkway is all-weather hard-packed gravel, suitable for certain wheelchairs

Elevations: 60–85 feet
Type: partial loop
Dogs: yes
Restrooms: none

Description: The levee protecting Fortuna from Eel River flooding also serves as a popular multi-modal path. A short loop can be walked north along the levee before returning via the sidewalks adjacent to Riverwalk Drive. This walk can be combined with all or portions of the Riverwalk South route. At the far southern end, it is possible to leave the levee and follow a well-established dirt road either to the Eel River or along the banks to or near the confluence with the Van Duzen River, depending upon water levels. In mid to late summer and well into fall, typical low water levels allow pedestrian access to virtually all of the flood plain.

Getting there: Drive south on US 101 18.1 miles to Exit 688 (12th Street). At the end of the exit ramp, following signs for Riverwalk Drive, go straight. In 0.6 mile, there will be parking on the right around the River Lodge Conference Center. There is a pleasant picnic area and overlook near the parking area. Approximate driving time, 25 minutes.

The route: North - Turn right (north) on the path on the top of the levee. The path makes a sharp right turn (0.8) and proceeds away from the river through an industrial area to Riverwalk Drive (1.1). At Riverwalk Drive take a right turn. The route relies on sidewalks (except for the last block) as it completes the loop with the final leg (1.7).

South – Turn left (south). Follow the levee until exiting through a gate (0.9) and continuing on the paved Sandy Prairie Road for a short distance (1.2). The route forks right past a gate and again becomes a hard-packed gravel road atop the levee. The levee moves farther and farther away from the Eel River and parallels a large,

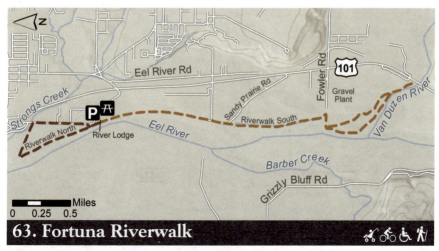

well-established grove of alder to the west and cultivated fields to the east (2.0). The trail is crossed by two gravel roads, the first one emerging from between to fields to the east (your left) and the second one (unmarked Fowler Road) from the nearby rock crushing operation to the east. Turn right on this second road and follow the right fork to the Eel River bar (2.3). It may be possible except in higher water conditions to walk south along the river bar to the confluence with the Van Duzen River (2.6) or even the US 101 bridge (0.4 each way). A modest loop can be created by following a gravel road that parallels the north bank of the Van Duzen near the confluence and taking that back to the levee (0.6).

64 · Fortuna Architectural Walk

Length: up to 2.5 miles
Total ascent: 270 feet
Elevations: 90–280 feet

Type: loop
Dogs: leashed
Restrooms: yes

Description: This short walk through northern Fortuna passes five houses of special interest and includes some views out over Fortuna. You could easily add the Depot Museum. Although Fortuna has neither the quantity nor the quality of historic homes found in Ferndale, Eureka, and Arcata, this is a pleasant walk through areas of the 'Friendly City' unfamiliar to most Humboldt County residents.

Getting there: Take US 101 south for almost 17 miles to Fortuna's Main Street (Exit 689) and follow Main Street for 1.2 miles until reaching Park Street. There are Rohner Park signs at the corner of Main and Park. Turn left on Park Street. Park across from the Fireman's Pavillion. Approximate driving time, 25 minutes.

The route: Just west of the Depot Museum (open seven days a week in the summer and Thursday – Sunday from September through May; free), take the paved walking path across the Rohner Creek bridge and continue west on 'O' Street for one block to 15th Street (0.1). Turn left on 15th and right on 'N' Street for three blocks. Turn right on 12th Street. Turn left on 'O' Street and follow it all of the way to 9th Street (0.5) where you need to jog left and right to stay on 'O' Street. Just past

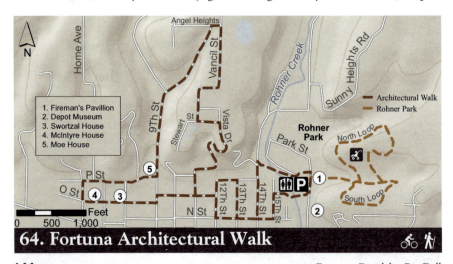

Fortuna - Ferndale - Rio Dell

the Calvary Chapel at 9th and 'O', notice the bird houses that have been attached to the west side of the garage on the south side of the street. Continue following 'O' Street. On the corner of 8th and 'O' Street is the Swortzel House, built in the 'Stick' architectural style with its use of prominent boards to frame windows, geometric patterns, and featuring knobs, spindles, and other 'borrowings' from furniture. At 624 'O' Street is the McIntyre House with its distinctive entry columns (a return to Greek and Roman architectural forms occurred after the Chicago World's Fair in 1893). Turn right on 6th Street and right again on 'P' Street. Follow 'P' back to 9th (which includes one block that no longer allows vehicular traffic). (0.8) At 1010 9th Street is the Moe House, which contains many Queen Anne features.

O St. birdhouses

Turn left on 9th Street as it makes a long gradual ascent. Stay to the right as the road forks following Christian Ridge Road to the ridge top (1.3). Turn right on Angel Heights Drive following it less than 100 yards to its intersection with Vancil Street. Turn right on Vancil, following it as it winds through this hilltop neighborhood until it intersects with Stewart Street (1.6). Turn left on Stewart Street and right on Vista Drive as it descends and becomes 11th Street and on to 'O' Street (2.0). Enjoy the sweeping views from this aptly named street, taking care to watch for traffic as the road has no shoulders.

Turn left on 'O' and in one block turn left on 12th Street and right on 'P' Street to 13th Street. Turn right on 13th Street. Take note of the bungalow and Prairie (popularized by Frank Lloyd Wright) architectural styles incorporated into the shingle-sided house at 841 13th Street (2.2). This style emphasizes horizontal lines and exposed roof elements (beams and rafter tails). Another example of a bungalow is just off the suggested route at 843 'N' Street.

Continue to 'N' Street. Turn left on 'N' and proceed one block to 14th Street. Turn left on 14th and follow it north as it narrows until you see a footbridge crossing Rohner Creek back into the park, passing ball fields and a basketball court on your left en route to the parking lot (2.5).

Special thanks to Jerry and Gisela Rohde.

Rohner Park Trails

Rohner Park hosts a second growth redwood forest. Two loop trails – South Loop (0.6) and North Loop (0.8) – are reached by walking up a broad central road on the south side of the Fireman's Pavilion. They are in good condition and would make for good walking any time of the year. The North Gully Trail (off the North Loop), however, would benefit from some serious restoration work. The forest is surrounded by the community of Fortuna and that creates some unusual interfaces with the trails. For example, the South Loop looks into the backyards of a row of houses and both loops pass fences often in various states of repair and gates that tease the walker. The convenience of this resource is ideal for walkers living in the Fortuna area. But it is also worth a visit for others interested in trying a different urban redwood park beyond Sequoia Park and the Arcata Community Forest.

Getting there: As for the Fortuna Architectural Walk (Hike #64).

Region F:
Southern Redwoods

All but one of the walks in this section are within the boundary of the Humboldt Redwoods State Park. This sprawling state park, the third largest in California, follows the Eel River for much of the park's length and also encompasses the Bull Creek drainage. These walks offer access to a blend of majestic old growth redwood forests, mountainside prairies, and riverine landscape generally linked by the Avenue of the Giants or the Mattole Road.

Until 1960 when the current routing of US 101 was completed, the Avenue of the Giants was part of the main north-south Redwood Highway. The trip north

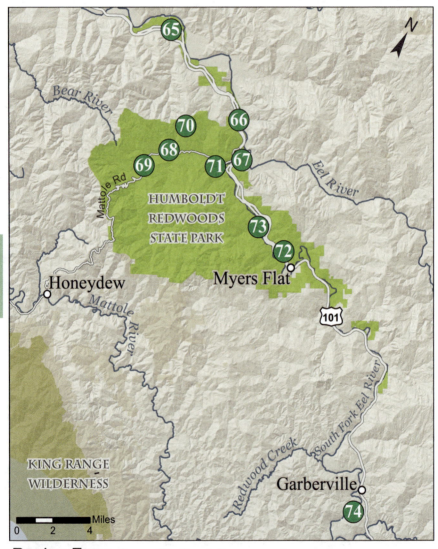

Region F: Southern Redwoods

from San Francisco was initially a three- and then two-day journey as the road was gradually improved. Roadhouses dotted the way, tourist attractions beckoned, and auto cabins and camps offered accommodation. Now, in many of the don't blink-or-you'll-miss-them hamlets, the sense of just hanging on is palpable. Some of the history has been washed away by the 1955 and 1964 floods, in other areas just overgrown by the fecundity of nature or the neglect of an economically bypassed population. The remaining eateries and attractions sprinkled along the length of the Avenue make for pleasant complements to most walks and offer glimpses into this past.

The Humboldt Redwoods State Park Visitor Center just south of Weott is worth a stop too. The Center's exhibits provide a helpful overview of the natural and human history of the area, including the fascinating story of Charles Kellogg. Kellogg's most lasting legacy, enshrined at the center, is the Travel Log. This is a hand-hewn redwood home he mounted on the back of a 1917 Nash Quad truck. From 1917 – 1921 Kellogg drove his eccentric mobile home across the country four times "to awaken interest in the great redwood forests of California, and to assist in their preservation." People like Kellogg and the Save the Redwoods League are among those we have to thank for the protection of this ancient forest.

View from High Rock

65 · Drury – Chaney Groves Trail

Length: 2.4 miles
Total ascent: flat
Elevations: 250–280 feet
Type: partial loop
Dogs: no
Restrooms: none

Description: In the massive flood of 1964, the once bustling community of Pepperwood was inundated by 30 feet of water. What remains on this floodplain of the Eel River are a few homes and farms, some vegetable stands, and a robust redwood forest. The Drury-Chaney Groves trail bisects the flat alluvial bench populated with redwoods that lie between the Avenue of the Giants and US 101. It is a flat walk and an accessible trail through several extensive groves of towering redwoods.

It was Berkeley paleontologist Ralph Chaney who first brought back 'dawn redwood' seedlings with him from China in the late 1940s. This deciduous sequoia joins the coast redwood and the giant sequoia as the three conifers known as redwoods.

Getting there: Drive south on US 101 for 32.5 miles taking Exit 674 (Avenue of the Giants/Pepperwood). Turn left onto the Avenue of the Giants for 2.7 miles. The road passes through what remains of the community of Pepperwood taking a bend to the south, quickly reaching the parking area for the Drury-Chaney Groves trailhead. Parking is available on both sides of the Avenue of the Giants. Approximate driving time, 40 minutes.

The route: From the parking area, the trail crosses a small open space and enters the redwood forest for the remainder of the walk. The level trail crosses the old Barkdull Road (0.6) -- a right turn here will take you to another access point from the Avenue of the Giants in half a mile; a left turn leads to the general location of the old Barkdull Ranch (0.1). After crossing the Barkdull Road, the trail reaches the loop trail (0.7). The loop is 0.9 mile long (1.6). The return to the parking area necessitates retracing your steps (2.4).

Extras. Once located between Pepperwood and Stafford, the town of Elinor had a railroad stop, hotel, post office, and logging camp on the east side of the Eel River

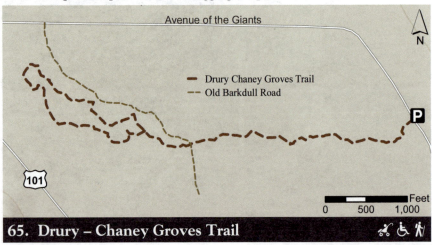

65. Drury – Chaney Groves Trail

and a collection of homes, store, and school on the west side. A ferry plied the river connecting the two sides of the town. However, when the 1964 floodwaters receded there was little of Elinor left. Just after you turn left onto the Avenue of the Giants from Exit 674, turn left again on Elinor Road and drive 150 yards to the concrete barriers that block old US 101. You can follow the old road for a short distance to the bridge (dated 1938) crossing Jordan Creek. During periods of low water, it is possible to wander east to the Eel River.

66 · High Rock and the Five Allens Trail

Length: High Rock - 1.4 miles; Five Allens – 2.7 miles
Total ascent: High Rock - 250 feet; Five Allens – 800 feet
Elevations: 190 – 975 feet
Type: out and back
Dogs: no
Restrooms: none

Description: The short walk to High Rock through the redwoods includes a spectacular turnaround point (High Rock) and the possibility of creating a loop. It also provides access to one of the better swimming holes along the Eel River. It can also easily be combined with a walk up the Five Allens Trail. That trailhead is just south of High Rock. The Five Allens Trail crosses under US 101 and then climbs consistently and, at times, steeply through viewless and modest stands of redwoods to two named groves: The Five Allens and Elisabeth Achelis. The trail provides for an excellent aerobic workout and pleasant walk but the trees themselves are far less impressive than those elsewhere in the park.

Getting there: Drive south on US 101 for just over 39 miles taking Exit 667A (Avenue of the Giants). Turn right onto to the Avenue of the Giants driving to milepost 8.7 (22.8) [mileage from the north end and south end of the Avenue of the Giants] which will be a little less than 1.5 miles from the US 101 exit. Turn left (east) on an unmarked but paved side road proceeding 75 yards to a parking area that serves as the High Rock trailhead. For the Five Allens trailhead, continue south on the Avenue of the Giants to milepost 9.4 (22.12). There is small pullout next to the trail on the west side of the Avenue of the Giants (there is a sign for

66. High Rock and the Five Allens Trail

the Maria McKean Allen Grove) and additional parking on the east side about 0.3 mile north. Approximate driving time, 50 minutes.

The route: The trail to High Rock begins inconspicuously on the southwest side of the parking area. Despite the density of the redwoods, fingers of poison oak touch the trail. A bridge spans a rocky chasm (0.3) before beginning a modest ascent following, at times, the old county wagon road that predated the Redwood Highway. Continue to bear right (although as you near the Avenue of the Giants several of the trails lead to parking areas on the Avenue). Several short switchbacks take you to the top of High Rock (0.7) with a protective railing and expansive views.

From High Rock, retrace your steps for the first 0.2 mile then stay right and drop down 150 yards to a sandy beach fronted by a pleasant pool near the base of High Rock. From here, in low water conditions, you can walk north (1.5) along the riverbed before turning west and completing the loop (1.6). The path from the riverbed back to the parking area is well used and easy to find.

To connect with the Five Allens trail continue south along the Avenue of the Giants about 100 yards past High Rock. A small sign ("Allen's Trail") marks the beginning of the trail on the north end of the small parking area. The trail crosses underneath US 101 (0.1) through a paved culvert. On the east side the trail climbs steadily (0.9) before leveling off. The trail forks (1.1) with the left option leading to the Elisabeth Achelis plaque (0.3 roundtrip) or the "The Five Allens" marker (0.2 roundtrip). The return requires retracing your steps back down the trail (2.7).

67 ·Founders Grove & Mahan Plaque Loop

Length: 1.6 miles
Total ascent: 100 feet
Elevations: 250 – 320 feet
Type: partial loop
Dogs: no
Restrooms: yes

Description: Although its majesty is slowly diminishing, the downed Dyerville Giant redwood still remains the most stunning attraction of this walk. Of course, the route also includes the impressive Founders Tree and a number of other old growth giants. The Founders Grove portion of this walk is particularly well-suited for families with young children or older members with limited mobility. The Founders Grove also has a self-guided nature trail. The Mahan Plaque loop trail is more root-bound with sections of irregular footing.

Getting there: Two trailheads offer starting points for this walk. To reach the Founders Grove trailhead take US 101 south 42.3 miles to Exit 663 (South Fork/Honeydew). Take a sharp left onto Bull Creek Flats Road and an almost immediate right onto the Avenue of the Giants as it crosses the South Fork of the Eel River. In 0.2 mile turn left onto the Dyerville Loop Road. The Founders Grove parking lot is on the left in about 0.1 mile.

For the Mahan Plaque trailhead, instead of turning onto the Dyerville Loop Road continue on south on the Avenue of the Giants for an additional 0.4 mile where there is a pullout on the east side of the road. This is at milepost 11.3 from the north (or 20.2 from the south). Approximate driving time, 50 minutes.

The route: It may be easiest to visualize this route as two distinct loops (0.6 each) with a connecting trail (0.2 each way) between the loops. The route is well signed and it would be virtually impossible to get more than very temporarily lost. The Dyerville Giant lies at the south end of the Founders Grove trail. This massive tree fell in March, 1991 shattering its top on a redwood that still bears the scar from the impact. It may have been in the 370-foot range which would have made it among the tallest in the world. The monument acknowledging the Mahans is located on the south end of the Mahan Plaque loop. The Mahans were instrumental in saving this grove of redwoods and protecting them in perpetuity. Rohde and Rohde (2004) provide more detail. The Pacific Lumber Company, which owned this land at the confluence of the two forks of the Eel River, began to secretly cut a railroad right-of-way in

Founder's Grove, photo by Michael Kauffmann

1924 with the intent of extending a spur line across the South Fork of the Eel and up into the rich redwood forests lining Bull Creek. Word of this reached the Mahans who journeyed down from Eureka to investigate. They sounded the alarm. The outcry was swift and within a few months a Save-the-Redwoods plan was in place. Although negotiations took six years to complete, the result was that the Dyerville and Bull Creek Flats were added to Humboldt Redwoods State Park in 1931.

Laura Perrott Mahan also willed her interest in Forest Lodge, the Perrott family's riverside retreat along the South Fork of the Eel, to the park which was eventually acquired in full by the state in the 1970s. Many of the Perrott clan are buried in the Table Bluff Cemetery near Loleta (see Hike #50).

Extras. Big Cut Trail continues further south from the southwest corner of the Mahan Plaque Loop. The trail climbs steeply to an earthen bench (0.2) engineered to protect the roadways now far below you. Soon the route takes you down and under US 101 (0.6). Cross the Avenue of the Giants (0.8) and arrive at the Women's Federation Grove and Julia Morgan's Four Fireplaces (1.0). From here you can further extend your hike by using the summer (only) bridge to cross the South Fork of the Eel and access the trail network there. (See Hike #71).

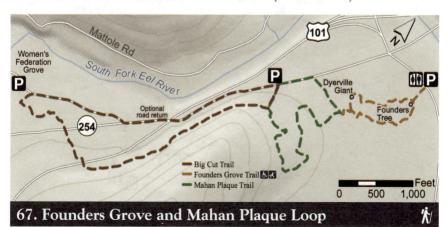

67. Founders Grove and Mahan Plaque Loop

68 · Bull Creek – Addie Johnson – Homestead - Albee Creek Loop

Length: 4.7 miles
Total ascent: 550 feet
Elevations: 380 – 800 feet
Type: partial loop
Dogs: no
Restrooms: yes

Description: This walk combines several shorter trails that could be considered standalone experiences. The Addie Johnson, Homestead, and the Bull Creek trails can be combined into a loop. The route climbs above the redwoods into oak woodlands to the historic gravesite of Addie Johnson. It winds through magnificent redwood giants that loom high above Bull Creek's flood plain. Although most of the hike is relatively flat, the route up to the gravesite climbs steadily on a well-graded trail.

According to Rohde and Rohde (1992), "A rancher named Tosaldo Johnson travelled from California to Texas to buy some cattle; while there, he married Addie Stewart. The couple came west, and in 1872 they homesteaded 160 acres on a sunny prairie above Bull Creek. One day several years later, Addie Johnson hiked up the prairie in search of a lost lamb; she eventually came to a lovely promontory that looked down on the family's homestead. Enchanted by the spot, Addie told her husband it was there she would someday like to be buried. Sadly, Tosaldo Johnson had to honor her request just a few months later when she died in childbirth."

Getting there: Drive south on US 101 for just over 42.5 miles to Exit 663. Turn right onto Bull Creek Flats Road and proceed west for 4.4 miles. On the left will be a turn into the Big Trees Day Use Area; parking is also available at the beginning of the Addie Johnson Trail. Approximate driving time, 55 minutes.

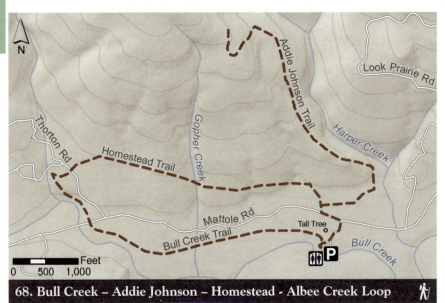

The route: From the Big Trees parking lot walk the access road 150 yards to Mattole Road. Turn left on Mattole Road and carefully walk to the trailhead parking area for the Addie Johnson Trail (0.1). Continue on the Addie Johnson Trail as it crosses the Homestead Trail (0.4) and rises above Harper Creek, exchanging redwoods for oaks and filtered views (1.3). The trail ends at the top of a wooded knoll where Addie Johnson's grave is marked by a wooden plaque surrounded by a picket fence. The route returns to the intersection with the Homestead trail (2.2). Turn right and follow the multi-use trail west to the access road to Albee Creek Campground (3.3). This is a popular equestrian route with riders coming east from Cuneo Creek Horse Camp. Turn left at the access road and follow it to Mattole Road (3.6). Turn right on Mattole Road and proceed west again being watchful for traffic (3.7). Turn left on the Big Tree trail as it follows Bull Creek, passing some of the most stunning old growth redwoods on the planet. The route culminates with Big Tree, one of the ten tallest trees, just before the parking lot (4.7).

Extras. The 4-mile Homestead Trail stretches from Harper Creek west past Albee Creek Campground, across two fords of Bull Creek and on to Cuneo Creek Horse Camp. The Big Tree Trail on the north side of Bull Creek or the Bull Creek Flats Trail can be taken from the Grasshopper Multi-Use Trail (MUT) the five miles to Rockefeller Forest Loop Trail (see Hike #39 in *Volume 1*). During the summer and early fall, a seasonal bridge is available and allows walkers to cross to the trail network on the south side of Bull Creek.

69 ·Squaw Creek – Baxter – Hamilton Barn – Homestead Loop

Length: up to 7.1 miles	Bull Creek
Total ascent: 1,100 feet	**Type**: loop
Elevations: 380 – 1,100 feet	**Dogs**: no
Access: three creek crossings of	**Restrooms**: yes

Description: This walk combines portions of longer trails (Squaw Creek Road and Homestead Trail) and the entirety of the Baxter Trail. The route climbs above the redwoods into oak woodlands with access to some stunning views over Pole Line, Cuneo Creek, and the upper Bull Creek drainage. The route includes the old homestead and orchards now part of the Hamilton Barn Environmental Camp.

Getting there: Drive south on US 101 for just over 42.5 miles taking Exit 663 (South Fork/Honeydew/CA Route 254). Turn right onto Bull Creek Flats Road which soon becomes Mattole Road and proceed west for 5.4 miles. On the left will be a turn into the poorly signed Grasshopper MUT/Grasshopper Peak Fire Lookout parking area. Parking is also available in the Hamilton Barn and Baxter Environmental Camps areas. Approximate driving time, 55 minutes.

The route: From the Grasshopper Multi-use Trail parking area, follow the trail/ road past the locked gate and continue to the fork in the road (1.0) with the left branch continuing the long journey up to Grasshopper Peak (3,373') and the right branch continuing 3.7 miles to the Whiskey Flat Trail Camp. [See *Volume 1* for the Grasshopper Peak day hike.] Follow the Squaw Creek Ridge Road to an intersection with the Baxter Trail, a junction that can easily be missed (2.7). A prominent sign notes the presence of an 'environmental camp' ahead (2.0 miles to Whiskey Flat) but the Baxter Trail sign is less apparent (to the right). Once on the Baxter Trail, the route gradually descends for the first half mile until it bends sharply back just before reaching the edge of the tree line (3.2). A faint trail continues on to the edge of the meadow (0.1) and offers a stunning panorama that is well worth the detour. The Baxter Trail continues its gradual descent until it reaches campsite #2 in the Baxter Environmental Camp and the first ford of Bull Creek (4.7). The alternative route (when the water is high) passes through campsite #2 and follows the trail to the Baxter Environmental Camp parking lot and on to Mattole Road. Those that elect to cross Bull Creek will then reach Mattole Road (5.0) just across from the road access to Hamilton Barn Environmental Camp. In high water conditions, the only option necessitates walking east on the Mattole Road to the Grasshopper MUT parking area.

There are two ways to walk through the Hamilton Barn area. One is to follow the access road to the Hamilton Barn Environmental Camp parking lot, crossing Mill Creek, and continuing through the campground to the second ford of Bull Creek (5.8). The second option is slightly longer and involves leaving the access road 100 yards from the Mattole Road, veering left, and intersecting with the Homestead Trail. In another 100 yards turn right and follow the Homestead Trail (it fords Mill Creek but the pedestrian bridge is just downstream and provides an easy alternative) to the same second ford of Bull Creek.

After completing this second crossing of Bull Creek the trail winds closer to and then further away from Mattole Road before crossing Bull Creek the final time

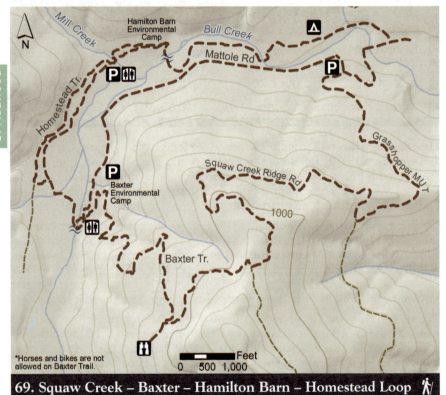

69. Squaw Creek – Baxter – Hamilton Barn – Homestead Loop

(6.2). The trail intersects with the Albee Creek Campground access road (6.4). Turn right and follow the road back to Mattole Road (6.7). Turn right on the Mattole Road and carefully walk west crossing Bull Creek on the highway bridge (6.9). Turn left on a trail just past the bridge. This trail joins Bull Creek Flats Trail in 0.1 mile (7.0). Turn right and follow Bull Creek Flats Trail back to the Grasshopper MUT parking lot (7.1).

For Hamilton Barn Loop: This 1.8 mile loop uses the Homestead Trail and the Environmental Camp access road to explore the ranch and aging orchards that Ruby and Hugh Hamilton worked for more than five decades.

see v2.hikinghumboldt.com/hikes

70 · Look Prairie

Length: 3.6 miles	Type: out and back
Total ascent: 1,000 feet	Dogs: no
Elevations: 360 – 1,360 feet	Restrooms: yes (nearby)

Description: This walk up the Look Prairie Road climbs quickly above the redwood forest through an extensive prairie and oak woodlands once the site of the ranch house and barn of the Look family. These days the most visible evidence of the homestead may be a handful of fruit trees midway up the prairie as the barn was lost to fire in the 1990s. If you do not find the views of Grasshopper Peak and Bull Creek valley breathtaking, the steep walk will be. Despite periodic tree cover, this walk can be hot and exposed in the heat of the summer. It is possible to reach the ridge top and Peavine Ridge Road in 3.3 miles and another 800 feet of elevation gain. See the Hike #40 in *Volume 1*.

Getting there: Drive south on US 101 for just over 42.5 miles taking Exit 663 (South Fork/Honeydew/CA Route 254). Turn right onto Bull Creek Flats Road and proceed west for 4.2 miles. On the right will be a turn into a small trailhead parking area for the Homestead Trail and the Look Prairie Road. Parking is also available less than a 0.1 mile east on Mattole Road at a picnic area. Approximate driving time, 55 minutes.

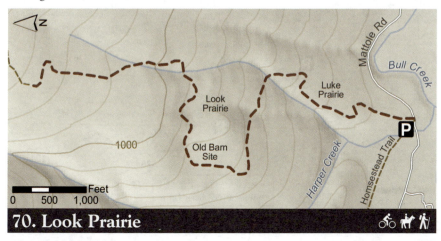

The route: The gated Look Prairie Road quickly leaves the forest and emerges briefly into the lowest prairie (which is actually called Luke Prairie after residents Bill and Mary Luke, who lived there beginning in the 1940s). The road passes the site of the Look barn (0.8) and homestead before taking a short dip and resuming the climb crossing the prairie to its east side (1.2). It re-enters the mixed conifer and oak forest and touches the upper portion of the prairie (1.6). The prairie is continually under assault by encroaching conifers. Without grazing and fire in its toolbox, the State Park relies on cutting these trees to maintain the prairie. The road again disappears into the forest (1.8) and continues its long ascent to Peavine Ridge. Most hikers will be satisfied to turn around here as the upper portion of the road is devoid of prairies and views.

71 · Rockefeller Loop – Women's Federation Grove

Length: 0.6 miles or longer	(Rockefeller Loop)
Total ascent: flat	**Type:** loop
Elevations: 300 feet	**Dogs:** no
Access: wheelchair accessible	**Restrooms:** yes

Description: In the summertime, when a network of summer footbridges are in place, the Rockefeller Loop serves as an excellent trailhead for a variety of walks extending far beyond this short trail that circles through this grove of redwood giants. (1) To the east, across the South Fork of the Eel River, is the Women's Federation Grove, Julia Morgan's famous 'Four Fireplaces', one of the better swimming holes along the South Fork, and a rare albino redwood. (2) Upstream along Bull Creek is the Big Tree Trail that reaches the Big Trees Day Use Area in about 4 miles. This option is not dependent upon a summer footbridge. (3) Crossing Bull Creek (on a summer footbridge), you can follow the River Trail along the South Fork of the Eel River for a mile to the confluence of Decker Creek or nearly 4 miles to another summer footbridge with access to Burlington Campground and the Visitor Center. (4) And, lastly, also across Bull Creek, the Bull Creek Flats trail

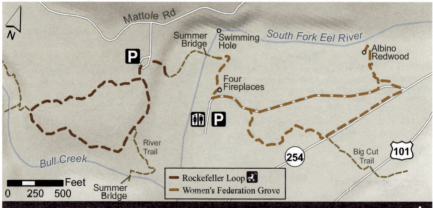

71. Rockefeller Loop – Women's Federation Grove

follows the south side of Bull Creek upstream to the summer bridge crossing to the Big Trees Day Use Area (3.2 miles). See Hikes #38 and #39 in *Volume 1* for more detail on Options 2 – 4.

Getting there: Drive south on US 101 for just over 42.5 miles taking Exit 663 (South Fork/Honeydew/CA Route 254). Turn right onto Bull Creek Flats Road and proceed west for 1.3 miles. On the left is a narrow but paved access road that is obscured because it drops so steeply down to the parking area for the Rockefeller Loop Trail. Approximate driving time, 50 minutes.

The route: This short, accessible trail can be taken either direction. Apart from the magnificent redwoods, there are two notable features, each about one third of the way around the loop. Proceeding counterclockwise, the first landmark is the junction with the Big Trees Trail that diverges to the right and leads to one of the summer bridges that crosses Bull Creek. The next highlight is the plaque commemorating the role of the Rockefeller family in funding the protection of these trees. Nearby is another trail to a summer crossing of Bull Creek. The loop is completed when the trail follows a rather narrow channel left by two fallen redwoods.

Departing from the east side of the parking area is a trail that leads to the broad bed of the South Fork of the Eel River. During the rainy winter, this can be a raging torrent unimaginable during the dry summer and fall when it shrinks to a shallow trickle. The summer footbridge crosses to the California Federation of Women's Clubs Grove and Day Use Area on the other side (0.5). In addition to popular swimming holes downriver, the Day Use Area features the iconic 'Four Fireplaces', a connection to the Big Cut Trail (0.1 mile east on the Women's Federation Grove access road) that leads under US 101 to the Mahan Loop Trail and Founders Grove (1.5), and the unique albino redwood. The albino redwood is located on the banks above the Eel River not far from the intersection of the access road and the Avenue of the Giants. No signs exist to assist you; only informal, social trails that lead to the tree. Unlike other redwoods, the albino is not a towering specimen but small with silver, white needles depending upon an adjacent tree for much of its nourishment (since it does not have chlorophyll). (0.9)

72 ·Williams Grove – Hidden Springs

Length: 5.1 miles with options
Total ascent: 1000 feet
Elevations: 250-750 feet
Fee: Hidden Springs and Williams Grove Day Use Area (summer)
Type: partial loop
Dogs: no
Restrooms: yes

Description: This walk offers the possibility of access to the Eel River on either end of the journey. However, the trail connecting these two popular areas is through second growth forest, the loop includes 0.6 mile of walking through Hidden Springs Campground, and much of the first mile immediately south of the Williams Grove Day Use Area is affected by traffic noise from nearby US 101. While these realities may diminish the overall desirability of the walking experience, the trail is very pleasant and much of route is well away from US 101. The opportunity to incorporate the Hidden Springs Beach Trail or the Williams Grove Day Use Area and Children's Forest Trail can be an added bonus.

Getting there: Drive south on US 101 for just over 50.2 miles to Exit 656. Turn right (north) on the Avenue of the Giants for about 1 mile to the Williams Grove Day Use Area or left (south) for 0.9 mile to the entrance to Hidden Springs Campground. There is substantial parking in the Williams Grove Day Use Area. During the winter when the area is gated, there is limited parking adjacent to the Avenue near the entrance to the Day Use Area. Approximate driving time, 55 minutes.

Hidden Springs Beach Trail, photo by Nancy Spruance

The route: From the Williams Grove Day Use Area the trail climbs through the redwoods to a culvert that allows hikers to safely cross under US 101 (0.3). On the east side of the freeway the trail parallels the busy thoroughfare below climbing to an open bench with views of Myers Flat and the Eel River (0.7). The trail continues its undulating traverse through a forest largely of second growth redwoods and tan oak crossing the Williford Road MUT (1.4). (See Hike #36 in *Volume 1*).

Continuing east on the trail from the Williams Grove to Hidden Springs Campground, the trail reaches fork (1.7) with the left fork proceeding to the upper campground emerging at campsite 74 (2.3). Going right, the trail emerges on the west side of Hidden Springs campground in 0.4 mile near campsite 134. By walking through the campground, the two ends can be connected to complete a loop (3.4) and then return to Williams Grove Day Use Area (5.1).

Extras. Hidden Springs Beach Trail. Across from the vehicular entrance to Hidden Springs Campground from the Avenue of the Giants is a poorly marked trail that descends to the river. The trail crosses Nelson Road (once part of the original Redwood Highway) and reaches a walkway of hand-set stones (0.4) that can be submerged during times of higher water. The trail soon reaches a bend in the river (0.5) and a popular summer swimming and sunning area. This area was also the location of a Native American village many years ago. The trail loops above the beach returning on the opposite side of the point via the bed of an old wagon road and

72. Williams Grove – Hidden Springs Campground

Nelson Road. The trail intersects with the trail back to the Avenue of the Giants (0.9) and returns to the Avenue (1.1).

Children's Forest Trail. From the Williams Grove Day Use Area a summer bridge (0.3 mile upriver) provides access to a quiet, seldom-used trail that heads south along west side of the Eel River to an alluvial flat (0.7). Here a short loop trail circulates through this old-growth grove (1.0). Return the way you came. (1.7)

73 · Garden Club of America Grove

Length: 4.2 miles with options	bridges
Total ascent: 700 feet	**Type**: partial loop
Elevations: 300-550 feet	**Dogs**: no
Access Constraints: Summer	**Restrooms**: yes

Description: This summer walk quickly leaves the busy Avenue of the Giants corridor behind as it crosses the Eel River, climbing through a mature redwood forest to beautiful Canoe Creek. The trail then loops through the extensive Garden Club of America Grove before returning the way you came. This little utilized route offers a blend of aerobic climbs, pleasant forest walking, a smattering of views over the South Fork of the Eel, and a taste of delightful Canoe Creek.

Getting there: Drive south on US 101 for just over 44.6 miles taking Exit 661 (Weott). Turn right (Newton Road) for 0.5 mile and left on the Avenue of the Giants (CA 254) for about 3.5 miles to the Garden Club of America Grove Day Use Area. Turn right and park. Approximate driving time, 55 minutes.

The route: From the signed trailhead, follow the trail to the broad riverbed cross-

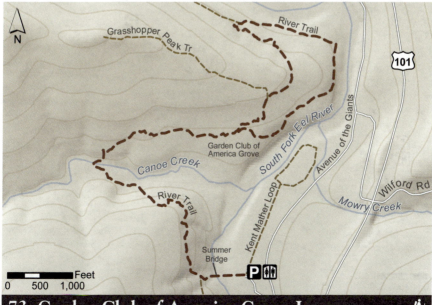

73. Garden Club of America Grove Loop

ing on the summer bridge (0.1). Climb the west bank to the junction with the River Trail (0.2). Turn right on the River Trail continuing as it climbs through a majestic redwood forest to a bridged crossing of Canoe Creek (0.9). At the intersection with the Grasshopper Peak Trail (1.4) turn left leaving the River Trail and climb to a signed trail junction (1.6). Turn right on the trail to Burlington until you rejoin the River Trail (2.0). Turn right and follow the River Trail south retracing your steps to the Garden Club of America Day Use Area spur trail, crossing the river and back to your vehicle (4.2).

Extras. The River Trail can be walked additionally north (toward Burlington Campground or Rockefeller Grove) or south (toward Williams Grove Day Use Area). The Kent Mather Loop trail (0.9) departs from the Garden Club of America Day Use Area.

74 · So. Humboldt Community Park Trails

Length: 2.4 miles with options
Total ascent: 250 feet
Elevations: 360-490 feet
Type: loop
Dogs: leashed
Restrooms: yes

Description: This 430-acre parcel, once part of the immense Tooby Ranch, of fertile bottomland adjacent to the South Fork of the Eel River was formally established in 2002. In addition to 3.5 miles of multi-use trails, the Community Park includes a riverside playground, a Frisbee golf course, skateboard ramp, picnic areas, and a community farm. Although the property is home to a network of trails connecting the meadows and woods, this suggested route follows the park perimeter.

Getting there: Drive south on US 101 for 67.0 miles taking Exit 639A (Sprowl

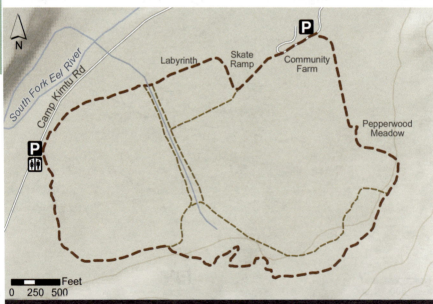

74. Southern Humboldt Community Park Trails

Creek) to Garberville. Turn right at the intersection with Sprowl Creek Road and descend toward the South Fork of the Eel River. In 0.9 mile watch for signs on the left for the entrance to the Southern Humboldt Community Park. Alternatively, continue on Sprowl Creek Road for 0.1 mile to the intersection with the Camp Kimtu Road. Turn left following Camp Kimtu Road for 0.7 mile to the west entrance to the Park. Both options have parking. Approximate driving time, 1 hour, 10 minutes.

The route: From the east parking area near the Community Farm residence and old ranch buildings, the perimeter trail proceeds west through the gate and on past the barn. For those unfamiliar with this trailhead, it can be somewhat off-putting as it feels like a private residence but the nearby house is the caretakers home. Soon you encounter several braids of trail, some staying in the fields and some meandering through the woods. There is a reasonable signage infrastructure. The trails converge in order to cross a seasonal stream on a small footbridge (0.5). The trail reaches to the west parking lot and trailhead (0.8). From the Kimtu Visitor parking area the trail bends around the west side of the park and turns east (1.3). Again the perimeter trail splits offering several choices with paths that stay in the trees and another that hugs the boundary of the meadow and woods. The various options again merge (2.2) at the Pepperwood Meadow (site of a performance stage) and complete the loop (2.4).

Other Options in the Area that Deserve a Short Mention

For many years the lake created by the summer dam of the South Fork of the Eel River at Benbow was incredibly popular. However, the dam is no longer and visitors tend to play golf, visit the luxurious Benbow Historic Inn, or enjoy the sunny weather. There are also several possible walks. *Volume 1*, Hike #35, describes the walk from Benbow to Kimtu Court and Alice Avenue west of Garberville. The currently closed State Recreation Area campground is the trailhead for the **Thrap Mill, the Pioneer, and the Ridge Trails**, a 2.5 mile network of trails along the hills above the west side of the South Fork of the Eel. Currently the only access to these trails involves either crossing the low-water bridge entrance to the closed campground (from Benbow Drive) or fording the river (not terribly difficult during low flow periods of the summer and fall) after walking south along the river under the freeway bridge. Continue along the gravelly beach on the west side to a path leading up the slope to the right. This takes you into the closed campground where you turn right on the paved road. Cross under the freeway again to reach the trailhead.

Walking from the Benbow State Recreation Area parking area or Benbow Inn, it is possible to cross east underneath US 101 to the Benbow Valley RV Resort and Golf Center and either follow along the East Branch of the South Fork of the Eel River through the Resort or head more directly to Benbow Drive. The **East Branch Road** extends past an arm of the golf course and above the river for almost 2 miles. The road passes an inactive quarry on the right and skirts a large rodeo grounds. Eventually the road passes Palomino Way, a small rural subdivision before crossing a cattle guard and becoming unpaved. This makes for a good turnaround.

Fleishmann Grove Trail (1.4) and Gould Grove Loop (0.7), located west of the Burlington Campground and the Humboldt Redwoods Park Visitor Center, are notable because both conform to Access Guidelines for trails. These level trails parallel the South Fork of the Eel River and offer summer bridge access to the River Trail. These two trails offer a convenient way to experience the big trees, to feel and smell a redwood forest if you have mobility or stamina limitations.

Region G:
King Range and Shelter Cove Area

Dominated by the 68,000-acre King Range National Conservation Area (KRNCA), the over 100 miles of trails in the KRNCA are generally too remote and rugged to be considered short day hikes. The day hikes in this region tend to be longer and are included in *Volume 1*. Several walks along the Lost Coast, accessible from Mattole Road, are in this section. Conklin Road just east of Petrolia and the short walk to Punta Gorda south from the mouth of the Mattole River, some walks in Shelter Cove, and the beautiful walk from the Needle Rock Visitor Center to Bear Harbor in Sinkyone Wilderness State Park round out the selections in this region. Savvy readers will wonder at the inclusion of any walks in the

Region G: **King Range and Shelter Cove Area**

Sinkyone as this 7,500-acre park lies completely in Mendocino County. However, realistically it is only accessible from Humboldt County.

The coastal mountains throughout this area shoot up steeply from the coastline, evidence of the tectonic forces at work here. King Peak, the tallest point in the range at 4,087', is just 3 miles from the ocean. In addition, these mountains are battered by intense winter storms that have further sculpted the terrain. The result is a dramatic and distinctive topography.

Poppies on the Lost Coast, photo by Allison Poklemba

Walk to Bear Harbor.

Punta Gorda Lighthouse, photo by Michael Kauffmann

Hiking Humboldt Volume 2

75 · Steamboat Rock to Sugar Loaf Island

Length: 3.2 miles with options	Durr creeks
Total ascent: flat	**Type:** out and back
Elevations: sea level	**Dogs:** yes
Access: high water at Singley and	**Restrooms:** none

Description: This beach walk departs from the Ferndale – Petrolia Road just after it descends the "Wall" near Cape Mendocino. It is possible to walk the beach for about a mile and a half south or north from this access point. Just offshore is the distinctive Steamboat Rock and visible to the north is 331-foot Sugar Loaf Island. If you are like me and wondering about why 'sugarloaf' ever became a popular name for geographical features, the answer is – before granulated and cube sugars were introduced in the late 19th century, a tall cone with a rounded top known as a sugarloaf was the traditional form in which refined sugar was produced and sold.

Getting there: Take US 101 south for 14.2 miles. Take Exit 692. Follow the signs to Ferndale. On the south end of Ferndale turn right on Bluff Street/Ocean Avenue. In less than 0.1 mile turn left on Wildcat Avenue to Petrolia and follow it to the coast. Local cyclists fondly refer to the final steep descent to the ocean as "The Wall", as they strain to finish the annual Tour of the Unknown Coast 100-mile bike race. Once the Petrolia Road reaches the base of "The Wall" and begins its six-mile ocean-side route, about one mile south is a parking area on the west side of the road just before a bridge (18.9 miles). Approximate driving time, 1 hour, 20 minutes.

The route: A plaque commemorating the Cape Mendocino lighthouse, located 1.5 miles north from 1868 to 1951, is adjacent to a trail that leads to the beach. To the right, the beach extends north reaching Singley Creek in about 1.1 miles. If the mouth of the creek is passable and the tide not too high, it is possible to continue another 0.5 mile to Cape Mendocino across from Sugar Loaf Island. Taken to the left the beach is walkable for about 1.7 miles. Sand is soft in both directions.

Cape Mendocino is the western most point in California and just offshore is the location of the Triple Junction, the seismic hot spot created by the point where the Gorda plate, the North American plate, and the Pacific plate all meet. Since 1983 this area has generated about 80 earthquakes a year of magnitude 3.0 or greater.

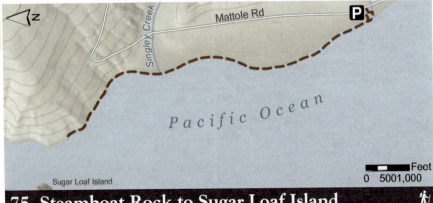

75. Steamboat Rock to Sugar Loaf Island

76 · McNutt Gulch/Creek

Length: 5.0 miles with options	McNutt Creek
Total ascent: flat	**Type:** out and back
Elevations: sea level - 30 feet	**Dogs:** yes
Access: high water an issue at	**Restrooms:** none

Description: This beach walk departs from the south end of the Ferndale – Petrolia Road just as it turns east from the coast toward Petrolia. This area lies near the center of a 15 mile stretch of shoreline between Cape Mendocino and Punta Gorda that experienced a 1 meter uplift during the April 1992 earthquake. It is possible to walk the five miles south to the Mattole River; however it is important to know that the mouth is passable. This stretch of beach shares many of the features of the more dramatic Lost Coast south of the mouth of Mattole River: high bluffs and hills rising from the shoreline, pristine beaches (apart from the carcass of an immense buoy beached along the route), prevailing northwest winds and soft sand. Aside from the seals that will keep a curious watch from the ocean, you are very likely to have the beach to yourself.

Getting there: Follow the directions for Hike #75 but continue 4 miles further south, about 23 bumpy miles from Ferndale. Limited but adequate roadside parking exists just before the bridge over McNutt Creek after which the road begins to climb and turn inland. Approximate driving time, 1 hour, 30 minutes.

The route: There is a pedestrian opening in the fence on the west side of the road and north side of the bridge to a trail that drops to a crossing of McNutt Creek (0.1). The flow in McNutt Creek ranges from impassable in high water to virtually dry during later summer and early fall. If impassable, then it is possible to walk south across the bridge on the road for about 100 yards, where the fence can be crossed, and you can scramble down the steep bank. The route follows the coast south eventually (2.1) approaching a stretch of steep bluffs pockmarked with several shallow caves. The beach continues south passing LaRue Gulch, where the coastline briefly flattens (and a primitive road may offer some temporary relief from the soft sand) before narrowing again as the beach rounds Mattole Point and reaches the mouth of the Mattole River (see the hike Mattole River North). However, because a one-way hike necessitates greater logistical arrangements and requires the mouth of the Mattole River to be closed, most hikers will be content to walk out and back.

Hiking Humboldt Volume 2

77 Conklin Creek Road

Length: up to 5.4 miles
Total ascent: 200 feet
Elevations: 60 - 170 feet
Type: out and back
Dogs: yes
Restrooms: none

Description: This road walk follows the south side of the Mattole River for several miles through diffuse residential areas and bucolic landscape. Several times the road rises above the river channel, providing views up and down the Mattole River. The road is not heavily used.

Douglas iris

Getting there: Take US 101 south for 14.2 miles. Take Exit 692 (Fernbridge/Ferndale). At the end of the exit ramp turn right onto Singley Road/Fernbridge Drive. In one-half mile turn right on CA 211, crossing over the Eel River on Fernbridge. In 4.8 miles (which takes you to the Victorian Inn at the south end of Main Street, turn right on Bluff Street/Ocean Avenue. In less than 0.1 mile turn left on Wildcat Avenue and follow it as it winds over several broad ridges to the coast and eventually east and inland to the small hamlet of Petrolia, 28.2 teeth-rattling miles from Ferndale. Continue through Petrolia for 1.3 miles to Conklin Creek Road, just before crossing the Mattole River. Although opportunities exist for roadside parking along the length of the road, I prefer to drive 2.5 miles and park near the end of the public road on a pullout overlooking the Mattole River. Approximate driving time, 1 hour and 50 minutes.

The route: The walk is a very straight-forward out-and-back road walk with the eastern half feeling much more rural. The western half of the walk follows the wooded riparian zone of the Mattole with the riverbank frequently just yards away. This area benefits from the warmer, sunnier climate of the Mattole River and can easily be combined with an ocean walk, just a short drive away, to enjoy the best of both worlds. From the suggested parking area, walk west along the road as far as the Mattole Road intersection (2.7). Return as you came.

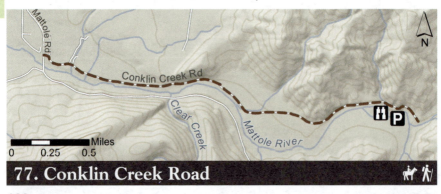

77. Conklin Creek Road

∞ The First Producing Oil Well in California

It was 1859 when the *Humboldt Times* first mentioned that petroleum springs, seeping "rock oil", had been located both at Bear River and five miles south of Cape Mendocino. Six years later, the Union Mattole Oil Company shipped six containers of oil to San Francisco, each container holding fifteen to twenty gallons, from the first productive well in California. This well was just several miles east of the current location of Petrolia. Although records indicate that shipments increased to as much as 850 gallons per month, oil was never produced in large enough quantities to be deemed a success. But for a time, the Mattole was the site of an oil rush. Companies were purchasing mineral rights to land throughout the region. Wells were drilled. Hope ran high enough that the original town name of New Jerusalem was soon changed to Petrolia. But within a year, the harsh truth had set in and soon the climate, access to water and land attracted new settlers with little mention of petroleum.

Moses John Conklin, the eponymous origin of Conklin Road, arrived in Sacramento in 1852 where he married and lived for several years before moving to the Mattole Valley. His wife, Margaret, was the first white woman to enter the region south of Cape Mendocino in Humboldt County. Conklin farmed and raised livestock, and was not only an active businessman, but served as assessor, justice of the peace, and notary public. ∞

78 · Mattole River to Punta Gorda

Length: 6.4 miles	Creek difficult with high water
Total ascent: flat	Type: out and back
Elevations: sea level	Dogs: yes
Access constraints: Fourmile	Restrooms: yes

Description: This is a popular gateway to the Lost Coast and the northern portion of the King Range. The 6-mile round trip to the remnants of the Punta Gorda lighthouse stays along the beach the entire way. The soft sand and the omnipresent northwest wind can make this walk a trudge although early starts help diminish the latter challenge. Hills rise steeply from the beach and help create the character that makes the Lost Coast one of the premiere backpacking experiences in Hum-

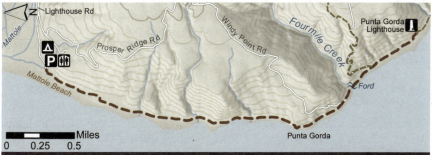

78. Mattole Beach to Punta Gorda

Hiking Humboldt Volume 2

boldt County. *Volume 1* covers some of the longer day hikes and a variation of this hike using the Prosper Ridge Road.

Getting there: Take US 101 south for 14.2 miles. Take Exit 692 (Fernbridge/Ferndale). At the end of the exit ramp turn right onto Singley Road/Fernbridge Drive. In one-half mile turn right on CA 211, crossing over the Eel River on Fernbridge. In 4.8 miles (which takes you to the Victorian Inn at the south end of Main Street), turn right on Bluff Street/Ocean Avenue. In less than 0.1 mile turn left on Wildcat Avenue and follow it as it winds its way over several broad ridges to the coast and eventually east and inland to the small hamlet of Petrolia, 28.2 bumpy miles from Ferndale. Continue through Petrolia for 1.4 miles to Lighthouse Road, just after crossing the Mattole River. Turn right on Lighthouse Road and continue 4.8 miles to its termination at the King Range/Mattole River Estuary trailhead and Campgroud. Park at the trailhead. Approximate driving time, 2 hours.

The route: From the parking lot, head south on an old jeep road which follows the base of the hills that rise steeply from the coastline. The jeep road offers brief

༄ California Coastal Trail

One hundred and fifty-four miles of the total 1,200+ mile length of the California Coastal Trail (CCT) lie in Humboldt County, more than any other county. It enters the county from the north on the Carruthers Cove trail (Hike #2) and Gold Bluffs beach and leaves on low-volume roads headed into the Sinkyone Wilderness State Park. The beginnings of the CCT can be traced to the 1972 Coastal Initiative. This Initiative established the Coastal Commission, required the development of a coastal plan, and created the California Coastal Conservancy. The Conservancy was empowered to purchase coastal land and develop trails, public access, and pursue habitat restoration. In 1976 the Conservancy was assigned the principal role in the development of the CCT. The CCT was defined as, "A continuous public right-of-way along the California coastline; a trail designed to foster appreciation and stewardship of the scenic and natural resources of the coast through hiking and other complementary modes of non-motorized transportation." The CCT has been described as "a yarn comprised of several different but roughly parallel threads – here widely separated, there drawn together." One strand may be for beach walkers, another for cyclists, another may be merely a temporary alignment.

In 2001, the legislature directed the Conservancy to determine what was needed to complete the CCT. The "Humboldt County Coastal Trail Implementation Strategy" was published in 2011. This report still classifies over 50 miles of the CCT in Humboldt County as "inadequate". Private lands necessitate some extensive and awkward detours veering well off the coast. Current alternatives are heavily dependent on walking along public highway corridors. For example, you take your life in your hands as you leave the access road to Skunk Cabbage Trail, dodging 101 traffic until you reach the levee system along Redwood Creek through Orick. From Ferndale, the CCT is routed south up and over the narrow, shoulder-less Mattole Road for 21 miles far from the coast.

A number of walks included in this book are threads of the CCT including Hikes #75, #76, and #78; the Hammond Trail (Hike #18), Arcata Bottoms (Hike #21), and portions of several others. Some day the Humboldt Bay Trail will fill a major gap in the CCT. ༄

respite from the soft sand of this broad beach. The beach narrows and becomes rockier. Continue on past Windy Point Road, an old ranch track, which climbs steeply up the bluff (2.5), just before rounding Punta Gorda. The route passes two cabins prior to fording Fourmile Creek (2.7). The Cooskie Creek Trail climbs steeply to the left (2.9) and soon (3.2) you reach the concrete ruins of the old lighthouse (1912 – 1950). Re-trace your steps for the return.

Extras. At certain times during the summer and early fall, the mouth of the Mattole River closes and it is possible to walk north. This is the companion hike to the McNutt Gulch/Creek hike south (Hike #76). The turnaround is arbitrary. From the parking lot, walk through the campground north to the Mattole River estuary or head more directly west to the beach. You will reach the mouth and the moment of truth (about 0.5). If the mouth is passable, you will soon round Mattole Point (1.0). From here the coast north to McNutt Gulch is visible with Sugar Loaf Island in the distance. It is a magnificent panorama. The walk continues past LaRue Gulch at the low point in the bluffs looming above the beach (1.8) and on to rather nondescript caves in the bluffs (2.5). See also the description for McNutt Gulch/Creek walk.

79 · Shelter Cove

Planned in 1965 as a community with a potential population of more than 10,000, the 2,500-acre, 4,000-plus-home community of Shelter Cove was the single biggest residential development in the state at the time. Full-page ads shouted this unique investment opportunity. Roads soon honeycombed the steep hillsides. Prospects flew in landing on the new 3300-foot runway. But, 15 years later, less than 100 lots had been built upon and most of the 43 miles of streets led to empty cul de sacs.

In the end, many buyers made their purchase sight unseen, 400-500 of the parcels were not buildable, and the development itself became a poster child for the need for coastal protections. When the Coastal Initiative was approved by voters in 1972, Shelter Cove, Sea Ranch (Mendocino County), and Pacific Shores (north of Crescent City) were cited by campaigners as evidence of the need for a coastal act. Among the issues with the Shelter Cove plans was that no provision was made for public ocean access.

That shoreline access stalemate was finally broken when the state bought out about 30 property owners who had not yet built on their land. Because of that Mal Coombs Park, BLM's Seal Rock and Abalone Point enrich a walk along Lower Pacific Drive. Having gradually overcome its shady beginnings, Shelter Cove has experienced steady growth over the past two decades. By 2010, 631 lots had been built upon and the census documented 693 permanent residents. There is a vitality long missing on this stretch of the Lost Coast with its plunging mountains, pristine beaches, and rocky shore.

79a · Shelter Cove Short Loop

Length: 2.2 miles
Total ascent: 215 feet
Elevations: 30 - 150 feet
Type: loop
Dogs: yes
Restrooms: yes

Description: With the exception of a broad coastal shelf, Shelter Cove is built on the steep hillsides of the King Range. Much of the coastal shelf has been allocated to the golf course and the Shelter Cove Airport. Basically, this walk, very popular among the locals, circumnavigates the airport and golf course.

Getting there: Drive south on US 101 for 64.0 miles taking Exit 642 (Redway). Continue south on Redwood Drive for 2.0 miles turning right on the Briceland Road (later becoming the Shelter Cove Road) toward Shelter Cove. In 21.2 miles, after climbing and descending steeply into Shelter Cove, you will reach a T-junction. Turn left on Upper Pacific Drive for 0.4 mile and right on Machi Road for 0.1 mile. The distinctive Mal Coombs Park, with the lighthouse featured prominently, provides an excellent place to park. Approximate driving time, 2 hours.

The route: Turn left from the parking lot onto Lower Pacific Drive with nice ocean views. The BLM has created two public viewing areas along Lower Pacific Drive ("Seal Rock" and "Abalone Point"). Abalone Point (0.9) offers superb views north along the Lost Coast and the King Range. After an additional 0.2 mile, note the sign for 'Nature Trail' on the right side (1.1). The Bill Franklin Nature Trail climbs to three access points on Seafoam Road and features prominently in the shorter walk option. Lower Pacific Drive intersects with Upper Pacific Drive (1.3). Turn right on Upper Pacific and follow it to Machi Road (2.1). Turn right on Machi Road to return to Mal Coombs Park (2.2).

Extras. The return along Upper Pacific Drive can be varied. Sea View Drive (on the right less than 0.1 mile from the turn onto Upper Pacific Drive from Lower Pacific Drive) offers a short variation. By turning left for one block on the Shelter Cove Road, you can turn right on Bambi and right again on Ocean View. This will eventually intersect near the south end of Upper Pacific Drive near the junction with Machi Road. And, lastly, just after turning on Machi Road is the Boat Landing and Harbor. It is less than 0.1 mile to an overlook.

79b · Bill Franklin Nature Trail and Sea Foam

Length: 1.4 miles
Total ascent: 350 feet
Elevations: 100 - 450 feet
Type: partial loop
Dogs: yes
Restrooms: yes

Description: This Nature Trail could easily be combined with other road walks as any number of variations exists on the Shelter Cove road network. However, I was surprised at just how few of the upper roads offered stunning ocean views. The Nature Trail has labeled plants in the lower section and several benches for resting throughout. The upper portion of the trail offers a short but rigorous aerobic workout.

Getting there: Drive south on US 101 for 64.0 miles taking Exit 642 (Redway). Continue south on Redwood Drive for 2.0 miles turning right on the Briceland Road (later becoming the Shelter Cove Road) toward Shelter Cove. In 21.2 miles, after climbing and descending steeply into Shelter Cove, you will reach a T-junction. Turn right on Upper Pacific Drive for 0.4 mile and left on Lower Pacific Drive for 0.2 mile to the beginning of the Nature Trail. Parking is very limited. Alternatively, you can drive 0.5 mile on Upper Pacific Drive and turn right on Redwood Drive. The road climbs steeply up. Take the first right turn (0.3 mile) and a right again on Seafoam Road (0.1 mile). Just as you make the right turn onto Seafoam is the upper entrance to the Bill Franklin Nature Trail. Again limited parking is available. Approximate travel time, 2 hours.

Bill Franklin Nature Trail.

The route: The Nature Trail has three access points to Seafoam Road (the lowest access emerges onto Duluard Road which quickly reaches Seafoam. The other two access points emerge directly onto Seafoam and are signed.

From the upper Seafoam Road access, the trail steadily drops to the crossing of Upper Pacific Drive (0.5). Continue west to Lower Pacific Drive (0.7). The final portion of the trail has a number of signs identifying common plant species. On the return, take the first spur trail to the right after crossing Upper Pacific Drive. This releases you onto Duluard Road (1.0). You will quickly reach Seafoam Road (1.1). Turn left on Seafoam Road and walk uphill to the starting point (1.4).

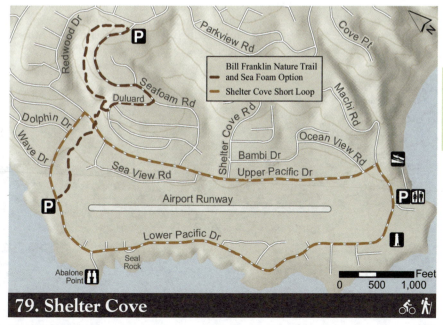

79. Shelter Cove

80 · Sinkyone – Needle Rock Visitor Center to Bear Harbor

Length: 5.4 miles
Total ascent: 900 feet
Elevations: 0 - 270 feet
Access: drive to the visitor center is long and daunting.
Type: out and back
Dogs: no
Restrooms: yes

Description: Admittedly, this walk is entirely in Mendocino County. However, because of its isolation, the only real access is from the Redway to Shelter Cove highway (either via Whitethorn or a white-knuckled ride along Usal Road over Chemise Mountain and through Whale Gulch). From Four Corners (the junction of Usal and Briceland Roads), the 3.5 mile access road to the Needle Rock Visitor Center should only be driven in a high clearance vehicle.

Once you reach the Visitor Center, the Sinkyone has a magical quality. Expansive views of the ocean from meadows that are again home to Roosevelt elk. Spring flowers, whale watching, isolated beaches, massive mountains thrust up from the ocean. That makes the trip well worth the effort.

Although the Sinkyone hosts the 22-mile Lost Coast Trail, the short trip to Bear Harbor offers a delightful sampling of this remote stretch of coastline. A second choice would be the 2.2 mile walk (each way) to Whale Gulch.

Getting there: Drive south on US 101 for 64.0 miles taking Exit 642 (Redway). Continue south on Redwood Drive for 2.0 miles turning right on the Briceland Road toward Shelter Cove. In 12.1 miles turn left on the Whitethorn Road (aka Briceland Thorn Road . . . although I have never seen signs using that label) for 9.5 miles. The road follows the Mattole River to its headwaters, gradually climbing to an intersection with Usal Road. Continue on an unpaved road following signs to the Sinkyone Wilderness State Park and Needle Rock Visitor Center (3.5 miles). Park at the Visitor Center. Approximate driving time, 2 hours, 30 minutes.

80. Sinkyone – Needle Rock Visitor Center to Bear Harbor

The route: Until a few years ago, it was possible to drive all the way to the Orchard Camp access to Bear Harbor. Now the narrow road has been converted into a walking path that hugs the bluffs gradually descending to Bear Harbor. The path begins just south of the Visitor Center. It soon leaves the meadow, passes the slide that ruptured the road, and weaves through a conifer forest that offers periodic views steeply down to the shoreline. In spring, this stretch is abundant with delicate Douglas iris. At about the halfway point (1.3) the trail descends to cross Flat Rock Creek before climbing one last time (1.8). The trail again descends following the east side of a valley that ends at Orchard Camp (2.5). Here the route leaves the road crossing a bridge and enters a daunting grove of ancient eucalyptus trees. After Railroad Camp (in the 1890s the Bear Harbor Railroad was built to haul tan oak), Bear Harbor becomes visible. Calla lilies, some evidence of the railroad, and some remnant rock work are about all that remains of a once thriving community that raised cattle and sheep and sent a steady supply of tanoak bark to San Francisco's tanneries. Several picnic tables dot this picturesque cove (2.8). Return as you came.

Option to Whale Gulch. Whale Gulch is a 2.2 mile walk (one-way) to the north. The route tends to stay in the open meadows north of the Visitor Center passing a primitive camp immediately north of the Needle Rock Visitor Center and again at Jones Beach. The access to Whale Gulch is subject to erosion.

Bear Harbor panoramic. Photo by Ryan Bourque.

Hiking Humboldt Volume 2

Region H:
Inland – Northeast

Once away from the coast, the climate becomes much more extreme. As locals know, the marine layer and fog that can blanket the coast during the summer months rarely penetrates past the first tier of mountains. Vegetation changes with oak woodlands replacing redwood forests. This part of the county touches on what David Rains Wallace calls the *Klamath Knot* – the confluence of Cascade and Sierra, a tumbling together of plant species, an unexpected abundance of biological diversity.

The best hiking opportunities are in the Six Rivers National Forest (SRNF), BLM's Lacks Creek Management Area, and along several rural roads. Sadly, the lack of support for and maintenance of trails in SRNF often requires a spirit of adventure. Several walks have also been included from the communities of Blue Lake and Willow Creek.

It is not unusual for inland county roads to pass through open range with privately held land on both sides of the road for considerable distance. As discussed in the Introduction, the public right-of-way is widely variable although generally extends a minimum of 40 feet. This does require care when parking and vigilance to keep from straying from the road. The intimidating signs often posted along rural roads are much more bark than bite. All this being said, the best strategy is avoid confrontation, explain your purpose when asked, and use common sense.

View to the Trinity Alps from Horse Mountain, photo by Michael Kauffmann

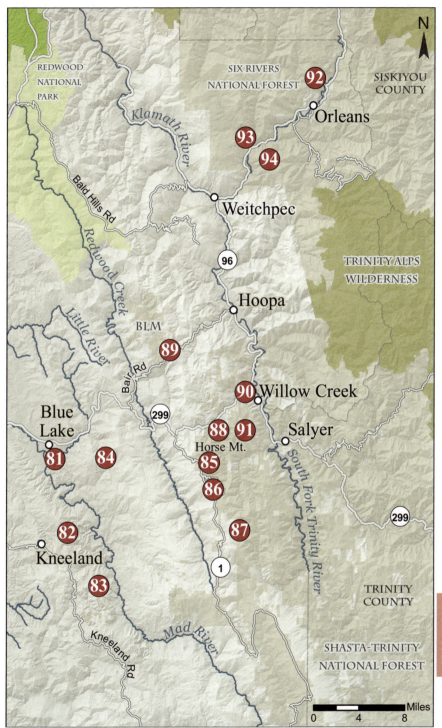

Region H: **Inland Northeast**

81 · Blue Lake

Length: up to 3.6 miles
Total ascent: flat
Elevations: 110 - 140 feet
Type: partial loop
Dogs: yes
Restrooms: yes

Description: This route combines two shorter walks into one longer walk around the Blue Lake Business Park and along the north levee of the Mad River. The north levee only periodically offers views of the river and makes for a pleasant stroll with a lush riparian zone on one side and broad pastures backed by the rising coast range on the other. Much of the walk around the industrial park is on a gravel path whose ambience may be diminished by its proximity to the power operation.

Getting there: Proceed north on US 101 for 9.5 to Exit 716A (east toward Weaverville/Redding). In 5.4 miles take the Blue Lake exit. Merge onto Blue Lake Boulevard through the traffic circle to Chartin Road and turn left on S. Railroad Avenue. Soon S. Railroad Avenue turns right and becomes Hatchery Road. In 0.2 mile, turn right on Taylor Way to park. The best parking may be found on Railroad Avenue (parallels South Railroad Avenue). Approximate driving time, 20 minutes.

The route: On the north side of the Mad River Brewery complex, about 0.1 mile from the point at which S. Railroad Avenue turns to become Hatchery Road, the **Industrial Park Trail** begins. A gravelled path proceeds west from an informational sign and map, crossing Taylor Way (0.4) and continuing south along the fenced west side of the Blue Lake Power property. The trail merges with the levee (0.5) and turns east continuing on the levee to Hatchery Road (1.0). Numerous social trails from the levee permit access to the Mad River. The shorter route turns left at Hatchery Road and follows the sidewalk back to the beginning (1.2).

Instead of turning on Hatchery Road, the **Mad River Levee** walk involves continuing on the levee. Cross Hatchery Road and follow the levee to a locked gate (0.7). The main channel of the Mad River is actually quite far to the west at this point. Return to Hatchery Road (1.4) the way you came.

81. Blue Lake Industrial Park and Mad River Levee

82 · Upper Fickle Hill Road

Length: up to 7.0 miles
Total ascent: 1,100 feet
Elevations: 1760 - 2380 feet
Type: out and back
Dogs: yes
Restrooms: none

Description: Fickle Hill Road stretches for 13 miles from Arcata to its intersection with Butler Valley Road. The narrow width and high levels of traffic make much of the length extremely pedestrian unfriendly. However, the final few miles pass through commercial timberland with just a handful of homes and almost no traffic. The road follows the ridgetop with views over the upper Jacoby Creek Valley, Kneeland, and, periodically, east toward Snow Camp Ridge. The relative proximity of this road walk to Humboldt Bay makes it an attractive option for those seeking respite from the fog in the summer.

Getting there: Proceed north on US 101 for 0.5 mile turning right on Myrtle Avenue. Follow Myrtle Avenue for 4.5 miles out of Eureka to the intersection with Freshwater Road. Turn right on Freshwater Road for 9.3 miles (it becomes Kneeland Road). Turn left on Butler Valley Road for 1.8 miles as it descends toward Maple Creek. A small amount of parking is available at the intersection of Butler Valley Road and Fickle Hill Road. Additional parking is available on the east side of Butler Valley Road just uphill from the intersection. There are also pullouts adequate for parking west on Fickle Hill Road. Since the views begin about 0.9 mile west of the intersection and that stretch of road is all uphill, walkers may prefer to park in the latter area to begin their walk.

It requires about the same amount of time to drive up Fickle Hill Road to this walk. However, Fickle Hill Road is in poorer condition than the Kneeland Road/Butler Valley Road combination. So, the Fickle Hill Road option makes sense only for those coming from Arcata and north. Approximate travel time, 40 minutes.

The route: From the southeast end of Fickle Hill Road, the first 1.6 miles are unpaved. The road climbs through thick forest emerging into an area cleared by

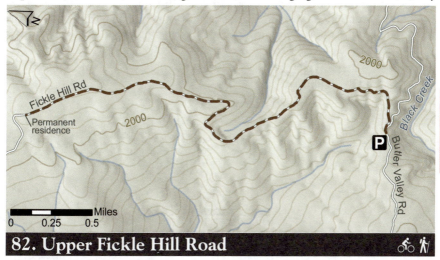

relatively recent logging (0.7). However, the views do not begin until a short distance to the west (0.9). The road descends to a minor saddle with views both to the southwest along the Jacoby Creek Valley and northeast across the Maple Creek Valley to Snow Camp Ridge and beyond. The road then resumes its climb reaching pavement (1.6) and again losing the views (albeit for just 0.3 mile) about a half mile later. A crest is reached (2.8) as the road passes through a broad prairie. The road passes the first permanently occupied roadside residence (3.0) shortly after the high point. West of the house, the road passes recent logging (3.2) and re-enters the forest (3.5). Although road walking certainly would be pleasant enough as Fickle Hill Road continues west, the views are limited and the habitation and traffic begin to increase. The recommended hike turns around here.

83 · Mountain View Road

Length: up to 5.6+ miles
Total ascent: 1000 feet
Elevations: 2680 - 2900 feet
Type: out and back
Dogs: yes
Restrooms: none

Description: For map lovers like me this is a great walk to come armed with a regional map, as much of Humboldt County is visible. This wonderful ridge top road walk offers abundant views in all directions as the road bends around Ashfield Butte and approaches the Iaqua Buttes. Although this route begins at the Kneeland Airport and follows Mountain View Road as it twists its way to the southeast, there is no reason not to walk the 0.9 mile back to the junction with Kneeland Road. It is all good up here especially on a foggy day around Humboldt Bay (the airport, which was constructed in 1962, was built here for just that reason). Do be aware that much of the route passes through open range and that area landowners have sensitivity regarding straying off the road.

Getting there: Proceed north on US 101 for 0.5 mile turning right on Myrtle Avenue. Follow Myrtle Avenue for 4.5 miles out of Eureka to the intersection with Freshwater Road. Turn right on Freshwater Road for 12.3 miles (it becomes Kneeland Road) as it climbs past the Kneeland Post Office and School to the intersection with Mountain View Road. Turn left on Mountain View Road for 0.9 mile to the Kneeland Airport. The airport has adequate public parking. Approximate

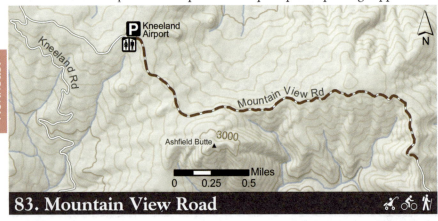

driving time, 40 minutes.

The route: Mountain View Road continues south around the end of the airport (0.3) following the ridge top as it approaches forested Ashfield Butte. The views in all directions are breathtaking. To the east the communication towers make Horse Mountain, a high point along South Fork Mountain, an easy landmark to identify. To the northwest television and radio transmitters clutter Barry Ridge. The road briefly enters the trees (0.8) on the north slopes of Ashfield Butte, descending to a saddle (1.3) and leaving the pavement, before crossing a cattle guard and climbing through meadows to the road's high point (2.0). From here, you will have superb views of nearby Iaqua Buttes, Board Camp Mountain off to the east, and even Black Lassic's distinctive point in the distance. The now unpaved road drops steeply returning to the trees (2.4) as it heads toward Iaqua Buttes. The intersection with a gated, private road on the left offers an arbitrary but reasonable turnaround (2.8). It is certainly possible to continue on south.

84 · Bald Mountain and Snow Camp Road

Length: up to 5.6+ miles
Total ascent: 1000 feet
Elevations: 2680 - 2900 feet
Type: out and back
Dogs: yes
Restrooms: none

Description: This road walk through commercial timberlands and working ranches offers spectacular views of the Mad River drainage, Humboldt Bay and the Mad River Bottoms and the ocean beyond as it follows Snow Camp ridge. The first 1.5 miles from the bottom of Bald Mountain Road rise steeply through open ranch and pasture land offering unimpeded views of the Mad River and Maple Creek drainage. Beginning about 1.5 miles the road enters long stretches of coniferous forest with more limited views. At 2.5 miles from the bottom most of the climbing is done and the road flattens out. So you can let your vehicle to do most of the 'heavy lifting' and park on upper Bald Mountain Road or at the intersection of Bald Mountain Road and Snow Camp Road. Although the 3.5 miles of Snow Camp Road south of its intersection with CA 299 offer additional magnificent vistas, the road is often narrow and constructed in a way that makes it difficult for pedestrians to easily get off the road.

Getting there: Proceed north on US 101 for 9.5 miles to Exit 716A east toward Weaverville/Redding. In 5.4 miles take the Blue Lake exit. Merge onto Blue Lake Boulevard and in 0.1 mile you will encounter a traffic circle. Continue on Blue Lake Boulevard through Blue Lake and Korbel (as it becomes Maple Creek Road) for 5.2 miles. Parking is available on the west side of the intersection of Maple Creek Road and Bald Mountain Road, although my recommendation is to drive up paved Bald Mountain Road and park at any number of pullouts once on the ridgeline (~2.5 miles). At ~6.2 miles Bald Mountain Road intersects with Snow Camp Road where parking is also available. Approximate driving time, 55 minutes.

The route: At about 3.3 miles from the bottom, the road crosses to the north side of the ridge. I suggest that your hike begin between here and 3.8 miles, where commercial logging has opened up vast panoramas to the north. For the next three miles, there has been enough logging to provide regular views as the road begins to bend more to the north, connecting with north-south Snow Camp Road at about

Lower section of Bald Mountain Road.

6.2 miles from the bottom. The first half mile north and south on Snow Camp Road are view filled and seems safe enough for pedestrians. (The remaining miles north should be avoided.) Return on Bald Mountain Road as you came.

Extras. The Fortuna Senior Hiking Group has hiked on unpaved Snow Camp Road beginning 5.5 miles south of the intersection with Bald Mountain Road and report little traffic, exceptional views, and relatively flat walking for about 3 miles.

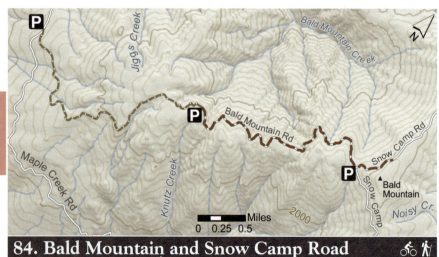

84. Bald Mountain and Snow Camp Road

85 · Walking in the Horse Mountain Area

Although there are actually no established trails in the Horse Mountain area, a number of interesting and view-rich walks are possible. The routes generally rely on maintained or abandoned Forest Service roads. Many of these walks occur in the 1,100-acre Horse Mountain Botanical Area, a designation that recognizes the unique nature of these high elevation plant communities of Jeffrey pine, western white pine, and Port Orford-cedar and other conifers. This area has been subjected to a high level of human impact as evidenced by the phalanx of communications equipment topping Horse Mountain itself, the old ski slope on Horse Mountain's north face, the nearby remnants of the Horse Mountain Copper Mine, and, all too often, shell casings and other trash.

In recent years, a coalition of trail advocates has been working informally to create an identifiable network of walking routes in the Horse Mountain area. Even though the Forest Service has not permitted the addition of any official signage or supported trail development, the coalition has identified several very pleasant walks that are reflected below. In all cases some level of route finding is involved and a map of Six Rivers National Forest is helpful.

Getting there: Proceed north on US 101 for 9.5 miles taking Exit 716A (CA 299) east toward Weaverville/Redding. In 28.0 miles take the Titlow Hill Road that exits right from Berry Summit. Follow Titlow Hill road for 4.6 miles to the broad Horse Mountain parking area that also serves as the junction for several roads. Substantial parking exists in this area for the Horse Mountain Mine walk. Turn left to reach the Indian Butte Loop walk and the Trinity Alps Vista walk. Continue straight along Forest Service 1 for the Cold Spring walk (Hike #86) and the Spike Buck Mountain walk (Hike #87). Approximate driving time, 1 hour.

∞ Port Orford-cedar

This rare conifer is found in a 200-mile swath of northwestern California and southwestern Oregon, rarely extending more than 40 miles inland. The Port Orford-cedar prefers cooler areas with ample winter precipitation. The trees that survive on Horse Mountain are at the southern extent of the species' range (Kauffmann 2012). The species is prized as a landscaping plant, as a finished wood product, and for its splendid aesthetic beauty in the wild.

Beginning about 60 years ago the Port Orford cedar has increasingly been threatened by a root rotting disease (*Phytophthora lateralis*). *Phytophthora* is the same genus as the disease that caused the Irish potato famine—with much the same results. When Port Orford-cedars are infected, the disease spreads around the base of the tree turning tissue to mush, effectively girdling and killing the tree. The resting spores can persist in soil for long periods of time and are easily spread through water. Soil on vehicle tires, especially during the rainy season, is considered to be primarily responsible for the spread of the infection but boots and mountain bike tires contribute as well. Efforts to control the spread of *Phytophthora* have centered on closing roads in the rainy winter months. Please observe these Forest Service closures. ∞

85a · Indian Butte Loop

Length: 2.0 miles
Total ascent: 700 feet
Elevations: 4450 - 4940 feet
Type: loop
Dogs: yes
Restrooms: none

Description: Like virtually all walks in the Horse Mountain area, the Indian Butte Loop is unsigned and necessitates some comfort with route finding. That being said, this is not a complicated walk and the ever-present landmark of the communication equipment atop Horse Mountain makes it difficult to get lost. The out-bound route follows a forest service road with periodic views to the west; the return includes a steep climb through the old Horse Mountain ski area, now with twenty-year old conifers dotting the slopes. From here the views of the Trinity Alps and distant Mt. Shasta open up. The final leg has southern views of Titlow Hill and the remnants of Horse Mountain Copper Mine. These west and northwest slopes of Horse Mountain include a healthy representation of Port Orford-cedar.

Getting there: From the Horse Mountain parking area noted above, take the first left. This gravel road continues to climb to a junction with FS (Forest Service) 06N18 (0.4 mile), which has ample parking and serves as the trailhead.

The route: Walk past the gate on FS 6N18 as it contours around the west side of Horse Mountain. The road offers filtered views to the west as it gently loses elevation. A dirt 4-wheel drive track departs from the right at the base of the old ski run (0.8). (FS 6N18 continues for a short distance.) Follow the 4-wheel drive track to the east. The road soon splits (0.9). Do NOT take the downhill option. Stay right and continue until the route turns uphill and begins a steep ascent to the top of Horse Mountain (1.3). The road borders the old ski run with its 20-year conifers now growing on the slopes. Enjoy the view out over the Trinity Alps as you catch your breath. From the communication towers on the top follow the main access

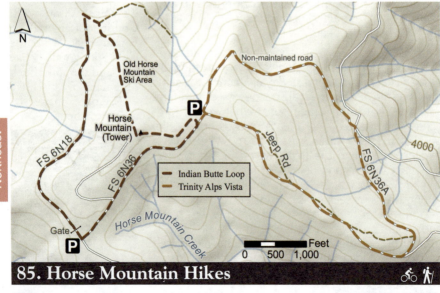

85. Horse Mountain Hikes

road to FS 06N36 (1.5). Turn right and complete the loop (2.0). From this road, you will have a view of the defunct Horse Mountain Mine to the south.

85b · Trinity Alps Vista Loop

Length: 2.1 miles
Total ascent: 550 feet
Elevations: 4400 - 4900 feet
Type: loop
Dogs: yes
Restrooms: none

Description: This relatively short walk offers outstanding views of the Trinity Alps, Mt. Shasta, the Bald Hills and the Klamath Mountains, the Brush Mountain Fire Lookout, as well as nearby geographical features. Although unsigned, the route utilizes a combination of a lightly used Forest Service road, rough jeep road, and inactive logging road that circumnavigate an east-trending ridge of Horse Mountain. The route concludes with an aerobic uphill leg.

Getting there: From the Horse Mountain parking area, take the first left. This gravel road continues to climb passing a junction with FS (Forest Service) 06N18 (0.4 mile) on the left. Stay right for the next 0.6 mile passing two access roads to the communications towers at the top of Horse Mountain. Just beyond the intersection with the second access road is an area on the left suitable for parking.

The route: I recommend that you walk this loop counterclockwise. Walk east continuing along the same Forest Service road you drove up on. At the top of the grade (0.2), you have a choice to either continue on the gravel road or to follow a rough jeep road that parallels the Forest Service road. Both drop steadily down and offer stunning views. The jeep road follows the ridge top and has unrestricted views but the final particularly precipitous 20 feet, as it re-joins the forest service road, require careful navigation. If you follow the Forest Service road from the top of the grade (where the jeep road diverges), turn left onto FS 06N36A (0.9). The jeep road connects directly with FS 06N36A a short distance north of the intersection. FS 06N36A contours to the northwest high above the East Fork of Willow Creek. Just after

∞ Horse Mountain Ski Area

In 1954 the Humboldt Ski Club opened up the first official Horse Mountain ski resort. It continued for the next thirty years. At the peak of operation, there were four rope tows and runs with names like The Bowl, Horse Trail, Bill's Hill, Gredigan's Hill, and Ridge Run. Jack Walsh, who ran the Horse Mountain Ski Area from 1962 - 1980 with the help of his large family and friends, built a two-story lodge and reportedly hosted up to 200 skiers daily. Classes were offered and races were held, but the operation remained a labor of love. The Horse Mountain Ski Area never made money. The slopes were always plagued by erratic and undependable snowfall and inconsistent crowds. In 1983 it closed for good.

Little evidence of all of this activity remains. Increasingly vegetation is returning to obscure the ski runs on the north side of Horse Mountain. The lodge was dismantled and the rope tows gone. The snow pack remains as unpredictable as ever. But when it does snow, crowds return to sled, cross-country ski, snowshoe, and play among the drifts. ∞

passing a boulder field of red rock lying above you (1.4), an inactive logging road climbs to the left (poorly marked with a couple of colored ribbons). Take this old road, regaining most of the elevation you have lost. The road bends left unveiling great views to the northwest to the Bald Hills (including the distant Schoolhouse Peak fire lookout) and west to the ocean (1.9). The final leg returns you to the saddle and the parking area (2.1), well-rewarded for your efforts.

85c · Horse Mountain Mine

Length: 3.4 miles or longer	**Type:** out and back
Total ascent: 530 feet	**Dogs:** yes
Elevations: 4160 - 4650 feet	**Restrooms:** none
Access: snow in winter and Port Orford-cedar closures (see sidebar)	

Description: This is entirely a road walk. The road descends past tailings, remnant foundations, and other evidence of the Horse Mountain Mine, now the subject of an extensive clean-up effort. While that is interesting enough, this hike has the added bonus of views out over the Trinity Alps and down the deep valley created by Horse Mountain Creek.

Getting there: See directions for Hike #85, **Walking in Horse Mountain Area**.

The route: Walk past the gate on FS 06N38 on the east side of the parking area [certain times of the year when the potential for spread of the Port Orford Cedar pathogen is at a minimum, the gate is opened]. The road descends past a hillside of mine tailings (0.3), the concrete foundation of a building (1.1), and the main processing plant (1.7). The road continues its downward descent at an accelerated pace. While it is possible to add more distance to the walk, there is nothing of special note.

Extras: Visit www.v2.hikinghumboldt.com to read about **Lookout Rock.**

Remnants of the Horse Mountain Copper Mine.

∞ A Brief History of the Horse Mountain Mine

Copper was discovered on Horse Mountain in the late 1800s or early 1900s. By 1908, several claims had been located in the area. The Horse Mountain Copper Company operated from approximately 1909 until 1929. According to the *Humboldt Historian*, the Horse Mountain Copper Company constructed several buildings, including a stamp mill, concentration plant, blacksmith shop, cookhouse, powder magazine, and several cabins. Ore (rock containing valuable minerals) and concentrates were moved primarily by pack train to Humboldt Bay, and then shipped to Tacoma, Washington, for smelting (production of metal). Ores from the site are described in historical accounts as being high in gold and tungsten.

By 1916, reportedly 28 men were working at the Horse Mountain Mine. However, on the last load of ore shipped to Tacoma, Washington, in 1916, the treasurer accompanied the load and, along with the ore, was never seen again. This reportedly "broke" the Horse Mountain Copper Company and the mine was closed for a time at the end of 1916. Mining activities resumed eventually and continued until 1929.

In 1958, a joint venture between Palo Verdis Mining Company and the Emperor Copper Company constructed mining facilities, including a copper mill, shop building, two residences, a laboratory building, a cookhouse, and a bunkhouse. Mining activities involved extracting copper and other minerals by electrolysis. Some limited open-pit mining also occurred. The company, however, apparently went bankrupt within a few years. Although there were several claim holders between the 1960s and 1988, no significant mining operation occurred at the site after about 1959. ∞

86 · Cold Spring Wander

Length: up to 2.5 miles
Total ascent: 550 feet
Elevations: 4650 - 4850 feet
Access: route finding skills needed

Type: partial loop
Dogs: yes
Restrooms: none

Description: Although a local hiking group has flagged a trail in the Cold Springs area, it is best to consider this an opportunity to explore a series of meadows, oak woodlands and rocky outcroppings, soak up some incredible views, and do some low-risk route finding. The area is bounded on the east by Forest Route 1, on the south by Cold Spring meadow, on the west by a steep drop into the Redwood Creek valley, and to the north by an extensive marshy fen. In the spring, the meadows are rich with wildflowers and later in the summer frequented by cattle, whose trails provide a network of walking options and are often part of the marked path.

Getting there: Follow previous hike's directions to the broad Horse Mountain parking area that also serves as the junction for several roads. Continue on paved Titlow Hill Road (Forest Service 1) for 2.6 miles, turning right on Forest Service 05N27. This dirt road is easy to miss so watch carefully. This is a short access road to Cold Springs (0.2 mile) where limited parking is available. Approximate driving

Cold Springs Meadow complex. Photo by Ann Wallace

time, 1 hour and 10 minutes.

The route: Option 1. Cold Spring Meadow: From the south side of the fenced spring, a trail follows the fence downhill joining an old road that descends gently through a mixed conifer and oak forest to Cold Spring Meadow (0.2 mile). This area has several old fire rings and has been the destination for spring wildflower fieldtrips. Although the far end of the meadow marks the boundary of Six Rivers National Forest (private land on the other side), there is ample opportunity to explore the rocky outcroppings and woodlands to the north.

Option 2. Split Rock: An informal trail has been marked with blue and white tape that begins by following the continuation of the road. However, the survival rate of the markers seems to be too brief to count on them for more than periodic affirmation that others have come this way before. Until the marking is improved, I suggest taking a west, northwest tack until you reach one of a long series of rocky outcrops divided by meadows and groves of oak trees (and encroaching conifers).

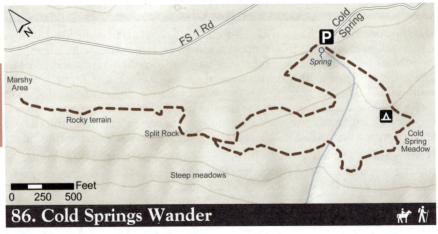

86. Cold Springs Wander

Once you reach these rocks and meadows, cow paths serve as good connectors as you explore your way north. A good turnaround is a marshy area roughly 0.5 mile north from the distinctive 'Split Rock', a large rock with a narrow passable channel on the west side.

From the north side of the Cold Spring parking area a trail (not the continuation of the road) leads northwest more directly (0.5 mile) to Split Rock and may be a preferred route until you have your bearings and understand the layout of this area.

As noted above, the area is bounded on the east by Forest Route 1, on the south by Cold Spring meadow, on the west by a steep drop into the Redwood Creek valley, and to the north by an extensive marshy fen. Understanding this will give you a greater sense of confidence as you explore.

87 · Spike Buck Mountain

Length: 1.9 - 3.3 miles
Total ascent: 450 - 850 feet
Elevations: 5100 - 5450 feet
Type: one way
Dogs: yes
Restrooms: none

Description: This walk is best for a more intrepid hiker comfortable with route finding. There are neither signs nor a well-trod trail. The route to the top of Spike Buck Mountain, one of higher points along South Fork Mountain, is an enjoyable adventure. The route relies on two logging roads: one very passable and one overgrown. A spike buck is a young male deer typically with unbranched antlers.

Getting there: Once at the broad Horse Mountain parking area (see directions in hike #85) continue on paved Titlow Hill Road (Forest Service 1) for 7.8 miles turning left on unsigned FS 05N18. En route you will pass the junction with the Friday Ridge Road (5.6 miles) on your left and FS 05N01 (7.3 miles). FS 05N18 is 0.5 miles after FS 05N01. Parking on the left side of FS 05N01 just after making the turn from FS 1. Driving time, 1 hour, 20 minutes.

The route: Walk east on FS 05N18. The road is in good condition as it contours along the northern side of Spike Buck Mountain passing through Russ Ranch prop-

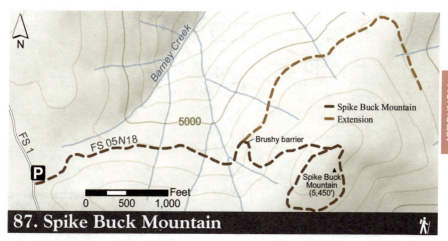

erty on both sides. You will reach a wider landing (0.5) where FS 05N18 continues east and to the right is an old logging road obscured by brush and a dirt berm. Staying on FS 05N18 will take you to a fork with the left branch descending and the right alternative contouring along the east side of Spike Buck Mountain until the undergrowth stops you (1.2). Clambering over the berm and pushing through the vegetation from the landing is your route to the top of Spike Buck Mountain. After fifty feet the old road becomes more apparent and serves as your route to the top. You will reach a broad landing with views toward the Yolla Bollys (0.8). From here, it is easiest to head directly up, picking your way through sparse undergrowth (0.9) although route options exist. The return involves retracing your steps.

88 · East Fork Willow Creek

Length: up to 4.0 miles
Total ascent: 1000 feet
Elevations: 1620 - 2600 feet
Fee: $4 day use

Type: out and back
Dogs: yes
Restrooms: yes

Description: The campground access road follows the East Fork of Willow Creek through the lush, shaded valley floor, passing 10 well-spaced campsites before climbing steeply on FS (Forest Service) 6N21 through a mature second growth forest to an area more recently logged. The first third of the walk is through the surprisingly delightful riparian zone with the remainder being completely aerobic. Once the route leaves the campground area, there is no regular maintenance so you may have to scramble around downed trees.

Getting there: Proceed north on US 101 for 9.5 miles taking Exit 716A (CA 299) east toward Weaverville/Redding. In 33.6 miles the East Fork Campground entrance is on the right. When the campground is open (typically June 15th-September 30th, call 530-629-2118 for updates) park to the right just past the entrance and at any number of places along the campground service road. When closed, it is possible to park safely outside the gate. Approximate driving time, 50 minutes.

The route: Follow the campground access road as it crosses the East Fork (0.2) and

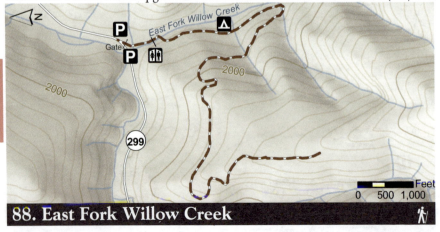

88. East Fork Willow Creek

parallels the creek and a series of campsites before making a sharp bend and commencing its climb (0.6). The road is unrelentingly up and eventually reaches an area more recently logged (2.5). No specific turnaround point exists.

Extras. There is a 0.8 mile walk from the **Boise Creek** National Forest campground (2.5 miles farther east on CA 299) to this beautiful tributary of Willow Creek. With pools perfect for wading, this is an ideal refuge on a hot summer day.

89 · Lacks Creek

The Lacks Creek Management Area is undergoing a dynamic transformation from industrial timberland to a multi-use environment that will include an extensive trail system. In 2006, with assistance from private conservation groups, the Bureau of Land Management added 4,500 acres in the Lacks Creek watershed to 4,100 acres it already owned. Although purchased primarily from Barnum Timber Company and Eel River Sawmills, the area had been intensively logged by a number of companies since the early 1950s. Now the emphasis is on restoration of this important Redwood Creek tributary.

A number of walking, hiking, and mountain biking options have been developed including the Beaver Ridge Trail included in *Volume 1*. Several shorter trails have been built off the Pine Ridge Road. I describe two walks here although more options are possible for those willing to explore.

The new trails along Pine Ridge are popular with mountain bikers (note the banked turns in many areas). Walkers should remain alert for downhill cyclists and bikers need to be aware of the multi-use nature of these trails.

89a · Pine Ridge

Length: up to 5.1 miles	**Type**: loop
Total ascent: 1020 feet	**Dogs**: yes
Elevations: 3460 - 4050 feet	**Restrooms**: none

Description: This landscape is dotted with open prairies and oak woodlands and the ever-encroaching fir forest. The walk, which can be an out-and-back or use Pine Ridge Road to create a loop, meanders through stands of oak and young fir as it follows the ridge crest. The trail offers wonderful views across the Lacks Creek drainage and far beyond the coastal range to the ocean, very visible in the distance. The Bald Hills, Horse Mountain, and Snow Camp Ridge can be identified.

Getting there: Proceed north on US 101 9.5 miles to Exit 716A (CA 299) exit toward Weaverville and Redding. Continue on CA 299 east for 18 miles. Once you are over Lord Ellis Summit, watch for the signed exit (Bair Road) on the left to Redwood Valley near the end of the first long, straight downhill grade (about a mile past the summit). Bair Road drops steeply down into Redwood Valley, crossing Redwood Creek, and intersecting with Stover Road at 3.7 miles. Bair Road turns right and climbs steeply up the east side of Redwood Valley in a series of torturous turns over the next 5.5 miles. This road can be very dusty in the summer, muddy in the spring, and snow-bound in the winter. Turn left on the access road with a BLM sign on your left into the Lacks Creek Management Area. In 0.6 mile the road splits three ways near an informational kiosk. To the left is Lacks Creek Road which leads to Beaver Ridge trailhead. Restrooms and camping are available. To the far right is the Pine Ridge Road. The middle of the three roads is the Mid-slope 4-Wheel Drive Road. For the Mid-slope/Pine Ridge Loop (see Hike #89b) this is a good place to park and begin. For the Pine Ridge walk, follow Pine Ridge Road 1.7 miles to a trailhead parking area with an informational kiosk. Although all roads to this point are passable by road cars, a high clearance vehicle certainly offers peace of mind. Approximate driving time, 1 hour and 20 minutes.

The route: From the trailhead, two trails diverge from the west side of the parking area. Take the Pine Ridge Trail veering to the right. The trail is very obvious as it winds its way north along the view-rich ridgeline. The trail tends to stay toward the west side of the ridge passing through groves of moss-covered oak and young stands of fir and tan oak. The trail drops down and crosses the Pine Ridge Road (1.6) at an intersection with a Forest Service road which heads east. This section of trail, called the Stormy Saddle Trail, continues from the southeast corner of the intersection and swings south before turning north, crosses the FS road, climbs

89. Lacks Creek

across a prairie and into the woods before switchbacking and crossing the prairie a second time. The trail again turns north and contours to the north side of a rounded peak with a bench and view (2.6). This is the highest point in the Lacks Creek Management Area. You can continue on the trail as it drops to the FS road (2.9) that you can follow (stay to the right at the one road junction) back to the intersection with Pine Ridge Road (3.7) that you crossed earlier. Turn left and either retrace your steps on the trail or stick with the road (5.1) although it lacks the aesthetics and views offered by the trail.

89b · Mid-Slope Road Loop

Length: 6.6 miles
Total ascent: 1320 feet
Elevations: 2910 - 3700 feet
Type: loop
Dogs: yes
Restrooms: none

Description: This loop begins (and ends) at the junction of the Pine Ridge Road, the Beaver Ridge Road, and the Mid-Slope Road, starting on the Pine Ridge Road and returning on the Mid-Slope Road. It combines road walking with a new trail designed for mountain bikers and hikers. The views from the Pine Ridge Road are especially grand with panoramas down Lacks Creek and out to the distant ocean. The trail down to the Mid-Slope Road gradually loses the views. The final leg, climbing back up Mid-Slope Road, a 4-wheel drive unpaved road, to the parking area is pleasant but without views.

The route: By walking counter clockwise, the uphill portions of the hike occur at the beginning and end of the walk and you face the best views. Follow Pine Ridge Road a marked trailhead and parking area (1.8). From here, take the marked Tomfoolery Trail on the left. You will soon intersect with a trail coming from the south (an alternate route to the Pine Ridge Road) and begin switchbacking down in long slaloms through meadows interspersed with stands of oak and conifer. Here it reaches the Mid-Slope Road (5.0). Turn left and follow the road through a dense, viewless conifer forest back to the original parking area (6.6).

Lacks Creek oak woodlands

90 · Willow Creek Walks

Note: Although plans exist, as of 2016 no trail signage has been put in place.

The small community of Willow Creek sprawls along both sides of the Trinity River valley. Often warm (hot) and sunny when the coast is beset by summer fog, there are some adequate road walks through and around the community. Summer can often be uncomfortably hot and winter can sometimes be cold and wet. I have identified several walks in this area. However, none of these walks warrant a special trip unless you are in the area. In the interest of space in this already overly long hiking guide, I have included only the Veterans Park and Camp Kimtu walk. On the companion website, details are posted of a walk through the Bigfoot Golf and County Club neighborhood, a mile-long Terrace Loop near central Willow Creek, and the Rowley-Wooden Trail in Creekside Park.

Although each of these walks has a different starting point, they all necessitate getting to Willow Creek. To do so, proceed north on US 101 for 9.5 miles taking Exit 716A (CA 299) east toward Weaverville/Redding. In 37.8 miles you will reach the town of Willow Creek. Approximate driving times, 45 minutes.

90 · Veterans Park and Camp Kimtu

Length: 2.2 miles
Total ascent: 200 feet
Elevations: 450 - 580 feet
Fee: $2 to park at Kimtu Beach
Type: out and back
Dogs: yes
Restrooms: yes

Description: The walk to Veterans Park and Camp Kimtu follows the normally quiet Kimtu Road past the pleasant park before dropping down to a popular summertime beach and swimming area along the Trinity River. With the option of walking over the terrace on the much busier Country Club Road (sufficient shoulder is present on the north side), this walk can easily be extended into commercial Willow Creek.

Getting There: This walk can begin at either end. Roadside parking is available on Country Club Drive, which involves a left turn from eastbound CA 299 one block east of the intersection with CA 96. Alternatively, utilize the Camp Kimtu beach parking area ($2 charge) or at Veterans Park at the north end of the walk.

The route: Walk northeast on the marked north shoulder of Country Club Drive as it quickly climbs the crest of the terrace (0.2) continuing on to the intersection with Kimtu Road (0.4). This road experiences considerable traffic that tends to move along rapidly so care must be taken. There is a reasonable shoulder. At the junction with Kimtu Road, cross over and continue along quieter Kimtu Road. You will pass Veterans Park (0.7) with its picnic area, bathroom, baseball fields, and children's playground, and continue as the road bends right and begins to descend. The road forks (1.1) with the right branch headed to Camp Kimtu and the left branch dropping to the beach. A bathroom is located in the beach parking area. This is a very popular swimming and wading area (1.2). Return the way you came.

WORD OF CAUTION – Swimming in the Trinity River always requires caution as the water is cold, the current is very strong, and it is easy to overestimate your swimming ability. Few summers pass without a drowning along the Trinity River.

Visit our website v2.hikinghumboldt.com to read more about the three other hikes in the Willow Creek Area.

91 · Brush Mountain Fire Lookout

Length: 4.9 miles
Total ascent: 950 feet
Elevations: 3150 - 3988 feet
Type: out and back
Dogs: yes
Restrooms: at lookout

Description: The top of Brush Mountain offers excellent views to the north and east; views to the west and south are limited by trees that do not inhibit views from the top of the lookout itself. The road walk from the entrance gate is a steady climb through a mixed oak and conifer forest until the final un-shaded 0.3 mile. On hot summer days the walk can still be reasonably pleasant with an early start. A delightful picnic table under a beautiful shade tree accompanies the panorama at the top

Getting there: Two ways exist to get to this trailhead. **Option 1.** Proceed north on US 101 for 9.5 miles taking Exit 716A (CA 299) east toward Weaverville/Redding. In 41.8 miles turn right on the Friday Ridge Road. This is just west of the bridge over the South Fork of the Trinity River and the eastern border of Humboldt County. Just after exiting CA 299, you will again turn right and follow the paved Friday Ridge Road (Forest Service 06N08) as it climbs over the next 7.0 miles. On the right is a large graveled pullout with FS 06N34 and FS 06N17

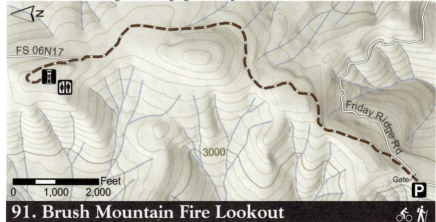

Hiking Humboldt Volume 2

diverging from the open area. A partially covered sign indicates the road to the lookout. There is parking just before the gate as well as in the large graveled turn-around. Approximate driving time, 1 hour, 30 minutes.

Option 2. If you have combined this walk with another hike in the Horse Mountain/South Fork Mountain area, from the parking lot (as described in Hike #85, p. 181) drive 5.6 miles south on FS 1 to the intersection with Friday Ridge Road. Turn left and drive 8.1 miles to reach the trailhead.

The route: Follow FS 6N17 past the gate and up the hill. The road is in excellent shape and is a steady but not exhausting ascent. The route stays in the woods as it continues to climb only to emerge for the final push to the cleared top of Brush Mountain. The return trip involves retracing your steps.

92 ·"Prospect" Trail

Length: 4.8 miles (one-way)	**Type:** one-way
Total ascent: 2100 feet	**Dogs:** yes
Elevations: 530 - 2350feet	**Restrooms:** none

Description: It seems that trails in the Six Rivers National Forest have experienced considerable neglect in recent years. Prospect Trail suffers from almost non-existent signage, limited maintenance, and abundant poison oak. Not too enticing especially in summer heat (this would be a better fall or spring walk). However, if you have an interest in the mining history of the region, this trail has much to offer. The extensive use of hydraulic mining often required transporting water long distances through elaborate networks of canals and sluices. Prospect Trail follows for some length several such canals. It also passes an old holding pond, test digs, and, no doubt, other evidence of past mining activity to the knowledgeable eye. Although the trail spends much of its length under a mixed conifer and tan oak canopy, it does break out for a view-filled stretch along a ridge high above the Klamath.

Getting there: Proceed north on US 101 for 9.5 miles taking Exit 716A (CA 299) east toward Weaverville/Redding. In 37.8 miles (Willow Creek) turn left on CA 96 and follow it north and east through the Hupa Reservation to Orleans. In

92. "Prospect" Trail

37.5 miles, just before the bridge across the Klamath River in Orleans turn left on Ishi-Pishi Road (just before the Six Rivers Forest Service compound). Follow Ishi-Pishi Road for about 1.8 miles just north of and around the bend from the Orleans Transfer Station (garbage disposal area). On your left is a somewhat obscured sign for the Prospect Trail marking the trailhead. Limited but sufficient parking is available on the right side of Ishi-Pishi Road just beyond the trailhead.

The upper trailhead is reached by taking Forest Service 15 (the G-O Road). This is 36.7 miles from Willow Creek on CA 96. Turn left just before the small airfield on the west side of Orleans. This paved road climbs steadily. The unmarked trailhead is 0.3 mile past the 6-mile sign (although 6 miles from the turn according to our odometer) on the right side. Park in a large graveled open area. The trail, again unmarked, departs from the southeastern corner of the parking area. Approximate driving time, 2 hours for either option.

The route: Many hikers will prefer to arrange their walk so that they begin at the G-O Road trailhead and end at the Ishi Pishi Road trailhead. The drawback of this approach relates to the absence of signage and challenge of locating the trail as it crosses a marshy flat (0.2). Once beyond this stretch of trail, however, the route, while at times overgrown, is generally obvious. The trail follows an old canal wall as it contours the ridgeline gradually losing just 120 feet of elevation (2.2). Some broad open expanses in this stretch offer grand views of the Klamath River valley and the Marble Mountains. The trail then descends rapidly along the forested ridgeline losing nearly a thousand feet of elevation that those climbing the trail will work hard to gain (3.3). The trail bends sharply to the northeast snaking along steep slopes for the remainder of the hike. The trail passes near the site of the Bonda Mine (4.4) and parallels another canal for 0.2 mile before its final steep descent to Ishi Pishi Road (4.8).

93 · Bluff Creek Historical Trail

Length: 2.4 miles (or longer)
Total ascent: 790 feet
Elevations: 450 - 1230 feet
Type: one-way (loop possible)
Dogs: yes
Restrooms: none

Description: Like many of the historic trails in this region, mining was the impetus for establishing the Bluff Creek trail. Unlike the 'Prospect' Trail (Hike #92), most evidence of this past has been reclaimed by nature. The rather poor condition of the first several switchbacks as the trail rises steeply above CA 96 belies the generally fine shape of this trail. Quickly, views of the Klamath River disappear and the remainder of the walk is in a mixed conifer and tan oak forest. Watch for poison oak. Several options exist for extending or varying this walk.

Getting there: Proceed north on US 101 for 9.5 miles taking Exit 716A (CA 299) east toward Weaverville/Redding. In 37.8 miles (Willow Creek) turn left on CA 96. Follow CA 96 as it makes its way north and east through the Hupa Reservation and along the Klamath River for 28.8 miles to Bluff Creek. Just past the highway bridge over Bluff Creek, a signed trail begins on the left. Parking is available on the right side of CA 96. Approximate driving time, 1 hour, 40 minutes.

The route: The initial steep climb (0.2) on deteriorating trail tread improves

∞ **Bigfoot**

Few legends have transcended cultures, eras, and regions like that of Bigfoot, Sasquatch, Yeti, or Ts'emekwes. Common to all is the notion of a species of shy, wild, hairy giants living in the remote wilderness. Periodic sightings and footprints over the years have constituted the primary evidence of the existence of Bigfoot – a record undermined by the abundance of hoaxes and the absence of fossil records.

Frame 352

No contemporary location has experienced a greater concentration of encounters than the mountains and forests of northern California. In 1958, tracks were found around a road construction site at Bluff Creek; and in the same region nearly a decade later, Roger Patterson and Robert Gimlin shot movie footage of a Bigfoot. The Bigfoot Country map reports that over 60 people have seen a Bigfoot and 70 sets of tracks have been documented in the Bluff Creek area. Nothing has been more dramatic than Patterson and Gimlin's experience.

As Patterson and Gimlin tell their story of the most incredible two minutes of their lives, they were on horseback in the early afternoon of October 20, 1967 when they "came to an overturned tree with a large root system at a turn in the creek, almost as high as a room." When they rounded it, they spotted the figure behind it "crouching beside the creek to their left."

Patterson's horse reared which made it more difficult for him to dismount and grab the camera from his saddlebags. He ran toward the creature as he filmed instructing Gimlin to "Cover me." Gimlin crossed Bluff Creek on horseback with rifle in hand. The resulting film (about 53 seconds long) is initially quite shaky as Patterson approaches the Bigfoot. In the steady middle portion of the film, the creature glances over its shoulder and walks behind a grove of trees, reappearing briefly then disappearing into the trees again as the reel of film ran out. Gimlin followed it on horseback, keeping his distance, until it disappeared around a bend in the road three hundred yards away. The men tracked it for three miles until losing it. They returned to the initial site, measured the creature's stride and made two plaster casts, and covered the other prints to protect them.

Even though most experts have branded the film and the encounter a hoax, this short clip (specifically frame 352) shot along Bluff Creek has become the iconic image of Bigfoot. ∞

quickly as the route enters the trees. The trail climbs steadily through forest to an intersection with a bend in the Slate Creek Road (FS Road 11N05) where you have several choices (1.2). You can return the way you came. You can walk downhill past a handful of homes on private in-holdings on Slate Creek Road for 1.6 miles to its intersection with CA 96 (2.8). This is a pleasant walk although it does necessitate walking back to the trailhead along CA 96 (4.0). Although CA 96 is not heavily traveled and offers nice views of the Klamath River, it is along the shade-less shoulder of the highway. The third, and perhaps most intriguing option for extending your walk, is to continue on the non-maintained trail as it continues up the Bluff Creek drainage. The only tricky maneuver is finding the continuation of the trail. Although overgrown for just a few yards, once you make your way forward on the south side and below the bend in Slate Creek Road you will find the trail continuing on a broad flat unused roadbed (that also hosts the waterline for private properties on Slate Creek Road and, I was told, was used by a now defunct fish hatchery). This route contours high above Bluff Creek providing regular vistas and can be followed until you are ready to turn back and re-trace your steps.

Hydraulic mining along the Klamath River from the Palmquist Collection, Humboldt State University Library

Extras. Klamath River Access. From nearby Aikens Creek Campground, there is a short, but interesting walk to the Klamath River. In the heyday of the Klamath River salmon and steelhead fisheries, this was a popular campground. From the end of the paved road, a gated and blocked road continues to the left. This once accessed a much more developed, full-service campground the vestiges of which remain. Remnants of a trail on the west side of the old campground now ends where a massive chunk of hillside slid into the Klamath River. The current unpaved access road leads to the river across an extensive boulder field.

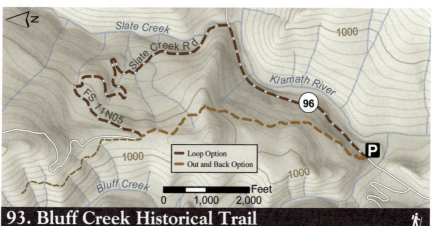

93. Bluff Creek Historical Trail

94 · Shelton Butte

Length: 4.6 miles with options
Total ascent: 680 feet
Elevations: 3000 - 3600 feet
Type: out and back
Dogs: yes
Restrooms: none

Description: Shelton Butte was once the site of an active fire lookout 3,000' above the Klamath River. Although vegetation limits the quality of the views these days, openings along the forest service roads leading to Shelton Butte allow you to see

Medicine Mountain, the western Marble Mountains, and Orleans to the northeast, the Salmon Mountains to the east, the coast range to the west, and the Klamath River snaking to the south. You can choose your preferred length of walk. All follow a seldom-used forest service gravel access road to the lookout site, now an automated weather station. It is a long drive through beautiful country.

Getting there (option 1): Proceed north on US 101 for 9.5 miles taking Exit 716A (CA 299) east toward Weaverville/Redding. In 37.8 miles (in the town of Willow Creek) turn left on CA 96. Follow CA 96 as it makes its way north for 15.3 miles to Mill Creek Road. Follow meandering Mill Creek Road (FS 10N02) for 12.7 miles where you make a left turn on FS 10N05 toward Hopkins Butte. After 4.7 miles you will reach a junction with FS 10N09 to Shelton Butte. The first and farthest walking option is from this junction. Ample parking can be found near the junction (FS 10N37). If you elect to drive closer to Shelton Butte, turn left on FS 10N09. In about 2.1 miles there is an open gate with parking options east of the gate. This is the starting point for the 4.6-mile walk. In another 0.9 mile, the road reaches a saddle with enough room for parking and turning around. Although the road continues up to the lookout site, walking further is not advised because of erosion. Take a current Forest Service map with you if you embark upon this adventure. Approximate driving time, 2 hours and 30 minutes.

Getting there (option 2): From Orleans, you spend less time on Forest Service roads and the route finding is not as challenging. After crossing the Klamath River bridge on the east side of Orleans, turn right on paved Red Cap Road. The road climbs above the Klamath River with territorial views of Camp Creek and Orleans. Shortly after crossing a bridge and passing a vineyard, the road turns sharply left and climbs up Rattlesnake Ridge. 4.9 miles along Red Cap Road, you reach a junction. Take the left fork (FS 10N01) and proceed for 1.4 miles. Take the unpaved right fork [FS 10N02] for 1.5 miles where you turn right on FS 10N05. This road continues to climb for much of the next four miles to the intersection with FS

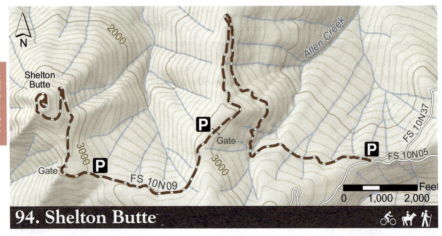

94. Shelton Butte

10N09. There is some road signage to assist with navigation. Driving time, 2 hours and 45 minutes.

The route: The entirety of this route involves road walking on FS 10N09. From the beginning of FS 10N09, the walk contours, gently climbing, to a crossing of the headwaters of Allen Creek (0.6) before turning north to begin a long switchback to the top of the grade and the first of two gates (2.1). This first gate is the starting point for the 4.6-mile walk. Along the northbound leg of this switchback there are excellent views of Medicine Mountain, the Marble Mountains, and the Salmon Mountains. The road then descends to a saddle (3.0) before beginning the climb to the lookout site. The road passes a second gate (3.3), this one uprooted, and turns north climbing more steeply. Near the top (4.1) a break in the brush offers the best views to the west. The final climb to the top (4.4) does not offer the reward that you would hope as the trees and shrubs have grown sufficiently to limit the views.

∞ Forest Service Roads

The U.S. Forest Service oversees an immense network of roads that often provide access to walks or serve as great walking routes. Six Rivers National Forest (and the Ukonom Ranger District it manages for Klamath National Forest) is crisscrossed by over 2,600 miles of roads. These roads are grouped into three classes variously referred to as 'roads maintained for passenger cars', 'roads not maintained for passenger cars', and 'closed roads' or primary and secondary (both maintained for passenger cars), local routes, and closed roads. The roads are marked by distinctive brown signs with white lettering.

The primary routes are assigned a one or two digit number and are often but not always paved. These and all roads assessed as suitable for passenger cars are marked on Forest Service maps by two solid parallel lines. These include forest highways such as Forest Service 1, which is an excellent paved road that runs from Horse Mountain south along the length of South Fork Mountain. A second class of forest routes are maintained to low-clearance standards for passenger cars. These secondary roads as well as those roads not maintained for passenger cars have identifying numbers that are posted vertically on 3-inch wide fiberglass signs (e.g., 6N08 or 5N10 or 10N09) and are graveled or dirt. Spur roads will be designated, for example, 10N05A, 10N05B, etc. off of road 10N05.

The 'Roads Not Maintained for Passenger Cars' are indicated on the map as dashed parallel lines. These roads are best for high clearance vehicles and are more likely to be subject to downed trees, rocks, washouts and other hazards. They tend to receive much less maintenance.

Motor Vehicle Use Maps (MVUM) of the Six Rivers National Forest are available on line or for free at Forest Service District offices and the Supervisor's office in Eureka. MVUM also indicate seasonal closures (such as for the prevention of the spread of the Port Orford-cedar root disease). Note that MVUM are difficult to print on conventional home printers because they are 33" x 44".

Even armed with all available maps, navigating in the National Forest backcountry can be very challenging. It is not unusual for road signs to be missing, spur roads overgrown, and roads decommissioned or blocked since maps were printed. Ask often about current conditions. ∞

Region I:
Inland – Southeast

Walking in this region of Humboldt County is hampered by the dearth of public lands and the concentration of marijuana cultivation. Although far too many areas have been carved into 40-acre parcels, a number of massive ranches remain that survive by grazing livestock, timber harvests, and guided hunting. Without access to these private lands, several county roads provide the best way to experience this landscape of open meadows, deep valleys, oak woodlands, and broad vistas. The Dyerville Loop Road, the Fort Seward Road, and the Redwood House Road offer three such opportunities. The walk in the Lassics, protected by Six Rivers National Forest, has similar attributes and, despite the long drive, remains one of my favorite destinations.

Another unique feature of this region is the summer and low-water bridges that cross the Eel River. These seasonal crossings make for interesting walks to rich bottomland agricultural areas, once linked by railroad but now isolated by the river. And lastly, this section includes several short hikes in the Grizzly Creek State Park and the Swimmer's Delight County Park.

Fort Seward Road by Nancy Spruance

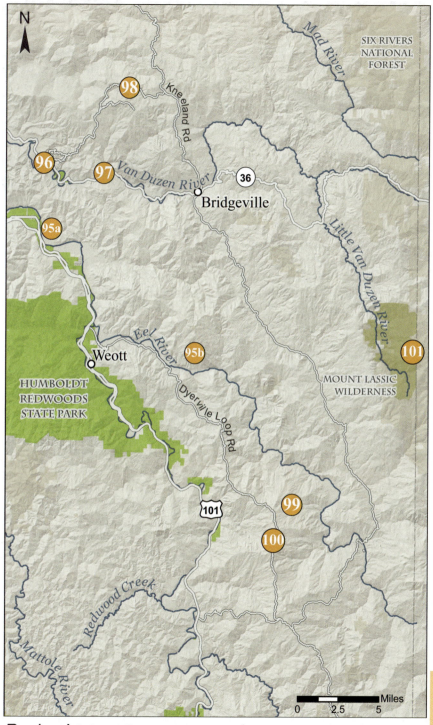

Region I: **Inland Southeast**

95 · Summer Bridge Options

Each summer, temporary vehicular bridges are put in place at several locations along the Eel River. In the case of Shively and Larabee, these bridges provide a more direct route to US 101. Upriver in McCann, where a low water bridge is permanently in place, the county operates a small ferry during periods of high water. If the term 'ferry' conjures up images of the Madaket that still plies the waters of Humboldt Bay, you would be sorely disappointed. This ferry, the remaining one of three such ferry services that once crossed the Eel River, accommodates a few passengers and no vehicles. For the last half century the county has operated this service because there is a county road on the other side. Efforts to construct a permanent, year-round bridge have been swept away by periodic floodwaters or dismissed as much too expensive to justify given the sparse populations.

Photo by Nancy Spruance

On the east side of the Eel are three unique, seasonal road walking opportunities. Each year from June 15th to October 15th (or later depending on water flow) a summer bridge is installed across the Eel River that dramatically shortens the drive to Shively and makes for a pleasant walk. Similarly, there has been a low-water bridge for decades that spans the river between Holmes Flat and Larabee. However, that bridge has deteriorated to the point that it is impassable for vehicles (but not for pedestrians during low water periods). Although the county has made a commitment to repair the bridge, until that is done a Bailey bridge has been installed during the summer and early autumn. And, the third non-traditional crossing is the McCann option noted above.

95a · Shively Road

Length: 4.8 miles with options	October 15
Total ascent: flat	**Type:** out and back
Elevations: 95 - 280 feet	**Dogs:** yes
Access: from around June 15 -	**Restrooms:** none

Description: Each summer the agricultural community of Shively, built on the flood plain of the Eel River, installs a temporary, railcar bridge over the Eel River. Access is from the Avenue of the Giants. The crude road follows the riverbed to the crossing and then bends south paralleling the river until it turns and joins the paved permanent roads of Shively. The route meanders through fields ending eventually in the rather decayed center of Shively and the old Northwestern Pacific Railroad crossing. Surprisingly little shade covers this route although the upriver afternoon breeze tends to keep the walking pleasant.

Getting there: Drive south on US 101 for 32.5 miles taking Exit 674 (Avenue of the Giants/Pepperwood). Turn left onto the Avenue of the Giants for about 3.0

miles. The road passes through what remains of the community of Pepperwood, taking a bend to the south, passing the Drury-Chaney Groves trailhead (see Hike #65). Watch for a sign pointing to 'Shively' at the south end of the Drury-Chaney parking area and a graveled road leaving from the left (east) side of the Avenue of the Giants just beyond. Roadside parking is available on the west side of the Avenue of the Giants just past the Shively Road or at the Drury-Chaney Groves trailhead. For a number of years the bridge has been sited in this general location, however it is always possible that the crossing will shift. Approximate driving time, 40 minutes.

> ## ∞ 1964 Flood
>
> Humboldt County often finds itself in the crosshairs of moisture-packed winter storms whose loads are unleashed on the coastal mountains. Floods remind us that our presence on the fertile river deltas and bottomlands is tenuous at best. The epic floods of 1955 and 1964 swept away the Eel River communities of Weott, Elinor, Dyerville, Pepperwood, Holmes, Larabee, and Shively. Most were never rebuilt and none regained their former status.
>
> Just before Christmas, 1964, over 22 inches of warm rain fell on the Eel River basin in a two-day period, compounded by quick melting of the heavy snowpack. By December 23, the volume of the flood at Scotia exceeded the average discharge of the entire Mississippi River basin. At Miranda the high water mark reached 46 feet (13 feet above flood stage) and signs in a number of locations document the unbelievable height of floodwaters (two of note include one high overhead at the old Weott town site north of Humboldt Redwoods Visitor Center; another is at the turn from the Avenue of the Giants east on the Dyerville Loop Road). Sixteen state highway bridges were destroyed along the North Coast, another ten county bridges were washed away in Humboldt County and the Northwestern Pacific Railroad was devastated. ∞

The route: The dirt road drops quickly out of the redwood forest to the broad and rocky bed of the Eel River. The road turns east from the Avenue of the Giants and crosses the main channel on a railcar bridge (0.3). The primitive road proceeds south until it turns east (left) and joins the paved Shively Flat Road (1.2). Follow Shively Flat Road along fences abundant in blackberries, fecund fruit trees,

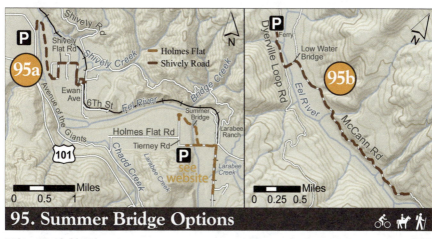

95. Summer Bridge Options

Hiking Humboldt Volume 2

and gardens of tomatoes, corn, and other vegetables. The road meanders across the farmland taking an indirect route into Shively, passing among other operations, the College of the Redwoods farm. Continue until you cross the moribund Northwestern Pacific tracks (2.3). This is as good a place as any to turn around. Take a right turn on Ewan Avenue which will rejoin Shively Flats Road (2.5). Retrace your steps (4.8). Note that Shively Flats Road changes names to Croco Lane or Crocco Lane along the way.

95b · McCann Ferry and Low Water Bridge

Length: 3.6 - 4.8 miles	water bridge
Total ascent: 320 feet	Type: out and back
Elevations: 190 - 350 feet	Dogs: yes
Access: high water closes low-	Restrooms: none

Description: McCann was once big enough to have a school and a store. All that remains is a diffuse community of small farms and homes. For most of the year, it is possible to cross the Eel on an elevated concrete low-water bridge. During those times when the Eel overtops the bridge, the only option becomes the nearby McCann ferry (limited hours). Starting from the unpretentious ferry terminus, this walk crosses the bridge and follows the east side road for about a mile and a half (farther is possible). The road rises above the Eel and provides excellent views up and down the river.

Getting there: Proceed south on US 101 for 42.3 miles. Take Exit 663 (South Fork/Honeydew/CA 254). Take a sharp left at the stop sign and an immediate right turn on CA 254. After crossing over a bridge of the South Fork of the Eel River, turn at the first left, the Dyerville Loop Road (0.2 mile). Follow the Dyerville Loop Road for 6.3 miles as it twists along the west side of the main stem of the Eel River. Turn left into the McCann Ferry parking area. Approximate driving time, 1 hour and 5 minutes.

The route: From the McCann Ferry parking lot, you should first take a brief walk around the accessible path and landing area. Then turn south on the road that will soon reach the concrete low water bridge (0.3). After crossing the bridge, the main route veers right (a smaller road veers left and services several homes downriver) and soon re-enters the trees on the east side of the Eel River floodplain. The road climbs past several homes and screening fences (0.9) offering river views up and down the Eel. The road rises higher with more views passing an intersection with a gravel road that heads off to the left (1.3). Stay right. You will reach a cattle guard and a reasonable turnaround point (1.8). Soon the main road deteriorates until it too is more gravel than bitumen. Stay right at the next intersection (2.2). The road ends at a turnaround (2.4). These are somewhat remote reaches of the Emerald Triangle and it is prudent to not stray from the road.

Extras. Camp Grant option. The paved Dyerville Loop Road (right turn from the Ferry parking lot) winds northwest through the forest and along Thompson Bluff for several miles before dropping back down onto open, broad Camp Grant Flat. The route crosses the floodplain to a Seventh Day Adventist Camp and a NWP railroad overpass (3.7), where the road begins to climb again as it re-enters forest.

Although the road is narrow at times and has limited shoulders, there is minimal traffic. Some of my walking colleagues prefer this direction. Turn around any time to shorten the walk.

Camp Grant, once the site of a short-lived Union Army regiment, became a logging outpost and staging area during the construction of the Northwestern Pacific Railroad through the early 20th century. Early settlers coming to Eureka from the south following the strenuous trails over Island Mountain (Bell Springs Road) and along the current Dyerville Loop Road passed Camp Grant on their way north.

Holmes Flat to Larabee. Like the low-water bridges that allow access to Shively and McCann, the walk across the decrepit Holmes Flat Bridge (or summer-only Bailey Bridge) follows a quiet road on the east side of the Eel River through pasture land, past old fruit trees, and a smattering of residences. (1.3 miles one-way) see v2.hikinghumboldt.com for more.

96 · Van Duzen County Park

Length: 4.5 miles with options	Swimmers Delight
Total ascent: 500 feet	**Type**: partial loop
Elevations: 280 - 500 feet	**Dogs**: leashed
Fee: $5 at Pamplin Grove and	**Restrooms**: yes

Description: This County Park occupies a narrow strip of redwoods along the north bank of the Van Duzen River. In the summer this area tends to be beyond the reach of the coastal marine layer and is home to several nice swimming holes. In the late summer armed with water shoes, it would be pleasant to walk the trail one direction and along the river on the return. The trail itself has suffered from neglect and necessitates some route finding and a spirit of adventure. This trail does have some of the most elaborate bridgework of any trail in the county.

∞ Strong's Station

Other than a rather forlorn sign, there is little evidence that this area was once the site of a bustling summer resort, hotel, and inn. Initially established by Samuel Strong between 1866-1875 as a stop for the overland stage, Strong's Station featured a large parlor with an organ and seventeen rooms. There were many fruit trees on this 426-acre retreat that offered, according to Charles Willis Ward's 1915 book about Humboldt County, "celebrated chicken and strawberry dinners, fine tomatoes, melons, sweet corn, and grand camp ground in the redwoods with good fishing and deer hunting." In 1936, Strong's resort was taken over by Steve Angeline and from then until 1960 it served as a boarding house and inn. It was demolished in 1969. Since then, nature has worked to return the area to a condition more like Samuel Strong encountered 150 years ago. ∞

Getting there: Take US 101 south 20.6 miles to Exit 685 (CA 36 East). Continue east on CA 36 for about 11.5 miles. A poorly signed turnoff exits right to Pamplin Grove at the west end of Van Duzen County Park. As of 2017, Pamplin Grove no longer permits day use parking. Parking is possible at Strong's Station at about 12.0 miles east on CA 36 (south side of the road) or

Epic Gully Crossing

at about 12.6 miles is the well-marked entrance to Swimmers' Delight at the east end of Van Duzen County Park. Turn right on the entrance road and proceed to the park tollbooth. Parking is available on the left near a trailhead. The trail will be described from Pamplin Grove. Approximate driving time, 40 minutes.

The route: The trail begins just east of the Pamplin Grove toll station. The trail is poorly signed or maintained in several sections. It is important to understand that the trail roughly parallels CA 36 and, with the exception of the Healy Creek crossing (0.2) stays well away from the Van Duzen. The Healy Creek crossing has been severely eroded and the trail obscured and may be challenging or impassable when water is high. On the west side of Healy Creek trail conditions improve (despite one aesthetically unpleasant stretch where the route hugs the outside of the bar-

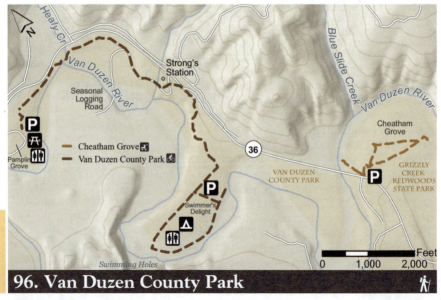

96. Van Duzen County Park

rier separating the trail and the highway). The trail joins an unpaved road that, in the summer crosses the Van Duzen on a low water bridge (0.8). It shares this road (although several side trails along the way dip into the trees and overlook the river before returning to this unpaved road) for a short distance (1.1). If you follow the gravel road to its intersection with CA 36 (the historic location of Strong's Station), you have gone too far. The real trail continues east from the gravel road about 100 yards back at an unsigned junction. The trail soon reaches an elaborate bridge system (1.3) spanning a gulch before reaching the Swimmers Delight entrance road (1.6). There are several choices at this point:

1) Turn right on the entrance road and turn left in 0.1 mile where there is a trailhead to the east side of the park. From this trailhead there are trails and a road through the campground that can be followed back to the entrance road as it nears the river access (0.6 from the start of the option).

2) Turn right on the entrance road and follow it to the river access (0.3 from the start of the option) with its well-established swimming holes.

3) Turn around and return the way you came.

Eventually the first two options necessitate retracing the route from Swimmers' Delight back to Pamplin Grove. However, during low water summer months armed with water shoes or uncanny balance, it is possible to follow the river back.

We elected to walk the trail to the gravel road (the one you joined 0.8 mile east of Pamplin Grove) and follow that road to the river. We returned to Pamplin Grove along the river. This did involve two crossings. **Note that poison oak is abundant along the trail.**

97 ·Grizzly Creek and Cheatham Grove

Length: 0.9-2.7 miles with options	trails are summer bridge dependent.
Total ascent: flat-680 feet	
Elevations: 280 - 500 feet	**Type**: partial loop
Fee: day use $8	**Dogs**: leashed
Access constraints: south side	**Restrooms**: yes

Description: Located on a bend in the Van Duzen River, Owen R. Cheatham Grove is a majestic patch of old growth redwoods spared by the founder of what would become the Georgia-Pacific Plywood and Lumber Company. The short hike loops through the grove. From the west side of the parking area two trails lead across the riverbed to the Van Duzen River.

Grizzly Creek Redwoods State Park offers a small network of trails on the north and south side of the Van Duzen River. A summer bridge crosses the Van Duzen to 1.5 miles of additional trails on the south side. The north side trails include a nature trail with interpretive signs, a meandering walk up and down the hillside east of Grizzly Creek, and a stretch of trail west of Grizzly Creek.

Getting there: Cheatham Grove - Drive south on US 101 for 20.6 miles taking Exit 685 (CA 36). Turn left on CA 36 and follow it east for 12.9 miles. The entrance to Cheatham Grove is on the left side of the highway, descending quickly to a parking area. The turn is just after a bridge over the Van Duzen but otherwise not well marked. Approximate driving time, 45 minutes.

Grizzly Creek Redwoods State Park - The entrance to Grizzly Creek Redwoods State Park is 4.2 miles east of Cheatham Grove on CA 36. The park entrance is on the right and provides access to day use parking, picnic tables, and a restroom.

There is a small parking area and trailhead 0.5 mile west of the entrance to the Park. This is on the right (south) side of CA 36 and provides access to the very west end of the trail system. No fee is required here.

Classic scene from Return of the Jedi was filmed here.

The route: Cheatham Grove – the trail through the grove begins on the north side of the parking area and winds through this stand of old growth. A few short spur trails can be confusing but the area is small and bounded by the river so there is little possibility of getting lost. A couple of trails lead to the Van Duzen River from the west side of the parking area. The full loop is about 0.9 mile. For Star Wars fans, Cheatham Grove has special significance as the location where the steadicam shots from *Return of the Jedi* were filmed. See map with Hike #96.

Grizzly Creek Redwoods. Access to the north side network of trails begins just across CA 36 from the Visitor Center. After a careful crossing of this busy highway, turn right. Stay right at the trail intersection (0.1) continuing on the Nature Trail as it climbs briefly and loops around to (0.5) an intersection with the 'Hikers Trail'. Turn right on this trail (or continue downhill for 200 feet to a reunion with the trail from the Visitor Center). The 'Hikers Trail' continues to a viewpoint above Grizzly Creek (0.9) before descending and looping back toward the Visitor Center (1.2). A connecting trail and a second option takes you underneath the CA 36 bridge over Grizzly Creek to a picnic area. From this picnic area, summer bridges cross the Van Duzen River to an additional 1.5 mile loop or cross Grizzly Creek to another 0.9 miles of trails (and the alternative parking area).

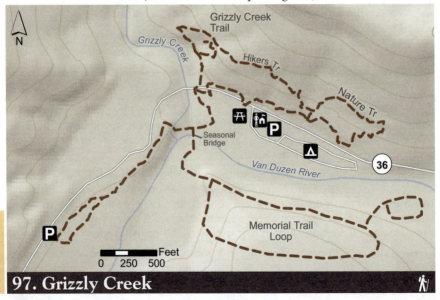

97. Grizzly Creek

98 · Redwood House Road

Length: up to 8.0 miles
Total ascent: 700 feet
Elevations: 2500 - 2770 feet
Type: out and back
Dogs: leashed (open range)
Restrooms: none

Description: Narrow, unpaved Redwood House Road follows nearby Yager Creek on the west end accompanying the watercourse through a narrow, wooded valley before emerging onto the exposed south face of Johnson Ridge. As the road rises above Yager Creek the views of Bald Jesse and the Yager Creek drainage improve. At the turnaround, panoramic views out to the ocean, the Ferndale Bottoms, and the east side of the Headwaters Forest reward you. Please respect the private lands and open range on both sides of the road.

Getting there: Drive south on US 101 for 20.6 miles taking Exit 685 (CA 36). Turn left on CA 36 and follow it east for 23.8 miles. Turn left on Kneeland Road climbing steeply 8.5 miles to the intersection with Redwood House Road. Turn left on Redwood House Road. Opportunities to park on the side of little-used Redwood House Road are numerous along the way although I would suggest not looking until you have gone a half-mile or so west. Going farther along Redwood House Road allows you to control the length of the walk. Approximate driving time, 1 hour, 30 minutes.

Most of Kneeland Road up from Bridgeville and all of Redwood House Road is unpaved. Kneeland Road and upper Redwood House Road are very passable for all cars. Although it is shorter to come from the west end of Redwood House Road, the lower sections of this route are in poorer condition and not recommended.

The route: The route is a straight-forward road walk. From the east side, assuming you parked your vehicle about two-thirds of a mile west of Kneeland Road, your route takes you through open pasture land before Yager Creek approaches the road and the road enters a narrow, wooded valley (0.7). On the left are corrals and pens for cattle. The road remains under tree cover and near Yager Creek (2.1), eventually emerging into open pastureland with periodic copses of oak trees. The road winds up the south side of Johnson Ridge climbing far above Yager Creek to the turnaround point (4.0) which occurs at a junction where a four-wheel drive

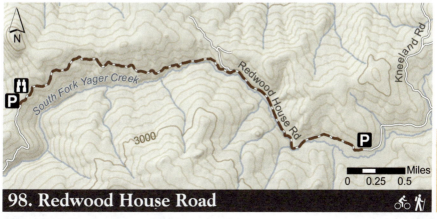

98. Redwood House Road

road turns right and climbs steeply up Johnson Ridge. The turnaround offers panoramic views to the west.

Kneeland – Bridgeville Road

Length: 7.0 miles (although walk can easily be shortened or extended)

The hike profile is very similar to the Redwood House Road.

Description: This road was once the primary land route into Humboldt County. Now, except for the ranchers and the few other residences in this rural area, it is rarely used. Following the climb out of the Van Duzen River Valley, the unpaved road follows the ridgeline north, offering unobstructed panoramic views to the south and east. On a beautiful spring day, the meadows and hillsides can be rich with flowers and the deciduous woodlands add color in the fall. One suggestion is to make a day of driving the loop from Humboldt Bay up to Kneeland and along the old road to Bridgeville and back on CA 36, leaving plenty of time for this walk and perhaps a part of hike #83.

Getting there and walking route: Instead of driving all the way to Redwood House Road along the Kneeland Road from Bridgeville, make the 4-mile long steep climb out of the Van Duzen River valley. Once on the gently undulating ridgeline, pull-out parking is frequent for the next 4.5 miles. Shortly before the intersection with Showers Pass Road (3.5 miles) the Kneeland Road descends into the Yager Creek Valley, losing the distant views. Although you can retrace your steps at any point, this intersection makes for a logical turnaround.

99 · Fort Seward Road

Length: 5.9 miles one-way
Total descent: 2620 feet
Elevations: 400 - 3010 feet

Type: out and back
Dogs: leashed (open range)
Restrooms: none

Description: This walk works best using a car shuttle or by parking part of the way between the top and bottom. The top offers views to the west to the King Range and along the South Fork of the Eel River and east to the Yolla Bolly Mountains, the Lassics, and Mad River Ridge. The descent offers amazing views of the Eel River Valley. Virtually every foot of this little used road is either downhill if you start at the top or uphill if you begin at the bottom. At the base of the road is the once vibrant, now quiet community of Ft. Seward.

Getting there: Follow US 101 south for 51.0 miles taking Exit 650 (Myers Flat). Turn left on the Avenue of the Giants (CA 254) and continue south for 1.9 miles. Turn left on Elk Creek Road and proceed east for 2.7 miles. Turn right on the Dyerville Loop Road and continue south for 11.4 miles on this partially paved road to the intersection with the Ft. Seward Road. Depending on your approach to this walk, you may wish to plant a car at the bottom (5.9 miles east) of the Fort Seward Rd. near the defunct railroad crossing or part of the way down to minimize the otherwise relentless climb. Ample parking exists at the intersection with the Dyerville Loop Road. Approximate driving time, 1 hour and 45 minutes.

The route: Ft. Seward Road is unpaved and all part of the Fort Seward ranch. The

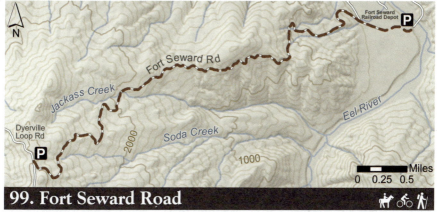

99. Fort Seward Road

walk is relatively steep for the first two miles as it descends through view-filled pastureland. During the winter and spring this area is lush and green but turns brown and sun-baked in the summer and fall. The road then enters mixed oak and fir woodlands interspersed with views and continues its relentless descent. For the final several miles the road is paved and for the final third of a mile is relatively level as it reaches the once thriving community of Fort Seward and the bridge over the Eel (5.9). This walk would be far less appealing in the heat of the summer.

Note: By following the railroad tracks south from the Ft. Seward Road crossing for 0.6 mile, you can visit the abandoned Ft. Seward Railroad Depot. The Ft. Seward area was once home to a hotel and, beginning in 1861, briefly a garrison of soldiers fighting in the Bald Hills War against area Native Americans.

100 · Southern Dyerville Loop Road

Length: 4.0-5.6 miles
Total ascent: 800 feet
Elevations: 2435 - 3150 feet

Type: out and back
Dogs: leashed (open range)
Restrooms: none

Description: This walk offers some advantages over the Ft. Seward Road walk in that this section of the Dyerville Loop Road follows Mail Ridge, the divide between the South Fork of the Eel River and the main stem of the Eel River drainages. As a result, it avoids some of the extremes of down or uphill while retaining the superb views. Not all sections of the Dyerville Loop Road are created equal, however. The best begins roughly two miles north of the intersection with the Ft. Seward Road and continues roughly 2.8 miles south of that same intersection. The road experiences little traffic. Summer can be hot and dusty along this stretch of exposed road. Spring can be magical.

Getting there: Follow the route outlined for Hike #99 to the intersection with Fort Seward Road where there is ample parking. From here you can walk the road in either (or both) directions. Approximate driving time 1 hour and 30 minutes.

The north end of the Dyerville Loop Road near Fruitland experiences more traffic and, while interesting, does not have the same quality of views that the road farther

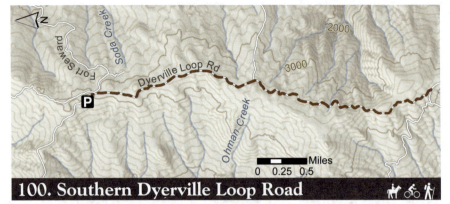

100. Southern Dyerville Loop Road

south offers. Once the road starts the descent to McCann, it is too narrow for safe walking until it reaches McCann (see Hike #95).

The route: The unpaved Dyerville Loop Road extends in both directions from the intersection with Ft. Seward Road. Northbound the road loses more elevation but both directions adhere to the ridge top and offer amazing vistas. Neither direction experiences much traffic and a walker can turn around at any point. Going south from the intersection, I turned around at the entrance to Tuttle Butte Ranch (4.2) as the road rapidly descends, soon becomes more tree-lined, and the landscape has been fractured more extensively by subdivision.

101 · Mt. Lassic and Black Lassic

Length: Black Lassic – 1.0 mile, Mt. Lassic – 1.8 miles
Total ascent: 450 feet (Black Lassic); 425 feet (Signal Peak)
Elevations: 5460 – 5876 feet
Type: out and back
Dogs: yes
Restrooms: none

Description: These three peaks lie astride the Humboldt and Trinity County line and form one of the most distinctive mountain landscapes in our area. From a distance, Black Lassic, standing at 5,876 feet in elevation, looks like an extinct volcano, but it is actually composed of fragments of black mudstone and sandstone. Mt. Lassic or Signal Peak, 5,860 feet, derives its name from a heliograph station once located on this peak around 1900. Red Lassic (5,856 feet), the only one of the three with no established trail to the top, completes this natural equilateral triangle (each peak is between .85 - .90 mile from each other). Six Rivers National Forest has designated this as a special botanical area encompassing 3,640 acres because of the distinctive geological and botanical features. Although the walks are short they can easily be augmented by walking along FS Road 1S07, which sees very little traffic and commands wonderful views in all directions. While the drive is lengthy, this is truly one of the special Humboldt County places.

Getting there: Take US 101 south 20.6 miles to the Exit 685 (CA 36 East). Continue east on CA 36 for about 46.5 miles (past Bridgeville and Dinsmore) to the Van Duzen River Road. Turn right on this paved road and continue south for 8.8 miles. Turn right on FS 1S07, a well-graded gravel road that climbs steadily to the

◦ The Lassik People (also spelled Lasseck, Lassek, and Lassic)

One of the few vestiges of the Lassik tribe in their historic territory is the name of the three Lassic Peaks. It is a tragic story, replicated frequently throughout the West, of the systematic extermination of a people by emigrants propelled by a sense of divine providence and manifest destiny. When European-Americans moved into the mountains and forests of the land drained by the Van Duzen River and Dobbyn Creek east of the main stem of the Eel River in the 1850s, the Lassiks lived in conical houses of bark and slabs in permanent streamside villages in the winter and camped on the ridges where food was more plentiful in summer. The majority of the Lassik people perished during the first few years of the occupancy of their country by settlers. A bounty had been placed upon their heads and trafficking in children for slaves was unrestrained. The few survivors were relocated to reservations in Round Valley and Smith River. ◦

west. At 2.7 miles from the Van Duzen River Road, the road forks with FS 1S07 continuing left. The first views of Black Lassic appear as the road climbs reaching the crest after nearly 7.6 miles. The access road to the Black Lassic trailhead and parking area makes a sharp left (east) turn at about the 7.2 mile mark. The short access road, however, is impassable for low clearance vehicles. Alternate parking is available just beyond the junction with the access road on the right side. Better parking still exists at the crest and about 0.2 mile beyond the crest where the road widens considerably.

The trailhead to Mt. Lassic, at the end of a short spur road impassable for low clearance vehicles, is off the right side of the road at just about 7.7 miles from Van Duzen Road. Parking is available at the trailhead for Mt. Lassic or along FS 1S07. Easy and enjoyable road walking is available as FS 1S07 continues on south. At about 8.1 miles a road departs from the right side of 1S07 that goes north before veering west around the north flank of Red Lassic to a seasonal lakelet. Snow can linger into June and can impact road and trail navigability. Call the Mad River Ranger District office for conditions (707) 574-6233. Approximate driving time, 2 hours and 20 minutes.

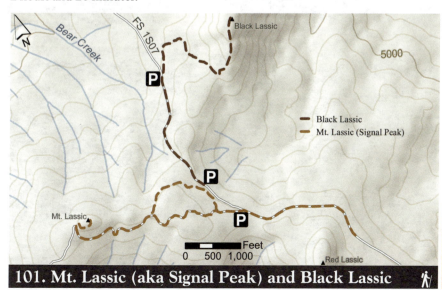

101. Mt. Lassic (aka Signal Peak) and Black Lassic

The route: Black Lassic – this short walk begins at the signed trail on the east side of the trailhead parking lot (about 0.1 mile east of 1S07 on the access road). The trail soon leaves tree cover (0.2) and switchbacks up a rock face before beginning the ascent up the south ridge of Black Lassic. The footing is surprisingly reliable and the gradient such that walking (versus scrambling) is possible to the top (0.5). The views east to South Fork Mountain and the Yolla Bollys, northeast to the Trinity Alps, and west to the King Range and the coast are stunning.

Mt. Lassic – this short walk begins at the signed trail on the west side of the trailhead parking lot (see above). Shortly after beginning the trail, the trail forks with the sign pointing both directions. In fact, both options rejoin in about 0.5 mile (right fork) and 0.3 mile (left fork) for the final 0.4 spur to the top of Mt. Lassic. The trail contours along the south face before turning north and approaching the top from the west. A weathered concrete monument marks the top. The panoramas from this summit rival those from Black Lassic with more south and west topography in view. Mt. Lassic is neither as exposed nor as steep as Black Lassic. Road walking on south along seldom traveled 1S07 is recommended and an easy way to extend your stay and broaden your exploration of this area.

Hiking in the Lassics Wilderness, photo by Allison Poklemba

Conclusion

"Every place needs people who will dig in, keep watch, explore the terrain, learn the animals and plants, and take responsibility. . . . No matter what the legal protections on paper, no land can be safe from harm without people committed to care for it, year after year, generation after generation."

- Scott Russell Sanders, *Coming to Land in a Troubled World*

The miles of trails and walkable roads in our communities exist only because of the commitment of many who came before us. Often these communities were hard-pressed to meet competing urgent needs but had the belief that, like parks and libraries and schools, trails were a critical part of a healthy community. When we walk in Humboldt County we should never forget that it was the effort of many who made this walk possible. Walk with gratitude!

I often hear about the challenge of finding resources necessary for adequate trail maintenance. For example, the annual allocation for the routine maintenance of the Hammond Trail is generally in the ballpark of $40,000. Money well spent, of course. But, there is no question that funds can be stretched further when paid staff efforts are supported by volunteers. Giving back can take many forms. Carry a bag with you that allows you to pick up some trash in the course of your walk. Teach your children trail etiquette. Join a program like the Volunteer Trail Stewards that holds regular workdays. Make a financial donation directed toward trails (e.g., Humboldt Trails Council). Serve as a board member for a walking, running, cycling, or equestrian group. There are countless ways to give back.

It is very important that we steward the resources we have with the intent to pass them to the next generation better than we inherited them. We each have a responsibility, a duty to do what we can to preserve these trails for those who walk in our footsteps.

References

Amato, Joseph A. (2004) *On Foot: A History of Walking*. New York University Press: New York

Anderson, Leslie Scopes (2011) *Unearthing Evidence of Creatures from Deep Time*. Humboldt State University: Arcata, California

Architectural Resources Group (1987) *Eureka: An Architectural View*. Eureka Heritage Society: Eureka, California

Brown, Scott (2013) *Eureka (Then and Now)*. Arcadia Publishing: Charleston, South Carolina

Jackson, Hal (1983) *Eureka: A Guide to the Architecture and Landscape*. Eureka Heritage Society: Eureka

Kauffmann, Michael (2012) *Conifer Country*. Backcountry Press. Kneeland, CA.

Rohde, Jerry (2014) *Both Sides of the Bluff: History of Humboldt County Places*. MountainHome Books: Eureka, California

Rohde, Jerry and Gisela Rohde (1992) *Humboldt Redwoods State Park*. Miles and Miles: Eureka

Rohde, Jerry and Gisela Rohde (1994) *Redwood National and State Parks: Tales, Trails, and Auto Tours*. MountainHome Books: McKinleyville, California

Rohde, Jerry and Gisela Rohde (2004) *Best Short Hikes in Redwood National and State Parks*. Mountaineers Books: Seattle

Rees Hughes - Author

Walked his way through some of the most stunning regions on Earth — from the top of Kilimanjaro to the arid interior of Australia, from the pilgrimage route up Sri Pada in Sri Lanka to the picturesque Cornish coast, from the Himalayas to the Andes — but has found little that compares with the magic of the Klamath Knot. Co-editor of *The Pacific Crest Trailside Readers*, he also serves as a volunteer trail steward coordinator, and is an advocate for the Humboldt Bay Trail.

Rees retired from a career in higher education after more than three decades at Humboldt State University, Seattle University, and the University of Kansas. He has a PhD from the University of Washington.

Jason Barnes - Cartographer

Originally from Michigan, Jason moved to Northern California to attain a certificate, and later a Masters in geographic information systems (GIS). He served as an officer for the Northern California region of the American Society for Photogrammetry & Remote Sensing (ASPRS) for five years. While living in Humboldt County, Jason discovered the Trinity Alps Wilderness and Klamath Mountains and began using his GIS skills toward citizen science projects involving lake bathymetry, glacier monitoring, and trail advocacy. When not hiking in the wilderness, he can be seen cycling the trails and roads of Humboldt County, exploring backroads on his dual-sport motorcycle, or capturing footage with his quad-copter. Jason is a co-author of the newest map set to the Bigfoot Trail.